Words of appreciation:

"I love this book because it is easy to read, easy to reference, easy to follow and easy to understand. It is clear, concise, the illustrations are great! The case studies are excellent. I recommend it a lot. The book enables a parent to see where changes can be made . . . an invaluable, simple tool for myself and my patients. As a pediatrician, the information is totally useful to me across the spectrum. Thanks for this incredible effort!" ~ Cornelia Franz, M.D., Pediatrician

"The children's artwork and accompanying dialogue throughout the book are real and easy for parents to relate to. The TIPS help you apply specific concepts to everyday life. I love the Self-Discovery chapter. The chapter on Hope is excellent." ~ Teresa Langston, Author, *Parenting Without Pressure*

"As grown-up children, there is an insatiable reservoir that longs to be filled with all the wisdom, practical applications, understanding/learning and humor that we can garner to support our untaught parenting skills. Dr. Messenger's book hits the nail on the head, comes in the back door and offers a cup of coffee and a good edible. Her creativity and expertise are refreshing in the text. I recommend the book to anyone who wants to embrace the privilege of parenting." ~ Jeanne Miller-Clark, Chaplain, Orlando Regional South Seminole Hospital, and more importantly parent.

"Whether a professional or a parent . . . this is a **must read** publication for everyone concerned with the growth, development and understanding of children." ~ Mark R. Brown, Director, Harbor School

"I love the concept of **Resilience** (throughout your book). To me it represents coping skills and ego strength. So many times, early trauma can rob a person of his/her ability to overcome. Why else do we see some people who seem to drown in a glass of water, while others can survive a tidal wave!" ~ Mark Williams, Ph.D., Clinical Psychologist

~ ❀ ~

"I read your chapter on **Listening** tonight, and I think it is absolutely fantastic. You think like a kid and a teenager. You relate very well to the problems of growing up. Most certainly, you understand what all us parents do that make it harder for children to grow up." ~ Dr. David Carr, Pediatrician

~ ❀ ~

"I have enjoyed looking at and reading *Secrets of the Third Little Pig: 7 Steps to Build a Child's Inner Strength*." If you just look at all the pictures in it, there is something to learn. The progression of the thoughts throughout the book are well presented at a timely pace. The examples are priceless. I found myself noting ideas just about every other page. There is something to share for everyone in reading this book." ~ Marsha M. Neilson Garzia, Parent

~ ❀ ~

"I enjoyed reading it as a parent and a professional. It is clearly written. The drawings by the children and quotations emphasize the message. The case studies are excellent. I was struck by its 'healing power.'" ~ José Quiñones, M.D., Psychiatrist

~ ❀ ~

"I enjoyed the examples of using positive imagery to guide the children out of their predicaments. By using words and stories that say "You **can do it**, here is an example of someone very much like you who **did it**," the child has a concrete thought of succeeding. This replaces the thought or image of failing and having the fear and conviction of failing. Hope is the greatest liberator and knowing how to instill it is a wonderful tool. Thank you. I just wish (the book) could have been longer." ~ Ginny Guyton, M.D., Pediatrician

~ ❀ ~

"This is a special book which offers numerous insights and ideas into children's needs. It easily lends itself to being read and used by **both** parents." ~Teri Marks, Ed.S., School Psychologist

~ ❀ ~

"I have read a lot of parenting books. This one had all the best parts of every book I've ever read." ~ Mrs. P.K., Parent

~ ❀ ~

"Children will suffer ... if the adults don't read this book." ~ Mr. W.W., Caregiver (Grandfather raising his daughter's daughter.)

~ ❀ ~

"I was given a whole stack of parenting books by the guidance counselor at my daughter's school. I tried to get through different ones and just ended up feeling more confused and depressed than ever. Then I picked up the **Pig Book**, and within ten minutes I had some helpful advice I could really use. Plus, it was fun so I wanted to keep reading." ~Ms. N.H., Single Parent/Working Mom

"It is clear that you bring a very special insight to parenting." ~D. Michael Mathes, Vice President, National Alliance for Mental Illness, Greater Orlando

"Dr. Messenger contributed her expertise to help parents overcome the psychological obstacles which prevent depressed children from getting the help they need . . . and established a sense of "hope" for the future." ~ Tracy McCommon, Producer, WMFE-TV 24

"I liked the layout. As a busy parent, it's hard to have the time to read more than a few pages at one time." ~ Mrs. K.C., Parent

"I like the presentation most — the pictures, quotes and stories are the best way to help parents enjoy the process of understanding and helping their children." ~ John Blankemeier, M.D., Psychiatrist

~ ✿ ~

"This is a wonderful book with such excellent information. Could hardly put it down. So much of the things I used right away." ~ Mrs. F.R., Caregiver (Grandmother raising granddaughter.)

~ ✿ ~

"It was **very** informative for parents as well as helpful to them. As a teacher . . . it was enlightening." ~ Julie Sanders, Teacher, Holy Family School

~ ✿ ~

"The book is so practical . . . for both parents and professionals. You can open it to any page and get a tip for immediate use. The artwork makes it! I love the analogies throughout to the "Three Little Pigs" story. Even kids can read it and get ideas to help themselves." ~Wanda Eppes, Ph.D., School Psychologist

Dear Dr. mesemger, I really loved that visit. My mom said that we might go again. And I've found a very few people who likes science. And I won the district spelling bee.
note by

love Adam

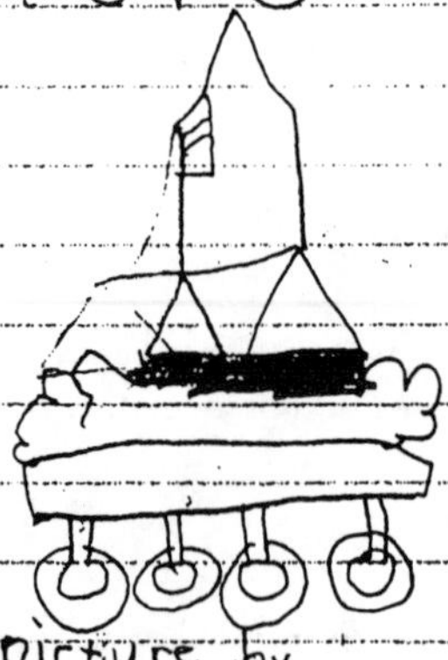

Age 7

picture by

Atom S.

To Margaret,
who has taught us all
infinite lessons about inner strength.

DAD

MOM

ALEC

OWEN

♥

FAMILY

Alec

Owen

The Horse stands
for caring on
the inner strength.

Alec

Margaret
(-"Mom")

Owen

"The greatest good you can do for another is not just to share
your riches, but to reveal to him his own."
— Benjamin Disraeli

Contents

Preface

There have been moments in your life
*   When you felt: What else could get worse?*
*   Then, perhaps, life did get worse . . .*

Through it all, you are the flower
*   That continued to thrive*
*   In the crack in the sidewalk of life.*

The sunny spirit continues to renew itself
*   Even though the container of life*
*   Seemed exhausted and worn out.*

—Verniece Wyles,
Psychotherapist and Friend
August 1, 1997 - Personal Correspondence

My deepest wish is that this book will touch the lives of children of all ages who are struggling to survive as flowers in the cracks of the sidewalks of life. The change will come through you as caregivers — parents, relatives, teachers, counselors, friends — who have made the commitment to help them thrive.

A Second Edition
Note from the Author

Like a mother who still reminds her independent adult child to put on a jacket before going out into the cold, I find myself having trouble letting go of this creation. *Secrets of the Third Little Pig* has been quite successful on its own for more than a year. For some reason, I keep wanting to improve the first edition just a bit more before the second edition debuts. It is especially hard to avoid completely redoing certain sections, since there has been such a strong recent surge of interest in the topic of resilience.

Nevertheless, just as an artist knows when to put down the paintbrush, I now put down my pen. I embrace the revisions as they stand. I have tried to objectively review the comments of colleagues and clients, friends and strangers alike, then weave them into a superior finished product. The recurrent suggestion that there be some type of accompanying workbook, game or activity book has been taken to heart. It is nearing publication itself.

My greatest learning experience has probably come from presenting book material to both professional and lay audiences locally and internationally. Just as "beauty is in the eye of the beholder," I have found that "wisdom is in the ear of the listener." At first, I was astonished at how discrepant the participant evaluations were. At the very same presentation, one attendee might describe me as "entertaining, enthusiastic and eager to help," while another would describe me as "a bit flippant and too directive." One person might love the morning topic and be bored by the afternoon session, while another would comment that the morning was worthless but I salvaged myself in the afternoon. Go figure.

In any event, I have been deeply moved by the reaction of parents and other caregivers to my work. Perhaps I am too sensitive, but I do get a lump in my throat when people tell me, "This book changed our whole family so we're not yelling any more" . . . "I've always loved my kid, but with your book it's

the first time in years I've really liked him" . . . "It's the only parenting
book my husband would actually read" . . . "It's the first non-fiction
book I couldn't put down . . ." My book has even been compared to
television. I've been told, it can just be turned on (opened up)
randomly, and something of interest will show up. It entertains and
advises yet has plenty of commercials (drawings and cartoons).

Perhaps the most dubious distinction, remarked on by a number of
people, is that *Secrets of the Third Little Pig* makes great bathroom
reading material. (Presumably for the same reasons mentioned above?)
But who cares! If that's where busy people have a few extra minutes to
read, what counts is that they use the information to enhance
children's lives.

And my final word to those confused souls who have asked me about
the title ~ no, this is NOT the pig that had roast beef. Although I
suppose it is possible, of course, that this third pig did enjoy roast beef
with her two brothers in the warm kitchen of the strong house that
stood against adversity and thus represents the bright pathway to
resilience . . .

"Life is like fording a river,
stepping from one slippery stone to another,
and you must rejoice every time you don't lose your balance,
and learn to laugh at all the times you do."

— Merle Shain

Acknowledgments

"To have played and laughed with enthusiasm
and sung with exultation;
To know that even one life has
breathed easier because you have lived —
This is to have succeeded."

— Ralph Waldo Emerson

For years when I have spoken with passion of my work, I have had people tell me, "You ought to write a book!" When I finally began to take the notion seriously, I realized what an arduous task it was. This book came into being only because of the synergy of many lives touching mine. I would like to thank a number of individuals for their inspiration and influence:

Maura Ramage . . . clearly the living definition of unconditional love. Thank you for your ability in transforming my scribbling into typed text; for your patience in accepting countless revisions; for your talent in illustrating and editing; and especially for your magic in weaving all the stray threads together. Who else could pull together a project of this magnitude and say, "I don't even feel like I'm working"?

Larié Messenger Ward . . . the greatest blessing in my life. Thank you for sharing your life and wisdom with me; for providing me so many opportunities for growth; and for contributing your love and talent through your poetry and drawings.

Marie and Glenn Messenger . . . my parents, who guided, supported and loved. Thank you for being the caring significant adults I needed in childhood and for being there during the ups and downs of adulthood.

Lorene Rictor . . . my sister, whose bonds with me are deeper than words can tell. Thank you for growing up with me, through all the years, even now.

Dr. Wanda Eppes . . . a friend and colleague for over two decades. Thank you for your optimism, honesty and encouragement, always when I needed them the most.

Verniece Wyles . . . a special cohort brought into my life through Divine absurdity. Thank you for modeling a life of dedication and caring and for giving me special messages of guidance and support.

Linda Johnston . . . my longest friendship in life. Thank you for the gift of always being there and for your brilliant insights in developing this book.

Ron Ferguson . . . our "consultant-on-call." Thank you for solving our mind-boggling computer crises along the way.

Clients, children and caregivers . . . people who have given me their trust. Thank you for allowing me to touch your lives and for showing me how much more I still have to learn.

Special teachers and mentors . . . guides who have shaped my view of the world. Thank you to Ms. Ann Cataldo, psychotherapist; Dr. David Parker, psychologist; Dr. José Quiñones, psychiatrist; Dr. Lewis Wasserman, pediatrician; Dr. Cornelia Franz, pediatrician; Dr. John Cleveland, instructor; Dr. Hannalore Wass, professor; Dr. John McGuire, professor; Dr. Kelland Livesay, supervisor; Mr. Joe McCawley, instructor; Dr. Tom Smith, compassionate professional (dentist); Ms. Margie Johansen, teacher; Dr. Waldron McLellon, author; Ms. Teresa Langston, parent educator; Mr. Michael Freeny, author; and Mr. Ned McLeod, attorney.

Special friends . . . blessings who have given me laughter, support and magic in both my personal and professional lives. Thank you to Mark, Simon, Natalie, Teri, Gene, Bonnie, Kathy, Andy, Calvin, Jill, Jim, Della, Chuck, Richard, Oriana, and G.N.O. crew.

Special workers . . . people who made this work complete. Thank you to Jenny, Trevor and Tyler Jackson, Gus Ramage, Michelle Clonch, Veronica Jones, and Tally Miller for the time and artistic talents they contributed. Thank you to Dr. John Blankenmier, Ms. Jean Anderson, Mr. Frank Vine, and Dr. Ginny Guyton for critiquing the 1st edition to make the 2nd edition better than ever. Special thanks to all the young people for the artistic inspiration they provided which has made the book so unique.

Inspirational Role Models . . . people who have led the way in displaying compassion and stamina and have thus spurred me to continue on this healing path. Thank you to Dr. Wayne Dyer, Ms. Oprah Winfrey, Dr. T. Berry Brazelton, Dr. Robert Wallace, Mr. Jack Canfield, Mr. Mark Victor Hansen, Ms. Ann Landers, and Dr. Violet Oaklander.

Loving pets . . . animals who have filled our home with warmth and affection. Thank you to the dogs, Heidi, Taffy, Sierra and Riley; the cats, Misty and Pepper; the birds, Patty and Percy; the iguana, Dustin; the fish (you know who you are); and all the other animals who have shared our home over the years.

Big, bad wolves . . . people and events that provided unsought challenges, disaster and pain. Thank you for providing me opportunities to learn, grow, rise above it and become resilient.

Higher Power . . . guidance from above and love in my heart. Thank you for everything.

Left to Right: Maura, Petunia, Charlene

About the Author:
Oinks & Squeals

Dr. Charlene Messenger obtained her Ph.D. from the University of Florida, Gainesville, in 1984. She currently holds licenses as a school psychologist and a mental health therapist. She has been a classroom teacher, then worked 14 years providing psychological services in elementary, secondary and exceptional education schools in Central Florida. In 1989 she was named "Psychologist of the Year" by the Orange County Association of Counseling and Development, and in 1984 received "Award of Recognition" from the Florida Association of School Psychologists.

In May, 1991 Dr. Messenger began her independent practice in Orlando, Florida, now called Brighter Pathways, Inc. Her office specializes in psychotherapy and evaluation for children and their families. The center includes independent consultants who provide tutoring, coaching, behavior management and life skills training.

Dr. Messenger has continued to expand her practice both nationally and internationally as an expert consultant to various institutions, including Walt Disney World, the Center for Drug-Free Living, Arnold Palmer Hospital for Children and Women, the National Association of School Psychologists and the World Congress on Child and Play Therapy in Kingston, Canada. She has appeared on numerous television programs, including "Petsburg USA" (Disney MGM), "Family Works" (PBS), "Ask the Family Doctor" (America's Health Network/Universal Studios), "Back-to-School Guide" (Global News and Entertainment/*Better Homes and Gardens*), and "Growing Up Sad" (WMFE-TV).

Dr. Messenger is also contacted regularly by Central Florida news reporters from NBC - TV 2, CBS - TV 6, WOFL - TV 35, Central Florida TV 13, and *The Orlando Sentinel* for expert opinions on breaking stories and issues involving children and families. In addition, she has taught as an adjunct professor at Valencia Community College and worked as a consultant to the Juvenile Detention Center in Orlando.

During the 1989-90 school year, Dr. Messenger wrote a series of articles for a local parenting newsletter which became the basis for numerous seminars and workshops. Audiences included PTAs, HRS groups, religious associations and parenting groups for exceptional children (i.e., those with Learning Disabilities or Attention Deficit Hyperactivity Disorder). The information, over the years, has been revised and expanded as the author has grown wiser as both a parent and a professional. Finally, the material has been pulled together in the current format to touch even more lives.

Of all her accomplishments, Dr. Messenger believes the creation of a new life — her daughter, Larié, born in 1985 — remains the highlight of her life. Because of a fortunate series of events, motherhood was able to take priority. She was blessed with almost a year of full-time maternity leave, followed by several years of half-time employment as a school psychologist. During those early years especially, she experienced both the inspiration and vulnerability of helping to shape a new life.

Perhaps just as important, Dr. Messenger remembers her own childhood. She still holds a childlike wonder and awe in her outlook. (There are those who would argue she never really grew up.) Yet she is also one of those individuals who rose above adversity in childhood to become strong. It is firsthand knowledge of childhood pain and resiliency which helps her guide others in their own healing process.

Tally, Age 14

The Sow:
A Piglet's Perspective

M O M

My mother has a kind
loving smile that is usaly covered
with a pink lip-stick. A bright lip-stick
that shines in the sunlight. It shines
like her goldened shimering
hair. Her eyes seem magical because
in the dark the are a earthy brown
yet a darkish jungle green
in the sun.

She is tall, allmost 6-foot.
Her height looks good when she
wears long, flowing dresses with
abstact disighs and colors on
it. She's also skinny.

My mother is almost always
late. Other than that she nice.
She is kind and always willing
to make friends,

Larie, 1995
(Age 9)

Introduction:

"If you want your children to be brilliant, tell them
fairy tales. If you want them to be very brilliant,
tell them even more fairy tales."

— Albert Einstein

Mike, Age 11

THE THREE LITTLE PIGS . . .

This classic fairy tale is a wonderful metaphor for how we prepare
ourselves to face day-to-day living. Each pig represents a combination
of temperament and attitude in life. Each house represents a level of
strength to handle adversity. The wolf, of course, represents the
problems and challenges that confront us along our way.

The first little pig values fun and freedom. While life should be
pleasant, it also requires work and responsibility. This little pig has lost
that balance. He focuses on convenience so he can have time to play
and amuse himself. His house reflects his shallowness. It is shoddy
and weak. This home is clearly insecure against outside challenges.
When faced with the first small problem, this pig is left helpless and
dependent on his two siblings.

The second little pig is somewhat more resourceful. He selects a better
building material and takes more time to construct his house.
Nevertheless, he does not make the effort to ensure its stability. This
home is only mildly secure. While it is initially strong, before long, it
too crumbles and falls. Now both brothers are dependent on their
remaining sibling.

The third little pig is clever. She carefully observes and sees the big picture. She prepares herself by reading and researching the best construction materials. She is diligent, responsible, and willing to delay gratification. This little pig visualizes what she wants in a home and makes it happen. She puts in the necessary effort up front so she can relax later. And she does it all with a sense of humor, remaining optimistic and hopeful even when teased.

In the end, this little pig's belief in herself pays off . . . her home is **resilient!** It stands strong against adversity. While she is not one to be taken advantage of, this little pig does have compassion. She understands her brothers' plight and opens her home to them. She is neither rude nor condescending to them. Instead, she is grateful for her blessings and is willing to share them with others. Everyone benefits from her approach.

In this book, we will look closely at the issue of **RESILIENCE**. Like the "little pigs," children are young and still developing. Caregivers have a major impact on their attitude and approach to life. What things can we adults do to bring out children's inner strengths? What can we do to help them face challenges without crumbling? If they do fall, how do we teach them to get up and move on with a sense of wisdom gained? In these pages, the resilient pig, Phoebe, is our model of inner strength against adversity.

Part One:

WISDOM TO WALLOW IN

OVERVIEW ~ My Story:
THE THIRD LITTLE PIG

A CHILD'S VIEWPOINT

NO PLACE TO TURN

BECOMING A TRUE EXPERT ~ A PARENT

WISDOM OF CHILDREN

My Story:
THE THIRD
LITTLE
PIG

I've shut the door on yesterday
and thrown the key away —
Tomorrow holds no fears for me,
Since I have found today."

— Vivian Yeiser Laramore

Doug, Age 7

The field of mental health with children became my calling at an early age simply because there was no one there to help our family when I was growing up. My older brother was diagnosed as paranoid schizophrenic at age eleven! This is generally an unheard of diagnosis at such a young age . . . unless there are severe, consistent symptoms which persist over time and across situations. And there were.

My childhood is filled with memories of horrors he inflicted on my younger sister, my parents and me. The stories are hideous and painful to recount. Yet I want you to know about the terror of living with a severely mentally ill person. Realize, too, that many adults have suffered through their childhoods with similar or even worse personal traumas. Some children are still suffering . . .

A CHILD'S VIEWPOINT

As a child, I did not at first realize that anything was really "wrong" with my family because I had nothing to compare it to. An analogy would be a child who assumed everyone in the class sees a blurry chalkboard because he does. It is only after he has his eyes checked and vision corrected with glasses that he can understand what is "normal" and what he has been missing.

Lisa, Age 10

The night of revelation came in second grade when I spent the night at a friend's house. All through dinner and into the evening, I was waiting and waiting for the explosion. I was stunned by the calmness and sane conversation. When would her brother start yelling and throwing food because a new brand of mayonnaise had been purchased? When would the screaming profanity start and her parents rush to close the windows so the neighbors wouldn't hear?

Or would my friend discover some evil trick he'd done that day? Perhaps he had picked his nose and wiped his boogers on her pillow case . . . or snuck into her room and put a deep scratch through each of her favorite record albums? Would he creep up and pound us unsuspectingly . . . or would he jump out and punch us then run off laughing hysterically while we cried? Perhaps he would try to hurt the family pet by putting a bag over its head or some other "experiment"? The worst was probably his wicked grinning and giggling to himself. It was clear something awful had happened — or at least was planned — and all that could be done was wait. Wait for the cruelty to reveal itself . . .

Sandy, Age 8

My friend, of course, had no idea what I was talking about. Those things NEVER happened in her house. They sometimes had arguments or got spankings or grounded. That was the worst. It slowly dawned on me that there was another reality out there I knew nothing about.

> "It is your understanding that is going to change your reality."
>
> — Deepak Chopra

Courtney, Age 8

My reality I had simply accepted. Over the years I developed coping strategies. I learned how to move my dresser in front of my bedroom door to barricade myself when my parents weren't home. I learned to express my rage with my portable chalkboard and colored chalk. I used to draw the ugliest pictures and write the nastiest curses about my brother. Later, when my frenzy had subsided, I'd erase the board feeling more balanced, often even laughing at my angry expressions. I learned to stay outside, away from him. I learned to take care of and enjoy my younger sister. I learned **intuitively** how to protect myself. That is what researchers are just now identifying as coping mechanisms for resilient children: PROTECTIVE FACTORS.

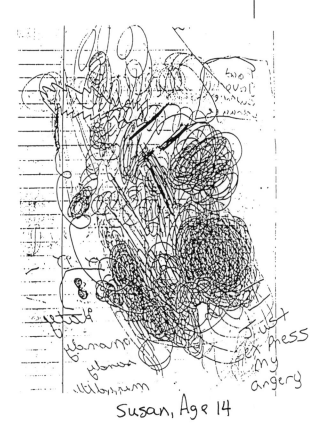

This "artwork" by an adolescent I was counseling shows how she modified my chalkboard technique by using a "scribble journal," different color ink pens and even backward writing.

Susan, Age 14

NO PLACE TO TURN

In the midst of all the family chaos, my parents did try to intervene. Their attempts were often futile and usually provoked even worse behaviors. My brother could be triggered easily from a relatively small issue into full-blown psychotic rages. Worst of all, **there was no place to turn for help.** I recall my parents hauling the family to various psychiatrists' offices and mental health centers. We would arrive with high expectations, only to leave bitter and disappointed yet again.

There was one child specialist in particular who had a very eminent reputation but a very difficult time with my brother in his office. My brother flung things off his desk, threw books off his shelves and clogged his commode with toilet paper. This man could not wait to get us out of there. His parting advice to my parents? "He'll grow out of it."

Little Terror

All Better Now!

FANTASY: "Growing Out Of It"

My brother, of course, never did grow out of it. He deteriorated. But somewhere along the way, I grew strong. I was resilient. As Rubin (1996) says, I fell down seven times but got up eight. I was later determined to **be there** for other families in need. My goals were, and still remain, to help heal maladjusted children, to give stressed (but not disturbed) children coping skills, and to share effective strategies for caregivers to help children to become more capable in life.

BECOMING A TRUE EXPERT – A PARENT

I was a psychologist with school children for eight years before I became a parent. Looking back, I don't think too much of my work was inaccurate at that time. In fact, I often received positive feedback. It's just that once I became a parent, I really understood children from a different perspective. I experienced firsthand the "fun" of taking 45 minutes to get a 2½-year-old to pick up crayons from the kitchen floor because of repeated sets of time-out to get the job done. It probably would have taken 30 seconds to do it myself, but what lessons would I have taught? "Be obnoxious enough and you'll get your way" or "Don't worry about your stuff, someone else will do it for you."

"You're so mean."
2½-Year-Old Version

Now, almost a decade later, it's *déjà vu*. Having helped my pre-adolescent feel more mature and ready for middle school by getting her ears pierced, her hair styled and her wardrobe updated, I figured I was in pretty good shape as a parent. Then "the conflict" hit. "EVERYONE is shaving their legs!" (especially her two best friends). "How can you be so mean?" I gently reminded her we had decided long ago that she could begin shaving on her 12th birthday which was only about a month away. She pouted, huffed, slammed doors and cried an entire evening — just like a 2-year-old!

"You're so mean."
11½-Year-Old Version

It would have been so easy to say that one little word of permission: "OK." Then I'd have been "so nice" and "such a great mom" for that time and place. But this was a battle I had chosen. It was a **limit** I had set. While sometimes I do negotiate, this time I was firm. There were too many potential bad lessons that were previews of coming attractions for the teen years: "Go along with the crowd" or "Mom can be manipulated."

Melissa, Age 8

Now I consider myself a "mommy-chologist," a term I first heard my daughter use at age four to introduce me to her new friend. I loved it and have used the title ever since. To all the caregivers — from daddy-gineers to mom-mattornies, from big-sis-coach to big-bro-guide, from grandpa-stodians to aunt-teachers — I invite you to enjoy the journey, even if the sidewalk is sometimes bumpy and cracked. You are the "care-chologist" for some special child.

WISDOM OF CHILDREN

Much has been written and said lately about "the inner child" within each adult. Now consider the reverse perspective: **Within each child, there is a developing adult.** Styles of behaving and getting along in life are established early. They can become life-long patterns.

When you look at a child — and mentally note strengths and weaknesses — ask yourself, into what kind of adult is this little one transforming? Gradually, but inevitably, this child will begin to see the world through adult eyes.

This book is not about re-creating children to become what you wish them to be. It's about **helping them recognize and use the wisdom that already resides within them.** Just as children's bodies have the capacity for self-healing physical injuries, their mental and spiritual selves have the capacity for self-healing emotional injuries. Our task is to listen to what they are SAYING, to sense what they are FEELING and to give what they are truly NEEDING.

This adolescent's drawing depicts her sense of struggle. She has depicted an angel on one shoulder and a devil on the other, highlighting the age-old feeling of being pulled in two directions.

"You can observe a lot just by looking."

— Yogi Berra

The book's artwork is based on actual drawings and paintings done by young people with whom I have worked over the years. To avoid any possible breach of confidentiality, I have chosen to have all artwork be reasonable representations from my practice done by the young people recognized under acknowledgments. I believe the pictures and accompanying dialogue often speak more eloquently than my writing.

As an author, I have found much resonance in previously published available literature. I have thus included quotes from many individuals, both living and deceased. These words of wisdom were carefully selected to be meaningful to you, the reader. Their inclusion in no way implies endorsement of the book itself, unless specifically noted. For the interested reader, sources are available in the book's very extensive bibliography, or I can be contacted directly.

The cases presented are composites of true stories, most of them from my work with children and their families over the last two decades. Special care has been taken to alter names and specific identifying features again to protect confidentiality. Any resemblance to any person, living or dead, is purely coincidental and unintentional. By using these examples, I do not intend to conjure an image of therapy as quick and easy. In fact, it is sometimes slow and frustrating. The REAL-LIFE anecdotes are presented to make a point clear for you or to show how the concepts can be applied to everyday life. For me, they highlight the essence of therapy: CHANGE.

For all the people who have shared their stories — the joys and pains, the successes and setbacks — I am deeply grateful. The process of my own growth and healing will continue as I am touched by even more lives. What's more, I would love to hear from you with your own stories and tips to share with other caregivers next time around. Together we will brighten more and more children's pathways.

"There are only two lasting bequests we can give our children. One is roots; the other wings."

— Hodding Carter

Bobby, Age 7

Good Intentions:
STICKS AND STRAW

OVERVIEW ~ Good Intentions:
STICKS AND STRAW

WOUNDS OF THE HEART

EMOTIONALLY DESTITUTE

A COUPLE OF CAUTIONS

LET'S GET ON WITH IT

A GUIDE BOOK

WHAT'S UP AHEAD

"Parenthood remains the greatest single
preserve of the amateur."

— Alvin Toffler

Ben, Age 6

*REAL LIFE: The voice on the answering machine sounded urgent.
Ordinarily, I do not listen to the messages that come in overnight, but my
office manager insisted because she did not want to simply take a message
this time.*

*"I think my daughter is being abused. Or if she's not actually being
abused herself, she may be witnessing abuse. I need to get her in to see
you as soon as possible." The rest of the message left the details of his
name and numbers where he could be reached.*

*I tried to recall this family as best I could while my assistant found the file.
It had been over five years since I saw them. At that time, Rachel was not
quite 2 years old. Her parents were going through a difficult divorce (is
there any divorce that's nice?), and I had done counseling with her two
older brothers, ages 6 and 7 at the time. As far as I knew, the boys had
adjusted as best as could be expected; Rachel of course had been too young
to participate. Although there remained much bitterness and resentment
between the parents, they had each moved on and found new live-in
partners. Mother had primary custody, and the children visited their
father on alternate weekends—a very typical arrangement. Now Rachel
was being abused? What kind of abuse? How did they know?*

Rachel's father was a powerful and prestigious attorney, but he sounded frantic when I returned his call. He was convinced somebody was doing something to his little girl. "She's just so different. She doesn't act the same anymore. She's afraid to leave her mother. I think she's afraid something will happen."

I still did not have a clear picture. "Tell me exactly what's happened, what kind of changes you're seeing that make you so concerned."

"Well," he replied, "the last two times she was supposed to come over to my house, she had a fit. She screamed and cried and said she didn't want to leave her mother. Maybe she's watching her mother be abused by her boyfriend and thinks she has to be there to protect her. I don't know, I just want some help."

Checking my appointment book, I had the choice of skipping lunch or staying late. We agreed on a 4:30 appointment. When I first saw 7-year-old Rachel that afternoon, I was struck by what a beautiful child she had become. My last image of her was as an infant. (Why is it we are always so amazed when children grow up, when they are doing exactly the thing they are supposed to be doing?)

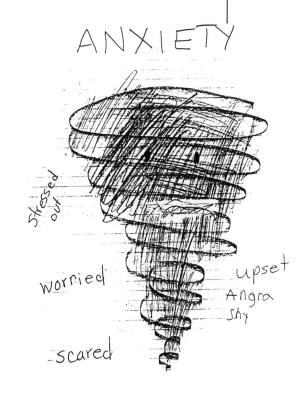

I spent some time with Rachel and her father together in my room. We drew a picture of "ANXIETY" and talked about how that felt inside. Rachel used the term "STRESSED OUT" a number of times, so we added this to our picture.

Then I spent some time alone with her. We utilized Shapiro's (1995) technique of Eye Movement Desensitization and Reprocessing (EMDR). Briefly, this is a fairly new counseling tool which is particularly effective with victims of trauma, especially PTSD (Post-Traumatic Stress Disorder). The intervention starts with a distressing image (in this case, Rachel crying when she leaves mom's house) connected to a negative belief ("I am afraid to leave my mother") and works through a series of eye-movement/visual tracking sets. This brings forward various images from the client to a final positive image and positive belief ("I am safe and brave. I can speak up for myself").

I had anticipated that we might uncover a major trauma. Instead, it turned out to be a set of little, tiny traumas that had added up. Rachel was not so much afraid of leaving her own mother as going to her father's home. She described his partner, Ellen, as extremely strict and rigid in her rules, saying "It's like I'm Cinderella and she's the step-mom."

KATHY, Age 7

As more and more came out, Rachel seemed helpless and trapped. She explained that her dad was "always tired" and laid around. "He seems like a stranger." Her brothers played together outside, but she could not go out without supervision, and she had no friends in the neighborhood. So, she mostly stayed in the back room because "Ellen would kill me if I made a mess." To make matters worse, Rachel witnessed much arguing and yelling between her father and Ellen. She concluded by saying she was afraid to sleep there because she always had nightmares.

Later when I spoke with Rachel's father, he was visibly relieved to find that no one was hurting his daughter, nor was she witnessing any abuse. On the other hand, I had to be the bearer of bad news: visits to his house felt terrible. Probably from her point of view it almost did feel like abuse — emotional abuse.

Rachel's father and I spoke about things that he could do to make her stay with him more comfortable. We focused on bonding especially. I suggested that they simply have some father-daughter time together. He looked at me miserably and said "I don't know how. I know what to do with my sons, but she's a girl. How do you play with a girl?"

This case speaks volumes about the pain children can suffer despite their caregivers' best intentions. This man would never have considered physically abusing his daughter, yet in his own way, he was neglecting her. He was depriving her of his love and affection — the things that she needed most from him. Moreover, his partner was cold and grumpy, so that there was no one to take up the slack.

Again we can turn to our original fairy tale. Rachel's father's good intentions were simply sticks and straw. They were not strong enough to hold up to her suffering.

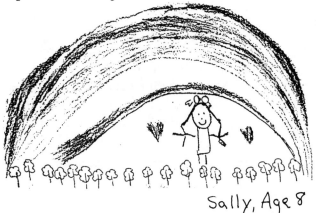

Sally, Age 8

WOUNDS OF THE HEART

Think back to your own childhood. What was it like on a day-to-day basis? Did people have good intentions, but were they just too frazzled running around to give you much attention? Did Dad come home from work with a six-pack and sit in front of the TV most of the evening? Was Mom too frantic making dinner and getting things ready for tomorrow? Did you have a sense that you didn't quite fit in? And what about your siblings? Were you the one who had to watch over them . . . or were you the one who was beaten up?

There are **so many ways to be cruel to people in our family without ever actually meaning to do it.** And patterns have a way of repeating themselves. In some cases, the very thing we promised ourselves as children to "NEVER do to my child when I'm a parent" is exactly what we do.

REAL LIFE: Lola sat in front of me with her eyes tearing. She was 25, had two small children whom she loved dearly and was married to a successful executive. He was rarely home, and most of the burden of child rearing fell on her. "I can't stand it that I hit my kids. I used to get hit with a wooden spoon when I was a kid, and I swore I'd never do it. Now I just get frustrated and that's the first thing I do, grab the wooden spoon."

"Remember, when **they** have a tantrum, don't have one of **your own.**"

— Judith Kuriansky

Danny, Age 4

I felt the hurt in her heart. But I also knew her children were hurting more desperately. I was not going to fall back on the psycho-babble of calling her a "dysfunctional parent" because she had grown up in a "dysfunctional home." Yes, Lola had grown up in pain. Most likely, she had left her own feelings locked up in a steel box deep inside. But we didn't have to focus on that. We could move forward. She could learn to be the kind of parent that she wanted to be to her children.

"If you were your own child, what would you do differently? See yourself as little Lola. How would you treat yourself?" *These questions started a self-exploration process which led to significant changes in Lola's home. The therapy was not extensive and analytical. It was brief and solution-focused. Lola had come because she wanted things to be different — she wanted* ***change.***

"Inside, there was this emptiness. There was no emotional core."

— Deborah Norville, *Back on Track*

EMOTIONALLY DESTITUTE

It is my belief that so many of us have grown up in painful situations that we sometimes feel numb to them. I have seen children from even very wealthy homes become **emotionally destitute**. Other children live in poverty but have a close-knit connection with family members. Some children learn and grow strong from their external stresses. Others slowly wither away or turn their pain into rage.

The desperation that can arise from days and days of emotional neglect is evident in the recent story of an adolescent (Mose 1997). By age 15, she had such a severe depression she began self-mutilation. That means she would inflict injuries on herself, usually cutting herself with razor blades or knives because "I just felt better . . . my life didn't feel so vague." What would cause young people to deliberately cut themselves just to see themselves bleed? You'd probably guess it was a major trauma. Wrong! **Inability to express feelings** is the root cause . . . and it can just be about small matters that build up. For example:

> "I felt so alone growing up. My mom and dad weren't bad people. It's just that no one in my family ever talked to one another. We were just supposed to be happy and pretend that everything was all right." (Mose 1997)

Although the phenomenon of self-mutilation is still fairly obscure, it was common enough in the detention center where I worked. There, I would ask the juveniles to roll up their sleeves and pant legs. There I would see the signs: pin scratches, self-inflicted burn marks, severe scars or still-healing deep cuts. More and more teenagers in my practice are presenting with these symptoms. Even celebrities like the late Princess Diana and Johnny Depp have been linked to this disorder. The self-hurt is usually cutting, but it can be biting fingertips until they bleed, burning the skin with cigarettes, or even breaking a bone. Always, the young people describe it as a **release** . . . "like opening a valve inside and releasing my frustration."

"Ruminating is one of the chief delights of the soul."

— Thomas Moore

Marlene, Age 15

> "If a child is to keep alive his inborn sense of wonder, he needs the companionship of at least one adult who can share it, rediscovering with him the joy, excitement and mystery of the world we live in."
>
> — Rachel Carson

Dennis, Age 12

It is time to move forward. It is time to heal ourselves and in that way heal the pain of our children. Whether you are a parent or a caregiver in some other capacity, you have tremendous power. Time and again, the research shows us **that the most mentally healthy children have at least one caregiver with whom they can bond.** If you are reading this book, THAT CAN BE YOU!

A COUPLE OF CAUTIONS

It is confusing, but I have to admit "THE EXPERTS" do not always agree. On the shelves of my office are at least a dozen parenting books by leading authorities. Their approaches range from logical consequences (such as, if your children are not ready for school on time, they simply go to school in their pajamas) to strict disciplinarianism (for example, spanking is a useful and appropriate discipline technique for a child who cannot be ready on time).

Compounding the issue is **temperament.** Just a sampling of available book titles refers to children who are "difficult," "strong-willed," "spirited," "angry," "defiant," "uncommon," "inattentive," "impossible," or "challenging." (I think these words could just as aptly apply to many adults!) Temperament will be discussed in more detail later, but the important thing to understand at this point is that children are not "blank slates" totally dependent on what happens to them. Far from it, their innate dispositions often affect how parents and others react to them.

Moreover, some children have a more difficult time of it than others just because of external circumstances. Some children grow up in homes where there is alcoholism, mental illness or physical impairment of a family member. Abuse can take many forms, from outright physical damaging of the body to more subtle neglect and rejection.

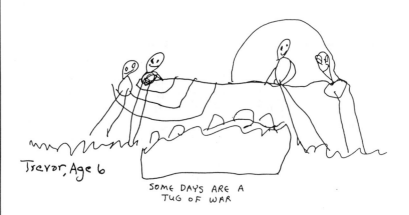

Trevor, Age 6

SOME DAYS ARE A
TUG OF WAR

LET'S GET ON WITH IT

Given that children and their caregivers each have their own temperaments and personalities, stresses and problems, needs and desires, how can we make the journey as pleasant — EVEN FUN — as possible? For I do believe childhood is a journey, and we must try to enjoy the trip without rushing our children to become "all grown up."

Along the way, we will travel peaks and valleys, and we will encounter bumps, potholes and even detours. Regardless, we have tremendous power to shape and mold children's experiences. It is a child's experiences and interactions with others, especially within the home, which lead to the sense of self — the perception of being successful and happy or the perception of being a loser in life.

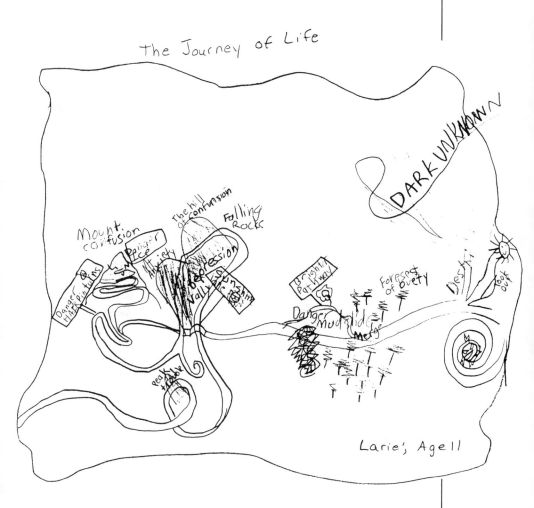

"All problems contain the seeds of opportunity,
and this awareness allows you to
take the moment
and transform it to a better situation or thing."

— Deepak Chopra

Steven, Age 7

Allison, Age 9

In the various settings in which I have worked, I have come to conclude that most well-intentioned caregivers are doing about 95% right. It's just that children are such experts at finding the 5% of glitches — the times when we are unsure and wavering, the times we are too stressed out with our own problems or the times we act in ways we regret later.

We each have a mental picture of ourselves, and that viewpoint in turn affects how we see the world and how we get along with others. To be successful in life, we must like ourselves. If we don't find ourselves acceptable, likeable, and trustworthy, who will?

Amelia, Age 7

Children who have a positive self-image are at their best. They have pride and respect in themselves and are accepted by others. They feel like **winners**.

A GUIDEBOOK

Rachel's story at the beginning of this chapter reminds me of numerous other stories where parents and other caregivers have sat in front of me lamenting that children did not come with "**An Instruction Manual**." These were people from all walks of life — from auto mechanics to heart surgeons. The idea does hold irony . . . if not merit. We would never want to trust our mode of transportation to an unskilled worker who was not trained in the complexities of transmissions, brake systems and electrical wiring. Nor would we trust our health to an unlicensed medical practitioner without experience in the complexities of the human body.

Yet most of us trust ourselves day in and day out with our most precious possessions — our children — with very little, if any, training. We shoot from the hip, gathering tips from more "experienced" friends and relatives. Sometimes we read magazines and newspaper articles, listen to talk shows or watch television shows giving advice.

"Be like a postage stamp.
Stick to one thing
until you get there."

to Mom

Callie, Age 7

— Margaret Carty

The focus of this book is on **WHAT WORKS**. Do not buy this book if you have good intentions but will just put it aside. Perhaps you already have other self-help books on parenting around the house. Maybe you bought one that looked promising or were given it as a gift by your mother-in-law. They are in your house somewhere collecting dust. Let's move beyond **GOOD INTENTIONS**. It's time to APPLY the ideas in this book.

Grab a pencil, and let's get going. Notice the pages are set up so there's room to take notes in the margins. Doodle, underline, make stars or circle things! That way, you'll remember better and use the information.

Have fun with this book and get smart at the same time. Be a kid. Open the pages at random and look at the quotations or drawings. The **children's art** speaks for itself with such power you may not even want to read the text at times. The children know what's going on in their lives. They will **tell** you . . . but not always in words. Listen with your heart. Remember your own childhood.

Look at the two completely different pictures below by two children going through completely different issues in their lives. Can't you just sense their emotions?

John, Age 12
"This is my step-mom. She is like a viper snake dripping poison."

Mary, Age 7

"Bunnies jump around in their moods. They jump happy to mad to crying to glad."

"But we still like them ♡"

Your purchasing/considering a book such as this one shows you are interested in doing young people right. To better use this book, please pay close attention to two special features. The *REAL LIFE* sections are composites of cases, mostly of children and their families whose lives have touched mine. More than likely, you'll recognize yourself or someone you know in these anecdotes. The *TIPS* sections are bonus ideas. They help you apply the concepts to everyday life. Much of the material here comes from years of making mistakes and learning what **NOT** to do!

> "Kids make their mark in life
> by doing what they **can** do,
> not what they can't. School
> is important, but life is **more**
> important. Being happy is
> using your skills productively,
> no matter what they are."
>
> — Howard Gardner, Ph.D.

Mark, Age 8

Sometimes you will read something that will border on the absurd because it is so obvious to you. You've known THAT for years, but maybe other parents have not. Other times, you'll read an idea or perspective that will touch you, and you will carry it around with you for days, thinking, processing, seeing it from all sides. Perhaps you will read something that just does not "feel right" to you, so drop it. Trust your instinct. There is no way we will agree on everything — life would be boring if we did.

REAL LIFE: I am delighted to tell you that Rachel's relationship with her father improved dramatically within just a few weeks. Dad was given several homework assignments: spend time with your daughter (a board game, a walk, a back massage, whatever) and do not fight with your partner in front of her (PERIOD, no matter what). We also decided he would look for other alternatives that would be interesting and fun. For example, since she had no friends there, is it possible that she could bring a friend over to spend the night? (When I had suggested this to Rachel, she had cringed, saying Ellen would never allow it.) Father said he would give it some thought. By the next session, Rachel came in beaming, sat on her father's knees and hugged him the entire time we talked. What a blessing!

Later that same session, Rachel and I spent some time alone talking about our feelings and how to speak up when we need to. We then took a sheet of paper, folded it in half lengthwise, and made two lists — one for things that made Rachel happy and one for things that made Rachel stressed.

Notice in the list below, how many positive things have to do with the change in the relationship between Rachel and her father. (Notice too that the divorce issue was still unresolved for Rachel. This would be the focus of future counseling.)

HAPPY

Might have friend
     spend night

Going to the movie

Dad going to make tacos

Dad going to make pizza.

Dad going to make banana
     pancakes.

Give my friends. E-mail on
     Dad's computer.

Played Clue

Played 13 Dead End Drive

Send E-mail to Daddy

No more nightmares

I love my mommy.

I love my daddy.

I love my family.

STRESSED

Pool boring because we
     go there every day.

Mom and Dad got divorced
     when I was a baby.

Ellen is so picky about
     us cleaning.

I wanted to play cards alone
     with Daddy.

Dad doesn't let me bring any
     clothes to mom's house.

I wish the divorce never
     happened.

JAMES, Age 8

"If we are brave enough to love, if we are strong
enough to forgive, if we are generous enough
to rejoice in another's happiness, and if we
are wise enough to know that there is
enough love to go around among us
all, then we can achieve a fulfillment
that no other living creature will
ever know."

— Rabbi Harold Kushner

Sally, Age 6

WHAT'S UP AHEAD

Think of yourself in a grocery store beginning your shopping. Right
now, your cart is empty, but as you go along, you see things you need
and pull them off the shelf to take home. It's time to fill your
"emotional shopping cart" with the ideas in this book. Here's what's "in
store" (oops — bad pun, but humor is important . . .).

As for the rest of Part I, the following chapter will explore what goes
wrong: RISK FACTORS . . . what things most contribute to a child
becoming a troubled adult? Happily, that is followed by a chapter on
what goes right: PROTECTIVE FACTORS . . . what things help a
child "beat the odds" to become a "winner" in life?

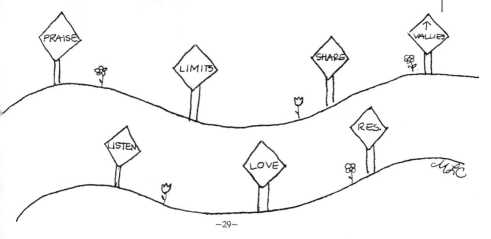

Once we learn what kids do and do not need, we as caregivers are ready to do something different. It's time for change. Part II of this book thus examines the SEVEN STEPS TO BUILD A CHILD'S INNER STRENGTH. Listed briefly, they are as follows:

1. **PRAISE** effort and accomplishment. ENCOURAGE more.
2. **LISTEN** with your heart. Hear "between the lines."
3. SET **LIMITS** to develop security and self-discipline.
4. SEND MESSAGES OF **LOVE** with smiles, hugs and notes.
5. SHARE **TIME** TOGETHER as part of the daily routine.
6. DEVELOP **RESPONSIBILITY** through chores and special jobs.
7. INSTILL **HIGHER VALUES** of compassion and optimism.

Part III extends Hope and Resources. I think of Hope as an optimistic belief in the future. Let's not forget that "the world offers us myriad healing turning points" (Butler 1997). That healing process and rising above adversity make up RESILIENCE!

To Charlene: Thank you for all the hope you have put in my life.

For years, investigators have studied maladjusted individuals and asked "what went wrong?" Friedman (1992) makes an analogy to physicians who consistently publish research on questions such as "Why did Ms. X become ill, and how can she be treated?" while "little is asked about why Ms. Y remained healthy."

In the mental health arena, only recently have we come to the point of looking at well-adjusted individuals and asking "what went right?" American Psychological Association President, Martin Seligman, Ph.D. believes that we are seeing a fundamental change away from **what damages people** toward trying to understand **what makes them strong.**

When a child who has the strongest possible predictors for future failure turns out fine, we need to ask "What can we learn from this? Why was this child resilient? What made this child rise above it?"

"The great thing in this world is not so
much where we are,
but in what direction we are moving."
— Oliver Wendell Holmes

Jennifer, Age 14

OVERVIEW ~ Risk Factors:
THOSE OLD HUFFS & PUFFS

WHAT'S THE SECRET?

NATURE vs. NURTURE

RISK FACTORS

1. Parental Absence
2. Poverty/Unemployment
3. Alcohol or Drug Abuse
4. Violence
5. Overcrowding
6. Instability
7. Trauma

SO WHAT DOES IT MEAN?

FINAL NOTE

Secrets of the
Third Little Pig

Risk Factors:
THOSE OLD
HUFFS & PUFFS

> "The world breaks everyone.
> Afterward some are stronger in the broken places."
>
> — Ernest Hemingway, *A Farewell to Arms*

Amber, Age 8

REAL LIFE: *Steven had said only two words to me so far, but they spoke volumes: "Stupid shrink." I watched my new 10-year-old client cruise around my room like a teen cruising the streets on a Saturday night looking for trouble. He would pick up various items in the room, look them over snidely and make an insulting comment. Within a few minutes, he had broken my talking troll, splattered water from the fountain onto nearby puppets and dropped the bucket of building blocks all over the floor.*

This was one tough young man. Each time he had an "accident," he'd look right at me and say "Sorry," with about as much sincerity as a rock. No doubt he was taking me on — challenging me. I knew what he'd been through. I'd read the reports, talked to his teacher, interviewed his dad. Steven had a childhood full of fear, anguish and isolation. He had become a survivor through the use of his "weapons" — angry words, a defiant attitude, destructive behaviors. By trying to protect himself, he had learned to hurt others.

My job now was to help him heal himself, to learn from his painful memories rather than relive them, hurting himself and others. He had to rise above his negative history and put his energy into living a happy life from here on. We had to shift his attention from the suffering of the past to the possibility of a stable, even positive, future.

Surprisingly, Stephen's brother had lived through the same pain and suffering but had emerged with a much different adjustment and outlook. Only two years older, Simon had taken the initiative to overcome rather than become a victim. He was a strong achiever in school. He had several active hobbies. When frustrated, he'd look for alternatives rather than explode. His "weapons" were charm and perseverance. He was resilient!

WHAT'S THE SECRET?

Why is it some children bounce back and some succumb? The story above portrays a topic that has intrigued me since my own childhood: RESILIENCE. Rubin (1996) asks "What makes it possible for some people to recover each time they fall, while others lie prostrate on the ground?" It is a question that haunts those of us who have risen above or escaped our painful pasts, yet we know others have not.

There are numerous examples from both public and private life where children have beaten the odds. John Edgar Wideman (1984) in his book *Brothers and Keepers* wrestles with this very issue. Why did he turn out to be a WINNER (a successful English professor and writer) while his brother is a LOSER (a convict

Lauren, Age 7

serving a life sentence for murder)? Or consider a poor, minority girl raped by a cousin at age 9, pregnant as a teenager, smoking cocaine in her twenties. Typically, you would expect her to become a prostitute, drug abuser or welfare mother. Why then did she become one of the most respected female role models of our time? . . . Oprah Winfrey.

REAL LIFE: Lillian Rubin, in her book The Transcendent Child, *describes her upbringing in a family confronted with overwhelming poverty, depression and death. Her mother's nearly psychotic rage determined daily life.*

*Rubin poignantly reveals, "I have lived with both the guilt and the wonder of being the transcendent child, the one who overcame the deficits of that past when my brother could not. **Why me and not him?** I asked myself a thousand times as I watched his painful — and often failed — struggle to manage his life successfully. . . . Then not long ago, he was killed in an automobile accident that looked more like suicide . . . . Why did he get stuck in our frightful past? How did I escape?"*

Alexis, Age 9   Alexandria, Age 11

SIBLINGS

The difference in self-concept is fairly evident in these two pictures by sisters only two years apart in age.

NATURE vs. NURTURE

For years, scientists and philosophers have debated the age-old question of which is more important: genetics or environment? New studies are weighing the effects of each more closely. Unfortunately, their conclusions sometimes clash.

On the one hand, researchers such as Dr. Thomas Lykken (1994), professor of psychology at the University of Minnesota, conclude that "There are genetic factors that influence most behavior . . . for most psychological traits, such as interests, talents and social attitude, being raised in the same family does not matter." In support of this view are the extraordinary case studies of identical twins separated in early infancy.

REAL LIFE: The "Jim Twins" who appeared on Johnny Carson in 1979 showed us mind-boggling similarities. Given the same first name by their biological parents, they were separated at four weeks, raised in separate adoptive homes, and reunited at age 39. One would expect the basic biology to match, and it did — health, weight, height and eye color.

But now, get this! Each had a former wife named Linda and a second wife named Betty. Each had worked as a deputy sheriff, owned a dog named Toy, chain-smoked Salems® and drank Miller Lite®. Each had the hobby of wood-working and had even built a circular wooden bench around a backyard tree and painted it white! (Efran 1998).

Alternatively, other researchers focus on the importance of environment and highlight the tremendous impact parents have on children. Dr. Patricia Cohen (1994), an epidemiologist at Columbia University, used extensive techniques in long-term research and found children who were routinely punished (spankings, threats, isolation, power techniques) were much more likely to exhibit disruptive behavior as adults (lying, stealing, yelling, hitting). Butler's (1997) retrospective research about "adults leading damaged lives" shows consistent themes of violence, alcoholism, divorce and incest in their childhood homes.

"Parents who are loving, attentive, supportive, firm and consistent with their children usually get the best results, but not all children are born with the same basic material. Genetics plays a big part in how children respond to the world around them. Let's face it, our world today is confusing, complicated and filled with dangerous choices."

— Ann Landers

Mary, Age 7

A recent White House conference on early childhood development focused on brain research. No doubt about it: the environment affects the brain and the child's future. Even during pregnancy, the brain is affected by outside factors — nourishment, stimulation, smoking, alcohol. Brain cells and neurons develop, and after the child's birth, they make connections with each other called synapses.

my blanket is warm.
mommy smiles.
MILK IS GOOD.
I like Books.
Red is pretty.

Age 2

I have lots of friends.
I am a good artist.
School is fun.

Maria

Age 7

Noted pediatrician, Dr. T. Berry Brazelton (1997) reports that "the first three years of life are when the vast majority of the connections are produced." A baby responds to environmental cues — a parent's smile, the sense of touch, warm milk, bright colors, exciting conversation, interesting toys and books. This is how the brain connections are supported. A child's "potential future wiring for intelligence, sense of self, trust and motivation for learning are laid down." After the first few years, a kind of "pruning" occurs and "unnecessary wiring" is eliminated.

REAL LIFE: How important the environment is becomes clear in studies of children who were put in institutions. Their basic biological needs were met. They had food, clothing and shelter. What they did not have was social, mental and physical stimulation around them. The effect? An estimated **drop of 5 to 10 points in the child's IQ for each year of institutionalization!** *(Bloom, 1964).*

RISK FACTORS

Child development researchers for the last several decades have investigated risk factors that help predict which children may end up in trouble. Children "at risk" can turn into high-school dropouts, juvenile delinquents, criminals, drug and alcohol abusers and chronic mental health consumers.

Looking at the patterns of these unhappy individuals, a number of risk factors have emerged:

1. Parental Absence

Children and adolescents are left unsupervised for long periods. Often one parent (usually the father) is not in the picture at all. Sadly, this phenomenon is especially evident in children of divorce. Or think about this: one-third of the babies born in the United States are born to unwed mothers! These children are usually starting out with a parent absent. Even worse, but thankfully far less prevalent, are those cases "in which happily adopted children were ripped from their parents' arms and delivered to some stranger" — the biological father who re-entered the picture (Parker 1999).

Mickey (5½) I'm playing on the playground.
Dad is small because he's far away.

Note that not only is father small and removed, but Mickey himself lacks arms. This may suggest feelings of inadequacy or fear of reaching out to others.

REAL LIFE: Absence does not have to be physical. Sometimes, children have the physical presence of their caretakers, but they are not there emotionally or psychologically. Sandy, age 14, is one such example. The product of a divorced family, Sandy lived with her father. Although he worked long hours, he was usually at home with her in the evenings and on weekends. She saw her mother in the same city about once or twice a month.

When Sandy came down with a severe bladder infection, neither parent was "available" to get her medical help. Her father was "too busy" with work to take off for a doctor's appointment. Likewise, her mother heard her pleas on the telephone, with Sandy crying how much it hurt, but she also was preoccupied with her own affairs. Sandy ended up beeping her psychotherapist every half-hour one day crying in pain, until the therapist herself took Sandy to a health clinic.

2. Poverty/Unemployment

When money is scarce, there is little hope to escape to a better lifestyle, and there is often fighting in the home about how to spend what few funds are available. One in five American children now live in poverty (Shapiro 1996). Both the children and adults tend to have low self-esteem, and almost everyone in the home is affected by the frustration of "empty pockets."

"All the things I want to get someday."
Joan, Age 18

Even relatively stable families can experience unemployment. Joblessness and underemployment have impacted millions of Americans as companies downsized to become more efficient. Desperation and anger go along with the changed lifestyle of scrimping and dipping into savings accounts to survive.

REAL LIFE: Years ago, I had agreed to work with Annie without charge. It was my investment in the future of her children. At age 19, Annie had two small sons, no job, no husband, no future. She did have a boyfriend sharing her apartment and helping with some expenses. Otherwise, she was a typical welfare mother with Medicaid and food stamps.

Annie told me constantly of the conflicts about how to spend what little money there was: the kids always needed new shoes, and the family could not afford their electricity bill if they used the air conditioner (which is miserable in a Florida summer!). My goals in therapy were fairly basic. I wanted to improve Annie's parenting skills and have her take the GED exam (to obtain a high-school equivalency diploma) so she could find a reasonable job.

The most fascinating part of Annie's story is how she unwittingly kept herself in poverty. During our work, she received a settlement from a previous car accident. She was given $8,000 cash. She was ecstatic, seeing all the things she wanted available to her now! Despite my strict cautions and attempts to help her budget, she spent the money immediately. At our next session, Annie was beaming. She showed me her new gold chains and watch. She talked about the new top-of-the-line computer and video game set-up for the boys!

Now, here is the reality. Two weeks later, she was in my office crying over her finances. She and her boyfriend had a huge fight the night before. There was only one can of ravioli in the cupboard. She wanted to give it to the boys. Her boyfriend insisted he wanted it because he was starving from working construction all day. Despite her windfall, Annie was back battling the primary need of hunger, in spite of all the "stuff" she now owned.

3. Alcohol or Drug Abuse

Adults in the home use alcohol or drugs excessively. Often it is a pattern repeated generation to generation. Some therapists believe the behavior is an attempt to "self-medicate" for feelings of depression. People who abuse drugs are much more likely to commit crimes and take from, rather than give to, a community's economy.

"I hardly get to see my dad and when I do, he drinks a lot of beer and goes to sleep."

Courtney, Age 11

Let's not deceive ourselves into thinking that drug and alcohol abuse is only in the lower socioeconomic-status families. I have had numerous cases where high-functioning, professional individuals were completely addicted to drugs, alcohol or both.

Alcoholism is one of America's most serious health problems. Its complications kill more than double the number of people who die of AIDS (100,000 annually). Fourteen million Americans abuse alcohol, and forty million more may be at risk of becoming problem drinkers. Alcohol is involved in forty to fifty percent of traffic deaths. It costs our country about **$99 billion** each year (Ferraro 1999). Sadly, research shows that alcohol abuse actually changes the structure of the brain, programming drinkers to return to it again and again

"Children of alcoholics are four times as likely as other children to become alcoholics."

~Dr. Robert Millman
N.Y. Cornell Medical Center

Many factors increase the risk of a child beginning drug use. In addition to exposure at home and genetic predisposition, peer pressure is critical. It is often hard to tell if the group itself leads a child to drugs or whether a child's drug use influences which group is joined. Studies do show clearly that if children smoked tobacco or drank alcohol, they were more than 50 times more likely to use marijuana and much more likely to use cocaine (Douma 1998b).

REAL LIFE: Mrs. V. and her husband were both respected and competent professionals. Because of repeated medical infections and operations, Mrs. V. was often on pain killers. Over time, even when she had no physical pain, she relied on the pain killers to "numb" her senses to

the everyday stressors of doing her job, running her own business and raising her children. The children themselves, however, would comment to me how they never knew what to expect from mom. Her moods undoubtedly depended on the level of medication in her system at the time. Ultimately, she went to an expensive drug rehabilitation center out-of-state to overcome the habit.

4. Violence

In the neighborhood, at school and with all types of media, children are exposed to disruptive, inappropriate and aggressive behavior. For example, you may go to a G-rated movie, but at the theater, you'll walk right past a video game where the advertising graphics display a man stabbed, his arms ripped from his torso, then his head sliced off, while blood spurts freely everywhere.

Most horrifying is a recent report about deaths from injuries to children less than one-year-old (Douma, 1999). You might not be overly surprised to see five of the top six causes of accidental death, in order of frequency: suffocation, motor vehicle accidents, choking (food or objects), fire and drowning. Now prepare yourself. **The most common cause of death to babies in America is homicide!** That level of violence in America ought to leave you speechless.

Compounding the issue of violence is how commonplace it has become to **pair sex and violence** in the media. Former FBI agent, Gregg McCrary (1999) points out that at a time when individuals are highly impressionable — adolescence — they are targeted for R-rated movies which bombard them with **intentional** pairing of sex and violence. What do you think that could lead to in the future?

touch me and die!

"A bad mood."

Ned, Age 10

REAL LIFE: Sadly, aggression is often portrayed as a reasonable way to solve problems. This dark reality was brought home by a new 5-year-old youngster in my office. Mark had just turned 5 — only a month ago, he would have been 4. After talking with him awhile, I asked a standard first-time question: If you could wish for anything, what would you wish for? For a 5-year-old, what would you typically expect? Usually, it's something concrete and monetary, such as a new toy advertised recently, a new big car, a million dollars or a hundred more wishes.

In this case, Mark looked straight at me and said "a gun." After a moment's pause, he added, "but it would have to be a __real__ gun." I replied simply, "Oh?" (This is an old therapist's trick of leaving it "open-ended." It also works when we are dumbfounded and do not know what else to say.)

Mark immediately brightened up. "Oh yes, it would have to be a real gun with __real__ bullets." I took a deep breath and answered, "Well, if you did have a real gun with real bullets, what would you do with it?" His reply: "I'd kill people, but only the people I didn't like." So this just-turned-5-year-old boy was deciding which people deserved to die. What a horrifying way to eliminate problems!

5. Overcrowding

Too many people live in too small an area. Private space and time are lacking. People get on each other's nerves. (Note that this risk factor is based on research in our Western culture. In other societies, such as Asian cultures, many generations living together in one home is a common and accepted way of life.)

"My apartment building and all the people that live there."
Jean, Age 5

REAL LIFE: Even children in roomy, comfortable homes can feel the crunch of phenomenal overcrowding at school. A survey of schools in central Florida, for example, found that in the 1997-98 school year, 77% (more than three-fourths!) of the schools "have more students than their buildings can hold" (Wertheimer 1997).

One middle school had more than 1,200 students on a campus that is supposed to have only 500. Another elementary school crammed 426 children into a campus built for 208. The result? Of course, there is the overflow of portables onto parking lots and athletic fields, and lunchrooms are so crowded, some students eat lunch an hour after they arrive so everyone can be fit into the schedule.

More importantly, the mass of human bodies leads to irritability and the opposite of feeling ready to learn. Teachers complain that they cannot walk between the tables and desks, and students complain they are jostled and have to "push through" everyone in the hallways. Now imagine yourself with a large brood of extra company (relatives perhaps?) overstaying their welcome at your house. Too many people everywhere . . . getting in the way . . . getting on your nerves!

6. Instability

Caregivers can be burnt out or depressed. When they are unstable in their moods, they switch rapidly from nurturing to rejecting. Some have chronic marital tension. Divorces and remarriages — or perhaps a series of live-in partners — all take their toll on children. When families move often, children have to keep changing schools. What's more, there is a lack of connection to extended family members like grandparents, aunts, uncles and cousins.

REAL LIFE: Betty drew the following picture on her own when she first started therapy. She brought it in to help me understand the "major players" in her young life. Unfortunately, she dropped out of therapy shortly thereafter.

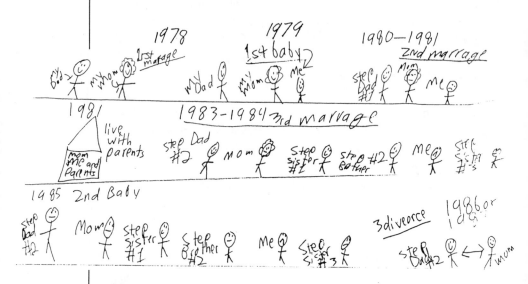

Notice in particular her own frowning expression at the key points of her mother's remarriages and the birth of her half-brother.

Several years later, I received a letter from Betty. She appeared to be repeating the pattern of instability into the next generation. At age 16, she had gotten pregnant, married the father and dropped out of school. Betty, her husband and infant moved in with her mother.

When Betty reached out to me after those years, I offered her free sessions because her finances were so tight. Although she scheduled several appointments, she never showed up. I can only conclude that she is stuck, and I wonder about this new baby . . . and what drawing he might make a decade down the road to describe his life.

7. Trauma

Life-altering traumas shake the very underpinnings of people's lives. These major devastations include death of a loved one, loss of home from disaster, and serious illnesses such as cancer. Sills (1997) describes such trauma as "a turmoil that you must continue to move through despite the fact that you see no beckoning light."

Prenatal and birth trauma fit in here, too. The sources seem endless. Problems can happen before birth (infection, illness, bleeding, toxemia, drugs), during birth (prematurity, lack of oxygen to the brain, forceps delivery) or right after birth (high fever, respiratory distress, accident, meningitis).

Abuse is a trauma that leaves emotional, if not physical, scars. Abuse can be physical (beatings, burnings), emotional (constant humiliation) or even neglect (not providing for basic needs). Sexual abuse can range from molestation by a babysitter to rape or incest.

REAL LIFE: John DeFrain (Blum 1998) and his colleagues utilized interviews with adults from traumatic family situations to study horrific examples of childhood abuse. One description from their study follows:

"One time I remember sitting at the dinner table when I was six or seven. My sister was told to say grace and when she finished, my dad slapped her across the face. He told her she said it wrong and to do it over. She started again and he slapped her again. This went on and on, over and over, faster and faster, for what seemed like half an hour. I remember sitting there across from her, paralyzed. I just kept praying, 'Get it right.' The problem was, she was doing it right, just the way we learned it in Sunday School."

"Rather than wondering about or questioning the direction your life has taken, accept the fact that there is a path before you now. Shake off the **why's** and **what if's**, and rid yourself of confusion. Whatever was ~ is in the past. Whatever is ~ is what's important."

— Vicki Silvers

Emily, Age 6

SO, WHAT DOES IT MEAN?

Even in different cultures and environments, similar risk factors have been found. For example, Werner & Smith (1992) concluded a forty-year study on the Hawaiian island of Kauai. They identified as high-risk those children who had been exposed before age 2 to at least four of the following:

- ♦ Mothers with low educational level
- ♦ Prenatal health problems/congenital handicaps
- ♦ Family alcoholism
- ♦ Family violence or instability
- ♦ Family discord or mental illness
- ♦ Poverty

Most recently, Doll & Lynn (1998) carefully reviewed previous studies and identified "Risk Conditions" and "Subsequent Outcomes." Their results are summarized in this chart:

Risks	Expected Outcomes
Poverty	Crime and delinquency
Low parent education	Lower IQ
Ineffective parenting	Teenage parenthood
Child maltreatment	Mental health problems
Poor health (child or parent)	Physical & medical problems
Parent mental illness/instability	Unemployment
Large family size	Less social competence

Be careful. One risk factor alone does not automatically doom a child to a life of misfortune. Rutter (1979) found that children with one factor developed about the same as other children without any risk factors.

Even so, risk factors compound themselves. Children who have a majority (4 or more of the risk factors) are **10 times more likely to be severely emotionally disturbed!** Maston (1998) points out that risks rarely come in single packages. She refers to "multiple adversities extending over time." Divorce is a good example. There are many changes and layers of change before, during and after a divorce. Or, think of the multiple risks for the many children and adolescents who spend their nights in homeless shelters. We as a society should be alarmed!

Can middle-class parents turn a blind eye and discount these risk factors because "it's mostly poor kids"? Can we defer it to social workers and other officials to set up community programs? It would not appear so. Look at the issue of **parental absence**. Parental absence is pervasive. In our country, **more than one-half** of all children will live in a single-parent family at some time while growing up. (Trafford 1992). Even more shocking, births to single women is skyrocketing. Births to unmarried women increased from 5% in 1960 to 34% in 1995 (Deisler 1997).

"The problem with people in this world is not what they don't know . . . it's what they **do** know that simply isn't true."

— Forrest Gump

Trevor,
Age 6

visiting

Mom's house

Dad's house

Every one has changes happen to them. Matthew's family has changed. Now his father does not live with his mother any more. They have decided to get <u>divorced</u>.

It is not Matthew's fault. He wishes his parents will get together again, but this is just a wish. It is not going to happen. Matthew will get used to visiting his dad in his house.

Page from a "Homemade Counseling Book" I made with Matthew, age six. Notice the focus here is on two issues:
① The divorce is inevitable;   ② It is not the child's fault.

Even in two-parent families, the adults are often overworked and exhausted leaving little time and energy for their children. (No kidding!) We would like our homes to be a place of solace after the toil of the day. Sadly, it sometimes becomes a battleground of frayed nerves and hurtful words.

"Mommy and Daddy are the grown-up dogs and we're the puppies. Everybody is always barking at everyone."

Roger, age 9, was asked to draw a picture of his family as **animals**. It is intriguing to note that in this drawing, no one has **ears**! All that "barking," but nobody can hear.

In suburban neighborhoods, children themselves report lack of parental attention and control — they are raising themselves! — at about the same rate as children in violent neighborhoods.

Kevin, Age 8

And as far as violence as a risk factor, recall that children do not have to experience direct aggression. It can be vicarious. Children are exposed to violence daily through television, movies and video games. Remember, too, that the pairing of sex and violence in the media leads to a paring of sex and violence in the impressionable mind.

This drawing was done when Andy
was asked to draw a picture of his family "doing something together."
Notice Andy's description of the TV show they are watching!

Wouldn't it be wonderful if we could inoculate children against
adversity the same way we vaccinate them against various physical
ailments? A simple vaccine, and they'd be protected from the effects of
childhood emotional traumas. While this analogy is obviously
ludicrous, the good news is that researchers are finding "antidotes" to
the risk factors.

FINAL NOTE

Review again the seven risk factors. How many are evident in your
own childhood? In your current family? With children you know or
care about?

1. **Parental Absence** ~ Children are alone and unsupervised for
    long periods.
2. **Poverty/Unemployment** ~ Empty pockets lead to low self-
    esteem and frustration.
3. **Alcohol or Drug Abuse** ~ This pattern is often repeated
    generation to generation.

4. **Violence** ~ Children are exposed to disruptive, inappropriate and aggressive behavior in the neighborhood, at school and in the media.

5. **Overcrowding** ~ Frustrations arise from too many people living in too small an area

6. **Instability** ~ Caregivers switch unpredictably from nurturing to rejecting; divorces and remarriages are common; relocation and school changes take their toll.

7. **Trauma** ~ Turmoil — disasters, illness, loss, abuse — can leave emotional, if not physical, scars.

"I have discovered
the meaning of life.
It resides in the
books I love and
the animals that
surround me;
in present friends
and in memories
of lovers and enemies,
too; in silk, champagne,
an applewood fire,
and Mozart.
It resides in what
I can wrest from
each day that I live."

— Nancy Thayer

Sammy, Age 8

OVERVIEW ~ Resilience:
THE BRICK HOUSE

PROTECTIVE FACTORS

INTERNAL PROTECTIVE FACTORS
Personal Characteristics

1. Temperament
2. Intelligence
3. Reading Skills
4. Positive Outlook
5. Talent
6. Gender
7. Age of Siblings

EXTERNAL PROTECTIVE FACTORS
Interaction with Others

1. Bonding
2. Impulse Control
3. Responsibility
4. Goodness
5. Sense of Humor
6. Locus of Control
7. Faith

FINAL NOTE

Secrets of the
Third Little Pig

Resilience:
THE
BRICK
HOUSE

"I like living, I have sometimes been wildly,
despairingly, acutely miserable,
racked with sorrow,
but through it all I still know quite certainly
that just to be alive is a grand thing."

— Agatha Christie

REAL LIFE: *In the early 1980s, I worked at an exceptional education center for children with severe learning handicaps and behavior disorders. There I met Benjamin. He was a student with a harsh history of abuse and neglect. His mother, only in her late 20s, already had 6 children. Plus, there was an infant in the home because one of Benjamin's teenage sisters had an unwed pregnancy. You can imagine the chaos.*

This family often subsisted on canned pasta or cold cereal. When money was tight, it would go for beer and cigarettes before food. In his younger years, Benjamin had sometimes been locked in a closet rather than having a babysitter. There was also a series of "uncles" who came and went. These live-in boyfriends of Mom's were often cruel, especially when drunk. Benjamin's cigarette-burn scars proved that.

At the age of 6, Benjamin had been removed from his home by HRS. He was evaluated and found to have an IQ (Intelligence Quotient) of 69. This score fell within the range called Educably Mentally Handicapped—or to the layman, Benjamin was **mentally retarded.** *His intelligence level was measured in the lowest 2% of the population. Typically, you would expect very little to become of his life. He would probably be another hopeless victim, repeating the pattern of destitution and dependency.*

Happily, fortune intervened. Benjamin was placed in a loving home with his grandmother, his aunt and her son (Benjamin's cousin). They provided not only affection and support but much stimulation. Although there was little money (they also lived on welfare), they took Benjamin to the library, read to him, played games and practiced homework skills. He also worked with a specially trained teacher in a small classroom.

"The game of life is not so much in holding a good hand as playing a poor hand well."

— H.T. Leslie

CALVIN, Age 8

At age 9, Benjamin was required by state law to be re-evaluated. When I tested his IQ, this time it had jumped to 85! This is considered Low Average. Now his intelligence level was above about ¼ of the population, instead of in the lowest 2% — at the retardation level!

Special education teachers and Benjamin's new family continued to work with and encourage him. When he was next evaluated at age 12, Benjamin's IQ was tested as 100! This is exactly in the middle of the Average range. He placed above ½ the population and below ½ the population. He was "NORMAL!" Opportunities for his life as an adult were multiplied. Here again, a blessing!

Dramatic jumps in test scores such as this are rare. But this case beautifully illustrates the power of intervention. What if Benjamin had stayed in his early environment? Would he still be "retarded" today? Would he be depending on taxpayers' dollars to just survive each day?

Benjamin, Age 9
Re-evaluation

Notice the bellybutton emphasized in Benjamin's drawing.
This is an unusual feature which may be a
"red flag" of possible sexual abuse prior to HRS intervention.
Also notice the developmental delay. This drawing is more reflective
of a much younger child.

In the last chapter, we explored the risk factors within the developing
child leading to a wounded adult. These are the warning signs that
predict a poor outcome in life.

Now it's time to take a closer look at the other side of the story. Let's
embrace the sunny, spirited flowers that somehow thrive in the cracks
of the sidewalk. What strengths do they have? What wisdom can they
share? The lessons here are all about RESILIENCE.

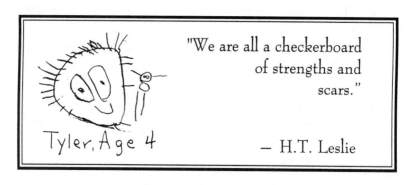

"We are all a checkerboard
of strengths and
scars."

Tyler, Age 4

— H.T. Leslie

Resilience does not simply mean self-reliance. It is much more than being stoic or determined. It is rising above adversity! It means finding the "flip side" of anguish to develop self-healing and self-respect. Be careful, though. Being resilient does not mean being invincible, invulnerable or emerging unscathed. Many resilient survivors hate their childhood, and some have residual effects of trauma — nightmares, trouble concentrating, depression or anxiety.

Even so, most people who survive major traumas, including war, abuse and personal misfortunes, believe the experience **strengthened them in the long run!** Certainly, no one would be expected to **choose** these experiences. Yet, in a recent study, 80 to 90% of the participants felt that they "coped more effectively" with new problems as a result. Many even claimed "increased confidence and self-esteem." The researchers concluded that people have "enormous ability to derive strength from past difficulty and loss" (Aldwin, et al. 1996). Moreover, those who overcome adversity believe they are kinder, quicker to help others, and often try to make the world a better place (Blum 1998).

"Resiliency is an interactive and systematic phenomenon, the product of a complex relationship of inner strengths and outer help throughout a person's life span . . . not only an individual matter. It is the outward and visible sign of a web of relationships and experiences that teach people mastery, doggedness, love, moral courage and hope."

— Katy Butler

PROTECTIVE FACTORS

So then, what is this "magic" that allows some children to translate and transform feelings of frustration, isolation, anger and fear into wisdom and passion for life? Such children have not only learned to survive — **THEY THRIVE!**

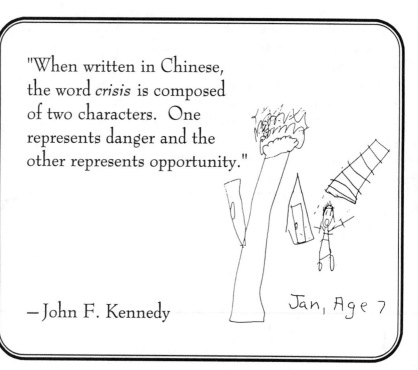

"When written in Chinese, the word *crisis* is composed of two characters. One represents danger and the other represents opportunity."

— John F. Kennedy

Jan, Age 7

After reviewing the work of various researchers and authors, I have chosen to break down protective factors into two groups. The **INTERNAL** factors generally refer to resilient children's unique make-up. **EXTERNAL** factors focus on the ways resilient children interact with their world. Learning how these children thrive will lead us to the **7 Steps to Build a Child's Inner Strength.**

INTERNAL FACTORS: Personal Characteristics

1. Temperament

This term refers to a child's characteristic style of approaching and reacting to people and situations. Longitudinal studies which have followed children from infancy to adulthood conclude that **temperament appears to be largely inborn or innate.** Researchers have even identified molecular sequences on human DNA that may correlate with fretfulness, anxiety, shyness, autism, impulsivity and aggression (Efran 1998 et al). By the year 2005, the federal Human Genome Project is expected to fully identify the 100,000 piece genetic "deck" from which our biological "hands" are dealt.

Some innate characteristics are positive, such as social leadership, striving for achievement and a cheerful disposition (Tellegran, et al. 1988). Others are much less pleasant, such as negative mood, distractibility and stubbornness (Tureki 1989).

Latest findings suggest that temperament is about 75% innate. In other words, **children come into this world "wired" a certain way.** Youngsters can be extroverted or shy, easygoing or demanding, calm or moody, active or passive. Many parents claim they could tell the difference among their children from birth. One child was fussy and wouldn't nurse while the other was pleasant and cooperative.

Sometimes mothers say they could tell a youngster was going to have a wild or mild disposition even in the womb. Many characteristics tend to run in families. Just as physical features can be inherited ("He has his daddy's nose") so can emotional qualities ("She has her daddy's temper").

Occasionally, I will emphasize the importance of temperament in a family by saying something like "Think of yourselves as two Cocker Spaniel parents trying to raise a Doberman puppy." Immediately the image is clear. We know even dogs have certain characteristic patterns of "personality."

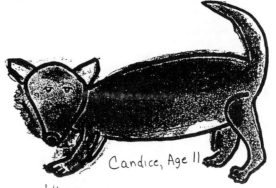

Candice, Age 11

personality is sweet, rambungtus, loveable, smart, stuborn

Response when asked to draw a **Pretend Portrait**.
"If you were an animal, what kind of animal would you be?" Candice
not only drew the animal, she described how its
personality matched hers. Notice the honesty in the descriptors!

Not surprising, the most resilient children tend to have more positive features in their temperament. As babies, they were described by their mothers as active, cuddly and good-natured; throughout childhood, they were more outgoing, engaging and likeable. Baseline happiness is "extraordinarily stable and primarily determined by heredity" (Efran 1998).

HINT 📖: For more details on **Pretend Portraits**,
see Step 1 - PRAISE.

2. Intelligence

The most resilient children tend to have average or above average IQ scores. This suggests they have common sense and practical judgment in everyday situations. Numerous studies reflect how severely a lack of early environmental stimulation impacts children; on the other hand, high IQs have been clearly linked with active environments in childhood (Dennis & Sayegh 1965; Dennis 1960; Engelmann and Engelmann 1966, Bloom 1964). Experts suggest children develop fifty percent of their intelligence by age four!

"The intelligence and organizing power inside you has overcome obstacles with effortless ease, despite all the struggle your conscious mind may think is necessary to keep life going."
— Deepak Chopra

Sam, Age 8

Resilient children have a more elusive intelligence as well — a sense of insight and intuition. As very young children, they learn to carefully observe and interpret others' behavior. They are able to identify patterns of behavior around them that predict trouble . . . and they learn to stay out of the way. As older children, they tend to label their families as "troubled" or different and to separate themselves mentally. They also learn where to find help and how to plan and set goals.

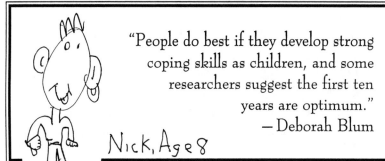

"People do best if they develop strong coping skills as children, and some researchers suggest the first ten years are optimum."
— Deborah Blum

Nick, Age 8

3. Reading Skills

Adequate reading ability is also a consistent theme with resilient children. Although they are not usually academically gifted, they do **read at least on grade level.** In fact, the ability to read on grade level by age ten is a startling predictor of whether or not poor children turn to juvenile crime. At least 70% of juvenile offenders were in need of remedial education by the fourth grade! (Blum 1998).

"No one ever told me I was loved. Ever, ever, ever. **Reading** and being able to be a **smart girl** was my only sense of value, and it was **the only time I felt loved.**"

— Oprah Winfrey

Resilient children are more inclined to use active tools for learning, such as games, puzzles, letters, tape recorders, atlases, maps and dictionaries as essential tools, rather than passively absorb TV. Cline (1980) claims reading improves when "the visual stimulation of television is absent." Without TV, the child is called upon to "simultaneously learn to exercise his imagination and depend more on language."

Julie, Age 10

Reading can be a source of solace as well. It can represent a roadway out of despair. This is especially true when a child identifies with characters in a book. One woman tells the story of how she kept the book *I Know Why the Caged Bird Sings* under her mattress where, as a child, she was repeatedly, routinely raped. This book, about Maya Angelou's abuse as a child, is credited with the woman's very survival (Johnson 1997).

"You have no idea what other people have gone through, and how a book connects with them. That's one thing I love about books."
— Oprah Winfrey

Suzie, Age 8

4. Positive Outlook

Resilient children avoid getting sucked into all the problems swirling around them. They look for the good in any situation. Psychologist Rebecca Sills, Ph.D. says, "Corney as it sounds, it eases pain to realize that you have gained from it . . . Payoff, however small, strengthens the spirit" (1998). People who bounce back are those who find the proverbial "silver lining" on the dark cloud. They look for a lesson to be learned or a gift to be offered others as a result of their adversity.

Projecting a positive future is important, too. Some children conjure up an image of themselves in the future, seeing a happy time and looking back on their suffering in the past tense. Resilient children seem to live by the mantra "This too shall pass." Although they may not use those exact words, they see the bigger picture and view adversity as temporary.

HINT 📖: For more about projecting a positive future, see Dr. Messenger's article "This Will Make A Great Story Some Day," in the section on Self-Discovery, page 369.

Jay, Age 6

"Definitely **act** happy. The way we act has a powerful effect on the way we feel."

— Dr. David G. Myers

REAL LIFE: I recall barricading myself in my bedroom to avoid my brother's madness. Although there were, of course, many tears, there was also a lot of positive thinking going on. I didn't kid myself "everything is wonderful," but I did imagine myself away from him, on my own and happy. I busied myself with various projects, usually drawing or crafts I kept in my room. Often I fantasized about ridiculous, but very upbeat themes . . . maybe I would marry one of the Beatles one day, who knows?

> *"If a family situation is insane, most people will build, within it, their own sanctuary and sanity. They learn the tricks of* **mental distance** *. . . They escape into music and books."*
> *—Deborah Blum*

Resilient people smile even when things are tough. The power of positive thinking has been reaffirmed in a recent study. Scientists found that the muscle movements necessary for a genuine smile actually "alter blood flow to the brain in ways that enhance a sense of well-being" (Hales 1997). While smiling does not make problems disappear, it does enhance pleasure.

5. Talent

Resilient children find a special hobby or skill. It can be anything: basketball, art, writing, dancing, karate. The point is this activity gives solace, develops a sense of mastery and helps them connect with nurturing, supportive adults.

As youngsters, resilient children often experiment with objects and mechanical things. They get involved in constructive projects or extra-curricular activities. As older children, they are typically industrious, looking for opportunities for paying or volunteer work. School achievement is usually good, sometimes above expectancy because of high motivation.

REAL LIFE: Basketball player Tyrone Weeks displayed an exceptional ability to rebound and block shots for his team, University of Massachusetts. His early life would hardly have predicted such success. He spent half his life separated from his mother as she repeatedly went in and out of drug treatment centers. Tyrone went to live with his basketball coach after his grandmother died. In addition to food and clothing, the coach encouraged his talent. Basketball gave Tyrone the self-confidence to carry himself through those dark days.

Paul, Age 7

"Hide not your talents.
They for use were made.
What's a sundial in the shade?"

— Ben Franklin

6. Gender

Believe it or not, girls tend to fare somewhat better in the resilience department than boys. This does not appear to be due to physical factors but rather to the way they are treated by others.

During infancy, there are very few physiological differences between male and female infants. Baby boys are slightly larger than baby girls, but there are no big differences on issues such as activity level, strength, sensitivity to touch, sitting up, teething and walking. Birns (1976) has concluded that physiological gender differences cannot be described clearly until age two.

The studies do, however, clearly show a difference in **the ways adults act toward infants based on gender.** Babies, even newborns, will be treated very differently depending on whether they are identified as male or female. For example, when the baby is labeled "male" (regardless of its true gender), strangers are likely to assume crying is due to anger. When the baby is labeled "female," strangers think crying is due to fear (Condry & Condry 1974).

Interestingly, adults are also more likely to encourage toddlers they believe are "boys" to become involved in active play, such as throwing a ball. Those same adults choose more passive play for "girls," such as talking, playing with a doll or giving a bottle (Frisch 1977).

Finally, research suggests mothers tend to show a wider range of emotion with baby daughters than baby sons. Thus, baby girls become better than boys in interpreting emotional expressions (Malatesta in Trottei 1983).

7. Age of Siblings

Both research and popular opinion have given credence to the effect of birth order. In general, we think of first-born or only children as independent and high achieving. The youngest child is often considered "the baby" and tends to be seen as easygoing and sociable. Middle children are often perceived as stuck or lost somewhere in between.

In fact, in the studies of resilient children, age of siblings was very important. The strongest children had a bit of space before the next baby came along. Werner (1992) found that in the group of resilient children she studied, many were the oldest in the family and none had a sibling born before they had turned 2 years old! Perhaps these several years gave the child a foundation of attachment compared to children who were "displaced" in the baby role while still infants themselves.

"Love yourself first and everything else falls into line."

— Lucille Ball

Amanda, Age 7

EXTERNAL FACTORS: Interaction with Others

1. Bonding

When we look closely at those children who were able to rise above their suffering, almost invariably there was **someone there** for them. The foremost element in transcending trouble is **not having to do it alone** (Blum 1998). If your parents believe in you, that is best of all. If not, there is someone else present — some kind of mentor or supportive surrogate — a neighbor, friend, teacher or other caregiver.

Resilient survivors actually **seek out** and "recruit" external nurturers. These children become adept at finding and enlisting the aid of adults such as teachers and coaches. Sometimes if parents are dysfunctional, children turn to extended family relatives such as a grandparent or an aunt or uncle.

Grandma, I'm So GLAD you always have time for me.

"There are the families we are born into, and there are the families we choose -- our circle of friends."

— Ronnie Polaneczky

Josh, Age 6

Sometimes the mentors are substitute families, such as the family of a girlfriend or boyfriend. Sometimes it is a low-paid worker for a group such as Four-H Club or YMCA. Often surrogate mentors are unpaid volunteers willing to give their time and care. Elkin (in Butler 1997) suggests such volunteer work benefits both the child and the volunteer who tends to become more involved and less depressed. Compared to matched control groups, children enrolled in Big Brothers and Big Sisters are:

- 52% LESS LIKELY TO SKIP SCHOOL
- 33% LESS LIKELY TO EXHIBIT VIOLENT BEHAVIOR
- 46% LESS LIKELY TO TRY DRUGS FOR THE 1st TIME

Franklin (in Butler 1997) studied resilient African-American men who grew up in poverty in rural Mississippi. He concluded that "each one of my men talks of somebody who stepped in at various points in their lives, took an interest in them and motivated them." Similarly, Werner and Smith (1992) found that at-risk children who drifted into juvenile delinquency tended to right themselves at the point some adult had taken an interest in them.

"My teacher. She gives big hugs."

Scott, Age 9

REAL LIFE: Here's a brief essay about a "hero" written by a sixth-grade student, letting us see the impact one adult can have at a critical time in a child's life. When the class assignment was to write about "a hero in your own life," Linda selected her third-grade teacher.

A True Hero

I think everyone liked Ms. Johansen. She was a very nice teacher especially because she had compassion for the kids. Especially me! That's why she's my hero. She even gave us a party every Friday if we earned it.

At this time, my parents were going through a divorce, and I had just moved. I didn't have many friends at school. Ms. Johansen helped me especially because she took me out for lunch in the middle of class while the other kids had a substitute. She and I talked about my parents' divorce while we ate at a sandwich shop. On a different day, she even took me out shopping. We got new clothes and my hair cut. It was like having an adult friend.

After third grade, I began to pay more attention to my appearance and my friends. Undoubtedly, Ms. Johansen still picks a favorite child of the year and becomes their friend. This special person was far more than a teacher. She was a hero.

What could have been a dark spiral downward was turned into a sad but liveable time by Ms. Johansen. This teacher goes out of her way to become a mentor, friend and special adult to emotionally needy children in her classes. Here's a lady who loves teaching . . . and is changing the world, one child at a time. (Way to go, Ms. Johansen!)

"We must never underestimate our own strength or importance. One person can make a difference, even when weakened by grief, despair and loneliness."

— Susan White-Bowden

Donnie, Age 12

"According to a 36-year study of 400 kindergartners beginning in 1951, **affection rather than strictness and discipline is the best guarantee of a child's healthy development.** Even stresses like divorce and alcoholism have less effect than tender loving care in predicting a satisfying life."

Carol Franz, Ph.D., Psychologist, Boston University

REAL LIFE: Examples of being "rescued" and given a "second chance" abound. Christopher Darden, for example, credits an African-American Studies teacher at his university with stopping his shoplifting and drift toward delinquency. Sheila Ballantyne, novelist, credits high-school music and literature teachers with rescuing her from her abyss with her alcoholic, con-artist father. Oprah Winfrey credits a stepmother with whom she went to live at age eleven as encouraging her career. Tyrone Weeks had his coach, Linda had her teacher.

I'm drowning almost, but grandma is coming to save me.

Vicki, Age 10

Having said all that about the importance of surrogate bonding, here's a word of caution. McCrary (1999) warns that there is sometimes a fine line between selflessness and selfishness. It may be very difficult to distinguish between a sincere, compassionate, giving mentor and a sexually predatory adult with ulterior motives. He reminds us that this is why the Boy Scouts now have in their handbook guidelines to identify and steps to take about inappropriate advances. What's more, leaders can only go on outings or camping trips in sets or groups, now, no longer singly.

It seems that resilient children have a great ability to build external networks. They learn how to be "likeable" and considerate of others. This is certainly consistent with earlier documentation of a good-natured temperament and positive outlook. Apparently, these survivors discover early on to develop "a winning personality." They learn social skills to **captivate the attention of others**. Moreover, they **choose wisely** those others who can offer stress resistance. Sensing the potential for healing that comes from bonding and attachment, they welcome the opportunity to be "adopted." They form a surrogate family of neighbors, friends, and colleagues, sharing joys and tragedies and a satisfying need to belong (Wolin & Wolin 1993).

"Instead of cursing the darkness, you lit a candle."
— Ann Landers

John, Age 9

Resilient children wish for something better than what they have (animosity, grief, silence), and they actually go out and find soothing company to share. In early childhood, they are on the lookout for chances to earn positive recognition. They look beyond their parents to other adults who pass through their house or who are available nearby. They intuitively develop skills to make and keep friends, both young and old.

"The resilient children drank up support promiscuously whenever they found it, the way a cut flower drinks water or a transplanted morning glory puts down roots and opens blindly to the sun."
— Katy Butler

Sharon, Age 7

As older children, they keep a lookout for people who can serve as substitute family members. They become adept at easily initiating new relationships and sustaining them over time. These relationships, in turn, help them release pain and disappointment in their own young lives. As adults, the resilient individuals continue to choose and cultivate relationships carefully. They are especially aware of the bonding value of rituals — celebrations, traditions and heritage.

We always do 3 jack-o-lanterns for Halloween - a funny one, a scary one and a happy one.

Maura

2. Impulse Control

The ability to restrain an impulse — or resist temptation — is a dramatic indicator of later adjustment. Those who can delay their gratification in childhood are remarkably more socially competent, self-reliant and trustworthy as adolescents and adults. They show resilience by facing stress rather than becoming frazzled (Goleman 1995).

Sadly, young children who do not control their impulses show a more troubled profile later. As adolescents, they are often described as stubborn, easily frustrated, mistrustful, irritable and indecisive. What is worse, poor impulse control in childhood is directly related to delinquency later in life (Block 1995).

> "We clearly see that choices are possible;
> we can say yes or we can say no.
> It is profoundly liberating."
>
> — Eknath Easwaran

Sarah,
Age 14

REAL LIFE: In what now has become a classic experiment started in the 1960's, 4-year-olds were given The Marshmallow Test. The dilemma was presented as follows: "Here is a marshmallow. You can have it right now if you want. BUT, if you wait until I run an errand (15 or 20 minutes), you can have **two** marshmallows when I get back!" Imagine the challenge for a 4-year-old. It would be a trial of patience, a struggle of self-control.

Some 4-year-olds quickly grabbed the marshmallow as soon as the experimenter left the room. Some would touch, smell or nibble it before giving in. Those with restraint, however, did active things to help them win their struggle. They covered their eyes. They sang or talked to themselves. Some played with their fingers and toes or even tried to fall asleep.

More than a decade later, the power of how the impulse was handled was evident when the preschoolers were tracked down as adolescents. Those who had resisted immediate temptation were much better adjusted. They were more capable of setting and achieving goals and were more personally effective and confident. They were also better students -- more eager to learn and more able to concentrate (Shoda, Mischel and Peake 1990).

Even achievement test scores were better. The experimental group was divided into thirds. Children in the most "grabby" group at age four were compared by their SAT scores to the group of children who were the most patient. The children who showed the most self-restraint scored an average of 210 points higher in their total SAT scores! (Goleman 1995).

Andrea, Age 5½

"The Bad Idea Monster"

Andrea drew this picture the afternoon she was sent home early from school for punching another student who accidentally bumped her. After an incident such as this, she would verbalize that it was a "bad idea" but then insists she "can't help it." Andrea has been diagnosed as hyperactive. One of our main tasks in counseling was helping her learn to control her impulses, specifically her "bad ideas."

3. Responsibility

In addition to actively seeking external support and bonding, resilient children are also called upon to be strong in their environment. Not out of choice but out of necessity, they are often given exorbitant amounts of responsibility at very young ages. Resilient children often practice quite early, usually by age 8 to 10, what psychologists call "required helpfulness" (Werner 1992).

Examples of this necessary stamina of responsibility are the teenager who is required to be the "stable parent" to younger children in the home and the high school student who takes her alcoholic father to the emergency room when he "accidentally" comes close to killing himself. Bleuler (1978) tells of a 12-year-old girl who dropped out of school to run the household and be a caretaker for her younger siblings.

By adolescence, many resilient children take on **the responsible role in an irresponsible family.** They do the housekeeping, such as cooking, cleaning and shopping. Many times they work outside the home so the money can be contributed to family finances. They help their younger siblings with homework or even attempt to shield them from the abuse they have suffered.

"I let my sister sleep in my bed when she's scared."

Julie, Age 12

REAL LIFE: Noreen was a strong survivor of childhood abuse. She recalls her teen years as protecting her younger siblings. "I saw all the suffering and I couldn't abide it. The worst was the way my father would go after the younger kids, the little ones who couldn't defend themselves. . . I felt I had to protect the little ones. It was a moral obligation, something I couldn't avoid, something any decent person would do" (Wolin & Wolin 1993).

These resilient children thus come to believe in themselves not because someone compliments them here and there for an accomplishment. Rather, they prove to themselves and to the world that they are competent and brave. They **feel their own inner strength and integrity.** What is more, children who take pride in helping **do not feel as trapped** (Brown, in Blum 1998).

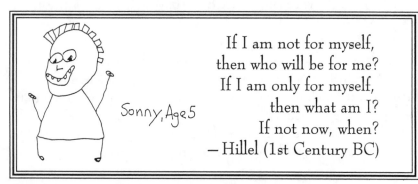

Sonny, Age 5

If I am not for myself,
then who will be for me?
If I am only for myself,
then what am I?
If not now, when?
— Hillel (1st Century BC)

As adults, these survivors almost invariably give of themselves and provide a sense of service for their fellow human beings in their daily activities. Responsibility helps give their lives meaning and smoothness.

Cherie, Age 15 (Painting) "My life is calm now."

"If you're looking for meaning
in the universe,
live a worthwhile life."

Mark, Age 7

— Carl Sagan

4. Goodness

Resilient children tend to "recharge" themselves by responding to the suffering of others. They value principals of decency, compassion, honesty and fair play. Resilient survivors dedicate themselves to good causes and pull for the underdog.

Apparently, the seeds of goodness are "sewn early when strong children in troubled families feel hurt, want to know why and begin judging the rights and wrongs of their daily lot" (Wolin & Wolin 1993). This sense of goodness or morality not only seeks to repair damage to the injured self but to improve the world, too. Here, survivors see not only how they can improve their own lives but how humanity as a whole can be perfected.

"Goodness is the
only investment that
never fails."

Jenny, Age 6

— Henry David Thoreau

This sense of morality and compassion is in stark contrast to the juvenile criminals mushrooming in our country in the late-1990s. "During the past decade the number of murders committed by teenagers has leaped from roughly 1,000 a year to nearly 4,000." Even worse, recent headlines suggest teenage crime these days shows incomprehensible callousness (Eftimiades 1997).

Children accused of acts of callous violence come from a variety of backgrounds. Blaming a history of poverty, broken homes and abuse is not enough to explain their behavior. Dr. Michael Schulman, a New York psychologist who authored the book *Bringing Up a Moral Child* sees it as a straightforward issue: "You need to teach the child that the family stands for goodness, not simply comfort and intellectual achievement, but that moral excellence is honored" (Schulman 1985).

"What it feels like inside. It's horrible."
Rita, Age 14

Because of that lack of goodness or morality, these violent youths are "without the capacity to make the connection with another life . . . they have no more reason for hurting another human being than they have for peeling an orange," says Dr. David Hartman, Director of Neuropsychology at the Isaac Ray Center for Psychiatry and Law in Chicago (Eftimiades 1997).

The good news is that resilient survivors exercise their conscience! They have a deep sense of morality and they make value judgments about the people in their world. Resilient children seem to be motivated by mercy and charity. They fight corruption within their own homes.

"Mom Yelling again."
Nancy, Age 9

Wolin & Wolin (1993) tell of an adolescent girl whose dysfunctional, alcoholic family could have made her incapable of accomplishing much in her life. She could have imitated her parents, mistreated her younger siblings or become a troublemaker or dropout. Instead, she was compelled by her **conscience** and her **compassion** to make a difference in her family. When questioned, she replied, "I couldn't turn my back. I felt that making a difference was my duty. And when I could see that I had changed things, I felt important and strong. That fed all my hopes that I would eventually get away."

In early years, these resilient children attempt to rise above the chaos. They question inappropriate behaviors even if they are done by adults. They start to define what is wrong and what is good, and they **make the decision to be different as adults**. As older children and young adults, they grasp on to concepts of compassion, justice, loyalty and fair play. They see hypocrisy and cruelty for what it is, and they stand up to it when they can. In the long run, resilient individuals are willing to sacrifice their own pleasure for the sake of justice and integrity.

Trevor, Age 6

"Statue of Liberty"

5. Sense of Humor

Resilient children use **humor** and **creativity** to cope.
They enjoy playing, laughing and composing. In
young childhood, they often lose themselves in
imaginative play. As older children, they often
become involved in arts, crafts or drama.
Many learn to use humor to
diffuse tension or relieve bad
feelings. These children are
often able to see the absurdity
of a troubled family or to
laugh at their troubles.

Ellen, Age 9

Ellen's sense of humor showed through in her comparison:
"All the fighting in our house is like touching a porcupine."

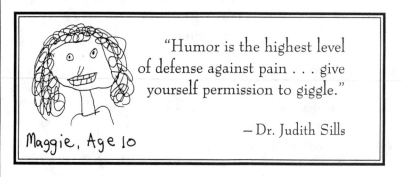

"Humor is the highest level
of defense against pain . . . give
yourself permission to giggle."

– Dr. Judith Sills

Maggie, Age 10

6. Locus of Control

Resilient children consistently show a sense of independence and belief
that they are in control of their fate. Weaker, hopeless children believe
that rewards and consequences are externally controlled, no matter
what they do.

Hope and **confidence** blossom in strong children. They have an abiding faith that their **troubles will be overcome.** They enjoy their independence and try to separate themselves from adversity physically as well as mentally. As young children, they often "stray" — wander off on their own, find enjoyable places to go and take solace in being alone (but not lonely). Older children stake out their own territory and look optimistically toward the future as a time of independence.

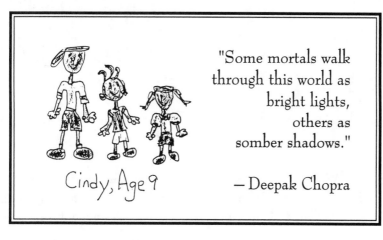

Cindy, Age 9

"Some mortals walk through this world as bright lights, others as somber shadows."

— Deepak Chopra

REAL LIFE: The following two cases demonstrate Locus of Control, with one child demonstrating strength and the other an attitude of helplessness. It is especially intriguing that the more resilient child came from a background of divorce while the more hopeless child was living in an "intact family."

Desmond was a bright, attractive young man from an affluent, extremely high-achieving family. An only child, he attended 6th grade at a private school where he was miserable. His grades were predominately Bs and Cs, but his parents couldn't understand why he didn't make straight As. His parents asked me to evaluate him to determine if he may have dyslexia or some other learning disability which would explain his "disappointing achievement."

*The testing revealed not only a superior intellect but strong school skills as well. The problem was not that Desmond was incapable. He was overwhelmed. Whatever he did was **never good enough** for his dominating father. Desmond felt he had **no control** over his life.*

My mom is a butterfly. She is very pretty and nice. But she can't do anything to stop the elephant or save me from the water.

This is my dad. He's an elephant because he's big and powerful! He keeps spraying more and more water on me. I think I'm drowning. Maybe he doesn't know.

That's me. I'm a giraffe who can't swim. I'm trying to keep my head above water.

When asked to draw his family represented by animals, Desmond portrayed his feeling of helplessness eloquently in his artwork. (The words were dictated to me by Desmond during session.)

Now compare this to nine-year-old Tracy's mental separation from parents' problems. After her parents divorced when she was a preschooler, there continued to be constant bickering. Each parent remarried, which just seemed to add fuel to the fire of hostility.

"I don't have to be a sponge and pull in everybody else's bad feelings."

Stepmother Dad   Me   Stepfather Mom

Tracy learned to separate herself from this. She was certainly aware of it, but her faith and hope allowed her to rise above it . . . or in this case "squeeze out of it." What a wonderful analogy she makes to not being a sponge!

Eddie Arcaro, one of the best
jockeys of all time, rode 250
losers before he won his
first race on a gelding
named "No More" in 1935.

— *The Orlando Sentinel*

Lucy, Age 7

7. Faith

Faith is an essential ingredient. Period.

Faith can be in some meaning or purpose of life. Faith can be in the
future, that bad times are temporary. Faith can be in a Higher Power,
to give one strength and diminish trouble. Staying connected to some
kind of faith keeps the spark of hope alive.

In the past, secular-minded scientists have shied away from spirituality
as a source of resilience. Even so, resilient survivors themselves will say
what a comfort it is to know that there is a Higher Power they can
turn to. Faith is an important protective factor regardless of the
specific religion: Buddhism, Catholicism, The Church of Jesus Christ
of Latter-Day Saints, or Jehovah's Witnesses. In one study, "people
almost unanimously said that they had received little help from people
in the church . . . but that they held to the idea of guardian angels or a
God who, as one man puts it, 'will always love me and forgive me'"
(Blum 1998).

"I had faith in God. I knew that somebody loves me,
somebody cares for me. When I felt like life
wasn't worth living, there was a God who
loved me and would help me come through."

— Kitishima, Kauai Child

Christina,
Age 12

"The child has no trouble
seeing magic where adults
find only mechanics
and practicality . . ."

Darren, Age 8

— Thomas Moore

REAL LIFE: When 8-year-old Darren was brought to see me by his grandparents, they informed me that he'd already been to several other therapists, yet they did not notice any change. They described him as increasingly withdrawn and depressed over the last year. Part of their concern was that they had no insurance and could not afford long-term psychotherapy.

Darren lived with grandparents because his mother had died and his father was a trucker, often away from home for long periods. Darren's history was that his mother was killed by a gunshot wound when he was only two years old. He had no memory of her, although he had seen photographs. Since he had grown up with his grandmother substituting as his mom, everyone assumed things had just evened out. Now, six years later, Darren was struggling with anger, resentment and confusion over not having a "real mom."

*Certainly, there are as many approaches that could have been taken here as there are therapists. Because of the family's spiritual beliefs and Darren's need for short-term, intensive healing, we utilized the **protective factor of Faith**. In three sessions, Darren was able to shift his thinking from preoccupation with "What might have been . . .?" to belief in his own Higher Power and his connectedness to his mother still, although in a different form.*

Part of Darren's healing included visualizing his mother and drawing a picture of her as an angel. We wrote her a letter with all the things in it Darren wanted to say now. Then we lit a candle, said a prayer, and carefully burned the letter so the smoke would go up to heaven. In many ways, this was a symbolic "good-bye" ritual very much like the traditional funeral Darren was too young to comprehend at the time. Finally, Darren was empowered to call on his mother at any time as we asked her to become his Guardian Angel.

HINT 📖: For more details on **Visualization**,
see Step 7- HIGHER VALUES.

"Searching is half the fun: Life is much more
manageable when thought of as a scavenger
hunt as opposed to a surprise party."
— Jimmy Buffett

FINAL NOTE

In our exploration of all the internal and external factors affecting
resilience in children, one thing is clear. There are myriad different
stages and different influences that impact when and where change can
occur. Various studies of at-risk children all conclude that second
chances do happen . . . and there are multiple opportunities along the
way to nurture a child's resilience.

"There is always one moment
in childhood when
the door opens and
lets the future in."
— Graham Greene

Matt, Age 9

Just as you did for Risk Factors, review now the Protective Factors.
Look for those in your own life . . . and in the lives of children who are
important to you.

Internal Protective Factors ~ Personal Characteristics

1. **Temperament** ~ Children come into the world "wired" a certain
   way, and the most resilient ones are good-natured and likeable.
2. **Intelligence** ~ Intelligence is average or above average, with a
   sense of insight and intuition.
3. **Reading Skills** ~ Reading is a source of solace and an active
   learning tool.
4. **Positive Outlook** ~ Lessons are learned and gifts are offered
   others as a result of adversity.
5. **Talent** ~ A special hobby or skill develops a sense of mastery and
   helps connect children with nurturing, supportive adults.
6. **Gender** ~ Girls tend to fare somewhat better in the resilience
   department than boys, due to the way they are treated by others.
7. **Age of Siblings** ~ The strongest children usually are either the
   oldest in the family or do not have a sibling less than two years
   younger.

External Protective Factors ~ Interaction with Others

1. **Bonding** ~ Children who rise above adversity do not do it alone; someone is there for them — a parent, neighbor, friend, teacher or other caregiver.
2. **Impulse Control** ~ The ability to restrain an impulse — or resist temptation — is a dramatic indicator of later adjustment.
3. **Responsibility** ~ Resilient children feel their own inner strength and integrity, and they take pride in helping others.
4. **Goodness** ~ Principals of decency, compassion, honesty and fair play are valued; pleasure can be sacrificed for the sake of justice and integrity.
5. **Sense of Humor** ~ Humor and creativity are coping tools to see absurdity in problems and laugh at troubles.
6. **Locus of Control** ~ Feelings of independence and confidence lead resilient children to believe they are in control of their fate.
7. **Faith** ~ This essential ingredient keeps the spark of hope alive.

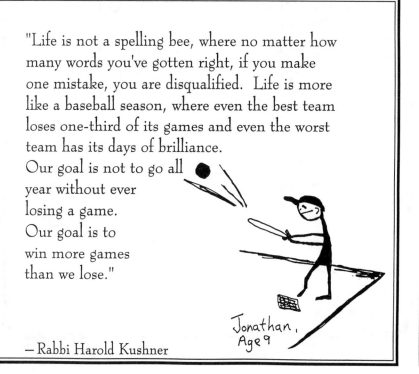

"Life is not a spelling bee, where no matter how many words you've gotten right, if you make one mistake, you are disqualified. Life is more like a baseball season, where even the best team loses one-third of its games and even the worst team has its days of brilliance. Our goal is not to go all year without ever losing a game. Our goal is to win more games than we lose."

Jonathan, Age 9

— Rabbi Harold Kushner

Part Two:
THE SEVEN STEPS

Secrets of the Third Little Pig

Step 1

Hip-hip-hooray!
Give each piggy 3 squeals a day!

OINK!

OINK!!

OINK!!!

PRAISE

Flawless

They tell me when I'm wrong.
I'm never ever right.
The impossible goal of prefection.
Is so far out of sight.

I always do my best.
I try and try.
It's all I can do.
I'm barely getting by.

I try to keep going,
But they push me farther.
It's never enough till I'm
FLAWLESS...

Larié, Age 11

1997

"Healthy families remind
each other of their goodness;
unhealthy families remind
each other of their failings."

— Matthew Fox

Dear Mom,
   I don't like it when...
you embarrass me in front of my
friends/other people

It is ironic that so many caregivers who want their children to feel good about themselves — to have positive self-esteem — unwittingly do just the opposite. In attempting to make children the very best they can be, these adults tend to focus on the negative.

Criticism, punishment or expressions of disappointment are used to point out mistakes. Usually when caretakers do this, they truly believe they are helping children to "improve" themselves. Remember the sticks and straw of good intentions? In reality, this practice can endanger the growth of character and usually generates ill will if not outright resentment.

"A child with high intelligence
but low self-esteem will not
achieve as well as a child
with average ability
and high self-esteem."

— Virginia Noiles

Neil, Age 6

What children need (in fact, what we **all** need) in order to truly blossom is support and encouragement. Many of us don't realize how much we need recognition, and how uplifted we are when we receive it. When we never hear from others whether our efforts are appreciated or not, it becomes increasingly difficult to hang in there and keep doing our best. How can we be certain we are needed or are doing a good job unless someone tells us?

TIP: Imagine yourself at work, perhaps sorting through a stack of papers left in your box. Suddenly you come across a difficult report you handed in to your boss two days ago. It has no response on it other than a yellow stick-on note which says, "Let's review this." What would your reaction be? Fear and dread? Or pride and eagerness? Most likely, your reaction would depend on the kind of working relationship you had already established with your superior. A relationship of trust and recognition will breed very different feelings than a relationship of criticism and degradation.

PRETEND PORTRAITS

A fun and often very revealing technique in therapy I call "**Pretend Portraits.**" The idea is that the child or teen draws the self or family as something **other than people.** Often these are plants or animals.

*REAL LIFE: Andy, age 11, used the **Pretend Portrait** technique to depict his feelings of constant criticism at home. Notice how his family picture speaks volumes about his sense of being the smallest and least competent member of his family.*

Perhaps in the home, more than anywhere else, the importance of praise is least appreciated. Despite the personal sacrifices required in family life, members tend to take each other for granted because of their frequent contact. They don't take the wonderful opportunities to build each other's self-image and self-confidence. Children especially are eager to hear praise and encouragement. Without it, family members can become negativistic and depressed. An important task for caregivers is to provide a great deal of nurturing to children's fragile egos. Recognition and encouragement have got to be two of the main ingredients in anyone's "emotional first-aid kit."

WITH PRAISE
(FERTILIZATION)

WITHOUT

The habit of giving credit regularly (even perhaps especially) in the little things will contribute to a happy home life. Recognition does not need to be a big production. In fact, it should be just a routine part of interaction with children. Informal words of praise in everyday conversation are natural and eagerly accepted. A simple "I'm proud of you," and an explanation of why, will go a long way. Other comments may be "You look so pretty when you smile," or "I really liked the way you . . ."

INDISCRIMINATE PRAISE

Generally, positive commenting does not spoil a child – unless the praise is extremely excessive or given **indiscriminately, that is, regardless of what the child does.** Effusive praise, bordering on child worship, can certainly lead to arrogance. Worse, children who are praised no matter what they do may grow up to believe they should be the focus of everyone's attention all the time, a most unhealthy attitude.

Unfortunately, these children come to believe that only they are important, and their feelings are easily hurt. They look the same as other children on the outside, but they seethe on the inside when they don't get the excessive, unearned respect they feel they deserve. When their demand for respect and attention goes unanswered, they may become rage-filled and violent. The tragedy of this pattern has become blatant in recent wanton, senseless killings by school-aged children.

Charlotte, Age 7

"When you're the only pea in the pod, your parents are likely to get you confused with the Hope Diamond."
— Russell Baker

Some studies in classrooms have shown that teachers who use praise in massive amounts can have a negative effect. Too heavy praise given without thinking can make a child dependent on external rewards, rather than developing self-satisfaction from learning. Most caregivers, however, do not err in this direction, but rather in withholding praise or giving insincere praise.

"We awaken in others the same attitude of mind we had toward them."

— Elbert Hubbard

Jennifer, Age 5

No, son. I didn't MEAN for your soup to spell that.

Gus

Honesty is critical if recognition is to succeed. Sincerity is what gives praise its power. Children are quick to recognize false praise, and it does more harm than saying nothing at all. Complimenting a chubby child for her great figure just won't make it so. But there is no child who is without some assets. Take the trouble to look for them every day. No matter how difficult a day it may be, a child will be sure to do **something** you can compliment. Show that you notice and that you care. Then encourage the child to go even further with it and to try new things. Soon there will be even more to acclaim.

PIGGY PORTION OF PRAISE SECRETS

Positive recognition is an art with far-reaching effects. Whether we always acknowledge it or not, children tend to be hard on themselves. Praise can help them focus — to develop into what we knew was there all along. In developing this art, here are some specific SECRETS . . .

✿ Oops Eavesdrop

Nothing carries more weight than accidentally overhearing something. Since you were not really **meant** to hear it, it must be true! Can't you think of an example of that from your own childhood or adult life? (Or how about that funny feeling when you think someone may have overheard something they were not supposed to know about?) When we "accidentally on purpose" have children hear something, that's an "Oops Eavesdrop."

Oh Ann! I wish you could see Laura's room. She cleaned it all by herself! It is just BEAUTIFUL!

*TIP: Put the **Oops Eavesdrop** in your toolbox of tricks. Set it up. **Make it happen.** Brag to Grandma on the phone about Jimmy when he just happens to be in the next room. Call your neighbor to boast about how well Laura's been keeping her room clean. Your child will be beaming . . . and even looking to do something else great.*

✦ Effort Approval

While it is easy to focus on a wonderful school paper or artistic drawing, try to remember that is just the final product. A lot of effort may have been expended along the way. By using "**Effort Approval**," we focus on **the process — the feelings and thoughts** that went into the work. Children glow when they see caregivers are as interested in what goes on inside them as in what they produce. Plus, emphasizing **how** it was done reduces pressure to produce a perfect product.

"It doesn't matter who you are,
where you come from.
The ability to triumph begins with you.
ALWAYS." — Oprah Winfrey

Lynn,
Age 7

TIP: Next time you look at a child's school papers notice how your eyes are automatically drawn toward the "red marks." There are the errors boldly pointed out by the teacher's marking pen. Take a deep breath and look again. Talk about how proud you are of the child for practicing the math facts or studying the spelling words, then talk about the grade. Can you "reframe" something? Try something unexpected like "I remember 6 months ago you didn't even know how to do multiplication. Now look how many you got right." For very young children, talk about the colors or feelings that went into painting a picture or building a block tower.

➤Kid-Creed

We want to build children's **confidence in themselves, not just their ability to please others.** So, in addition to stating your own pleasure, make sure you recognize the child's sense of pleasure too, i.e. "I can see how proud you are," or "You must be very happy with this." It is children's own self-satisfaction which will later help them follow through on independent projects. We want children of all ages to carry around a positive "**Kid-Creed**" even when we are not with them.

~ Kid-Creed ~
I am a good person.
I try hard even if I make mistakes.
I like myself.

REAL LIFE: Working at a middle school, I was referred a teen who was failing miserably. His records showed he had an IQ of 135 — he was Gifted! By testing him, I discovered his academic skills were excellent, too. Reading, writing and math achievement scores were well above grade level. Jack should have been an outstanding student. Why was he underachieving?

We simply sat and talked. It became clear Jack had given up on himself because his "product" was never good enough for his parents. No matter what he did, there was still something else he could have done better.

I believed at first this would be an easy case — just re-educate the family on how they perceive and praise him. Was I shocked when I was told by his parents that Jack was indeed the black sheep of the family! Both parents and both brothers (and even his aunts and uncles) all had IQS in the 140s and 150s! Poor Jack. He was inferior because his IQ was only in the 130s . . .

> "Praise is like sunlight to the human spirit:
> we cannot flower and grow without it."
>
> — Jess Lair

❥ Detail Magnifier

Too often children hear global praise such as "That's good." Comments that are too general have less impact. They also can lead to uncertainty about what actually is being complimented. Try to **be specific.** Use a **"Detail Magnifier,"** especially of the process, that is, the activity and the effort. For example, instead of "Nice job," try saying, "I know you worked really hard picking up all those clothes and putting them in the hamper." This helps children feel that they have truly earned the praise. (And maybe next time, they'll be less likely to leave their clothes all over the room or stuffed under the bed.)

I am so proud of you for folding those clothes so neatly.

❧ Sentence Seeds

Using "**Sentence Seeds**" is a great way to jump-start recognition.

*TIP: Try these **Sentence Seeds**.*

I really like it when you . . .
       You seem so grownup when you . . .
              I enjoy it so much when the two of us . . .
                     It wasn't easy, but you sure . . .
                            I'm amazed at how you . . .

HINT 📖: For more details on **Sentence Seeds**, see Step 1 -
         PRAISE, Step 2 - Listening Times, and the Dignity
         section in Step 4 - LOVE.

❧ Instant Replay

Immediate recognition is powerful, but so is **reliving the experience**. One of the best compliments a caregiver can give is to take the time to let children talk about the experience and share their own satisfaction. In this sense, then, praise is used to encourage and to think about what was accomplished. Think of it as "rewinding the tape" and watching an "Instant Replay".

TIP: A great time to do this is tucking them in bed. (Yes, even when saying goodnight to older kids.) Just bring up something great: "Remember today when we were in the kitchen and I was on the phone? You came up and interrupted me, but you stopped when I asked you and just waited. I could hardly believe it — and I just wanted to say thanks again."

❧ Invisible Signal

Nothing adds to the impact of praise like **getting close and smiling**. A hug is an added bonus. If you can, try to squat down so you are looking right into the child's face. Whenever I go in the waiting room to see one of my younger clients, I always drop down so we are eye-to-eye before I say a word.

Have fun with what I call the **"Invisible Signal."** This is a nonverbal sign of approval or perhaps a gentle reminder. Possibilities include affectionately rubbing a child's hair, patting the shoulder, winking or giving a thumbs-up sign.

*TIP: Make up your own **Invisible Signal** just between you and your child that says "Way to go!" Families I have known have used everything from sign language to clearing the throat as a special but private note of recognition.*

*REAL LIFE: When I was teaching third grade, I was assigned a particularly large class (40 students!) with an especially rambunctious student named Gilbert. In those days, children were rarely identified as having Attention Deficit Hyperactivity Disorder (ADHD), but I am certain now that would have been the diagnosis. After repeated attempts at traditional discipline failed, we decided on an **Invisible Signal.** I would wink at him when I "caught him being good." One morning, he was so focused and appropriate, I was effervescent in my winking to recognize him. At recess, another little girl from the class came over to ask me if I was all right. "You've been blinking so much today. I thought you had something wrong with your eye."*

❧ Kind Eyes

Take what you are hearing about the child and **rephrase the negative.** I call this using **"Kind Eyes."** If a neighbor says a child is "bossy," reframe it to "independent." Then look for opportunities to label appropriate (or somewhat close) behaviors as independent. You will be **shaping** this little person so that behavior comes more in line with what you expect. Soon the internalized "parent voice" will point out good characteristics even when you're not around.

*REAL LIFE: The very first week of kindergarten, my daughter's teacher demanded a conference. She proceeded to explain her concerns that Larié was "very spacey." I knew what she meant (my daughter was often "in her own little world"), but there was no way she was going to be labeled spacey. I insisted on using **Kind Eyes**. From then on, we called her behavior creative — which has the positive connotation of being ingenious, innovative and resourceful. I had to laugh at an "All About Me" second-grade paper in which Larié had described herself as "kreyatuv."*

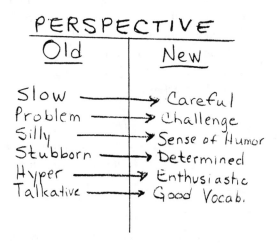

PERSPECTIVE

Old	New
Slow	Careful
Problem	Challenge
Silly	Sense of Humor
Stubborn	Determined
Hyper	Enthusiastic
Talkative	Good Vocab.

Certainly, this is an area where there are differing professional opinions. Brazelton (1996) suggests that "any label can hurt a child's self image." He perceives that even positive labels ("the brain" or "the jock") may place limits on a child. Such labels "may deter her from developing her other attributes and abilities." Even so, he acknowledges that a label of "feisty" he had given to a young mother about her baby "actually helped her to deal with her baby's temperament." In fact, she delightedly reminded him of this 30 years later.

My thinking is that had the doctor labeled the baby as "cranky," "bratty" or "difficult," this mother would have been less enthusiastic about interacting with her baby. "Feisty" was a positive attribute, implying alertness, zest and strength of character. I contend that people label each other all the time, either openly or subconsciously. Therefore, make it as happy an experience as possible. Transform **negative** labels to **positive** ones!

❥ Accomplishment Album

Show your child the progress that has been made by comparing it with previous work. **Focus on improvements** by using an "Accomplishment Album." Simply take a new photograph album with acetate sheets and put in all kinds of "good stuff." Sample items are a ribbon from a field day, a picture from art class and a principal award for behavior. You may even want to make a "progress graph" of some specific skill. Since children often have trouble judging their own progress, help them value their attempts.

*TIP: Make an "**Accomplishment Album**" for each one of your children. When a child feels down, this is the perfect friend to turn to lift up the spirits. You might want to "accidentally" leave these books out when family or friends drop by too. (Remember the power of* ***Oops Eavesdrop!***)

Mom, I'm GLAD you saved all this stuff.

❥ Hand Ruler

I often use a simple yet explicit technique to gauge progress in therapy. I call it the "**Hand Ruler**." Do this by holding your hands out in front of you, palms facing each other. Spread them only a few inches apart and say "I remember when you were only able to do this much" (multiplication, for example). Then spread your hands further, saying "Now you're doing this much!" Alternatively, you could hold your hands wide apart, arms outstretched, saying "I remember when the problem was this big." Move your hands in as appropriate to show "Now it's only this big."

FINAL NOTE

Growing up means that there are lots of challenges and disappointments that lie ahead. Fortunately, as caregivers, we have a powerful tool for helping our young people feel good about themselves. When we are supportive, positive and appropriately complimentary, we are making a valuable investment in children's sense of self.

"Healthy relationships imply supporting each other, yet there is no focus on 'fixing' the other person. Each person's process is respected and it is recognized that each must do what he or she must."

— Anne Wilson Schaef

Donna, Age 9

OVERVIEW ~ STEP 2:
LISTENING

WHEN TO LISTEN
> ❥ Listening Times
> ❥ Sensitive Times

HOW TO LISTEN
> ❥ Active Listening
> ❥ Body Language

DEEPER LISTENING
> ❥ Feelings
> ❥ Acceptance
> ❥ Self-Awareness
> ❥ Respect

A PIGGY PORTION OF
LISTENING SECRETS
> ❥ Ear Mirrors
> ❥ The Talking Stick
> ❥ Feedback
> ❥ Put It Into Words
> ❥ Recognition

FINAL NOTE

Secrets of the Third Little Pig

Step 2

LISTENING

Too Busy for Listining

"Mom, can we talk?
It's about school."
"Dont bother me now.
You know the rule."

"Dad, can we talk?
Something isn't right."
"Not right now;
How about to night."

We never talked last night.
Did he even care?
Mom never has time for me.
It isnt really fair.

Now Dad comes in.
He gives me chores to do.
"Not now, Dad,
I'm to busy for you..."

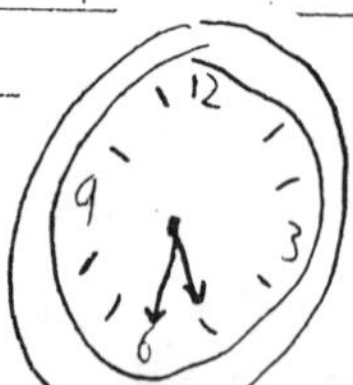

Larie, Age 11

1997

"The reason we have two ears and only one mouth
is that we may listen the more and talk the less."
— Zeno, Greek Philosopher
5th Century

Tom, Age 9

Caregivers often take great pleasure in buying surprises and gifts for children. There is a great deal of satisfaction in seeing their faces light up with the excitement of a new toy, even something relatively inexpensive. Unfortunately, one of the most important gifts we can give our children is often overlooked. This is the gift of ourselves — the gift of **listening**. Children who are listened to and who learn to listen become sensitive to others. They perceive their own ideas as important, but also learn to see others' perceptions. Out of listening grow the arts of negotiating and problem-solving.

On the other hand, poor listening can be the primary cause of personality clashes and poor communication. This can lead to poor morale and even depression, not only in childhood but in later adult life. Unfortunately the typical adult simply does not spend enough time listening.

"Fighting"
Andy, Age 9

All children have something important to say. It may not sound too important to exhausted caregivers who have worked all day and still have a slew of chores to do at home. Dinner has to be made, then the kitchen cleaned up. Later, the TV comes on, or we have an important phone call, or we need a few minutes to ourselves, and then it is time for bed. Despite our best intentions, a child may get the message "I'm too busy to listen to you right now."

Guaranteed, if we wait until later, it will be too late. Time after time, parents of adolescents complain: "No matter what I try, they just don't **listen!**" But we cannot expect young people in this independent, often rebellious stage to magically respond when we want them to.

"Banana In The Ear"
Syndrome

The give-and-take of good listening must be established early in order to carry over into later years and other relationships. Barriers to communication that are established early in a child are hard to break later — remember the adult is developing within. This does not mean it is ever too late for change, but it is often more difficult.

WHEN TO LISTEN

✦ Listening Times

In laying the foundation for listening, be aware of **when** to listen. Certainly, when a youngster is eager to share some exciting news, we want to be an attentive audience. But beyond that, we need to try to set aside a time each day to spend listening to each child. **Listening**

time when no other distractions, such as newspaper or TV, are allowed is great! Ideally this listening time would become as routine as times to eat or sleep. Think about what fits best for you . . . snack time? a quiet time after reading? a few minutes before bed? You might even think of this listening time as a version of our school-days "show-and-tell." If the idea seems awkward or uncomfortable to you, that could be a "red flag" that your communication together needs work.

REAL LIFE: In one family I know, each parent goes into each child's room separately every night before the lights go out. No matter how chaotic the day or how difficult the children have been, these few minutes are reserved. The children look forward to this special, personal time even if they haven't "earned" it. Plus, they can wait to share private things then, if needed.

TIP: Try a "listening game" to get started. "Sentence Seeds" are especially good. In the car or at the dinner table, take turns throwing out a Sentence Seed stem and see how other people answer. Examples:

> *My favorite vacation ever was* _____.
> *The worst part of my week so far has been* _____.
> *If I could wish for anything, I'd wish* _____.
> *The one thing I'd love to change is* _____.
> *Our family would be better if* _____.

It's OK to stop and talk about something you just found out about someone. The object is not to win by keeping score, but to win more broadly by communicating.

❥ Sensitive Times

On the other hand, there are times when it is most important to simply **allow the opportunity**. Be ready to listen without forcing a child to reveal. Do not turn listening time into an inquisition. **There are times to be quiet**, and we caregivers must develop a sensitivity to that, too. With a teenager especially, we can show we are available and be patient until the teenager is ready to talk.

"There's nothing wrong with teenagers that reasoning with them won't aggravate."

— Anonymous

Becky, Age 11

When children have had a bad experience, they may just need some time to think it through without being bombarded with questions. If there is a touchy subject that you want to address, pick a good time and a private place. Most important, don't try talking with a child when either of you is angry. At that point, feelings are out of control and not much will be accomplished. In fact, feelings can be hurt.

HOW TO LISTEN

❥ Active Listening

Now that we have a sense of when to listen, let's focus on **how** to listen. Much research has been done on the importance of "being with" or "attending to" the other person when we are listening. Many counselors and therapists receive years of training on just this subject of listening to their clients when they are talking about their problems. Mental health professionals use the term "active listening" — that is, **being a part of the speaker's world**, not just sitting passively.

> "When we communicate,
> 55% is BODY LANGUAGE,
> 38% is TONE OF VOICE,
> only 7% is THE WORDS."
>
> — *Psychology for Kids II*

GKS

❥ Body Language

Sometimes it takes a conscious effort to understand and care about what a child is saying. Make your concern obvious to the child through body language. Notice your **facial expression** and tone of voice, remembering that **actions speak louder than words**.

Susan, Age 10   Tone and expression
without words.

Gus

"Read the Bodies"
To Guess the Feelings in These 3 Different Interactions

If you seem bored, children will pick up on it immediately. They will probably react likewise to you. Make eye contact. Look directly at a child while listening, leaning forward and getting close to pay attention. There may be times, of course, when a child does not feel comfortable with strong eye contact, especially if it is a touchy subject, so don't force it.

> "No machine can replace the human spark: spirit, compassion, love and understanding."
> — Louis V. Gerstner, Jr.

Chris, Age 12

DEEPER LISTENING

❧ Feelings

When we are truly listening, we hear beyond the actual words (the facts). We attend to the feelings. Try to hear the **tone** and **quality** of what a child is saying. In counseling, some of the most important work a therapist does is to **"Hear Between the Lines,"** to get what a client really means but may not be able to express.

REAL LIFE . . . The power of simply being willing to listen was brought home to me recently by a new 12-year-old client. Tammy was brought in by her mother, who remarked "I don't really think anything is wrong with her, but her grandmother insists she is troubled so I finally agreed to bring her to someone." Tammy was delightful — pleasant, alert and energetic. She seemed very upbeat about her school, her friends, her dog, even her sisters.

*Then, without expression, she made a comment that just didn't fit. "I can't wait to move out of my house." I could **Hear Between the Lines** that there was some hidden trouble bothering her. By just **nodding** and **waiting** and repeating the main idea, "you're really eager to leave home," I gave her the **opportunity to share.** She broke down in tears and sobbed about her father's drunken fits and the terror with which she lived every day.*

Children's body language often speaks of feelings they will not or cannot put into words. **A giggle, a tear, or a shrug can tell a lot.** When children's legs are crossed and they are turning away from you, they are "closed down." Watch anyone's face closely and you will see many signs of the feelings within.

Be careful, though, not to jump to conclusions. Give children time to express themselves. Sometimes their feelings change so rapidly, it's hard to guess what's really going on. Teenagers in particular are known for their moodiness.

EXHAUSTED HAPPY CONFUSED

SAD GUILTY FRUSTRATED

Gus

❧ Acceptance

Show acceptance of a child's feelings, whatever they are — up or down. We are not saying we approve. We are simply showing we understand. We could say something like "I see you got really mad when the other kids said that. I think you're still mad just thinking about it." This shows children **we are truly with them but not necessarily agreeing**. No telling children how they "should" feel, either! Telling young people they should **not** feel what they already **do** feel tends to alienate them from us.

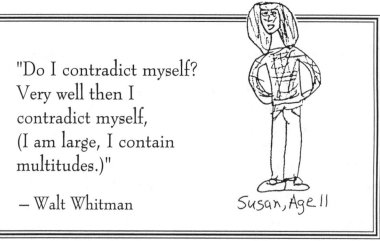

"Do I contradict myself?
Very well then I
contradict myself,
(I am large, I contain
multitudes.)"

— Walt Whitman

Susan, Age 11

What's wrong with this picture?

❧ Self-Awareness

Of course we cannot ignore our own feelings. Each of us listens differently, and our point of view affects what we hear. **Monitor your own reactions.** As you listen, be aware of your own attitudes and values and how they fit with what the child is saying and feeling. Being careful not to try to change the child's feelings, you can express your own feelings. It may work to say something such as "I feel worried and kind of scared for you when I hear you talk like that."

TIP . . . There are a number of different communication models available in the literature. I have been struck by the consistency among these models whether the setting is education, business or home. Typically a communication model starts with the word "I" as in "I feel . . . (confused, frustrated, worried, etc.)" This makes your point in a whole different light than starting with the word "you," which can feel an awful lot like an accusing finger being pointed, as in "You are . . . (mean, lazy, rude, etc.)"

Dear Mom,

   I feel disappointed when you yell at me.

Ryan, Age 7

❥ Respect

As adults with many more years of experience living, it is tempting to share the benefit of our wisdom through advice to children. We can express our feelings, but let's **avoid lecturing**. Don't tell children all the reasons they should listen to you. Even if you believe "someday you'll thank me for this," at this time, they probably won't understand or respond.

Avoid judgment or ridicule. Comparing a child to more capable or better behaved siblings or neighbors usually leads to resentment. Likewise, humiliation and criticism are sure-fire ways to get a child to turn you off, sometimes permanently. Think how you like to be treated, and how you react to being put down.

Do not pretend to have all the answers. **Allow some disagreement.** You may worry that a child who disagrees is showing disrespect. Not true, as long as there is no rudeness in the tone or comment. Children actually have more respect for caregivers who allow them to express their thoughts and feelings. **Allowing children to disagree shows we are STRONG; admitting we don't have all the answers shows we are HUMAN; and being willing to help find a solution shows we are SUPPORTIVE.**

POOR LISTENING

A PIGGY PORTION OF LISTENING SECRETS

The gift of listening is priceless when you consider the impact this energy spent has on our children. Here are a few more SECRETS to help you give the best of yourself as you invest in listening . . .

❥ Ear Mirrors

Unfortunately, people who live in the same house often have **sloppy listening**. We miss part of what is being said or (perhaps subconsciously) change it to hear what we want to hear. For example, "I'll **think** about it" is **misheard** as "I **promise!**"

Try using "**Ear Mirrors**", a technique developed in collaboration with my friend Dr. David Parker, Clinical Psychologist, many years ago. An **Ear Mirror** is like a regular mirror in that it **reflects back**. If you're wearing a green shirt, earrings and no hat, a mirror is not going to show you a purple shirt, no earrings and a baseball cap. "What you see is what you get," even if it's a bad hair day.

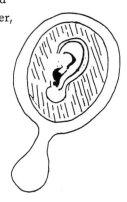

Saying the term **Ear Mirror** aloud is a signal. It means the listening person is **not allowed to answer** or tell their side of it until they have first "heard" the talking person's side by **repeating the main idea back aloud.** Remember, saying the other person's side only means you "got it." It does not mean you agree.

For example, if a child came into my room and said, "Dr. Messenger, you are so boring, and you have too many books and not enough toys and all you do is talk," I would not be allowed to say, "But all the other kids say I'm cool! They say I have neat stuff and I'm really smart. They like to come here!" I would only be allowed to repeat back the main idea of what the child said. "So, you think I'm boring and talk too much. You see too many books around instead of toys." The child has to acknowledge that I **got it**. Only then could I say my side. The child would have to listen and reflect back my view of it.

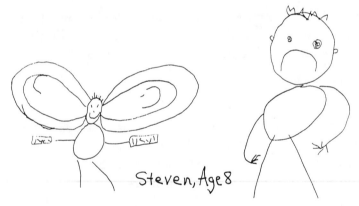

Steven, Age 8

DRAWING OF EAR MIRRORS
AFTER CONVERSATION WITH MOM
Notice the exaggerated ears are on a person with a big smile and a "reward" in each hand; the person with tiny ears wears a frown.

*REAL LIFE: Several years ago, I had a mother and teenage daughter walk into my office steaming mad. They'd had a huge fight in the car and couldn't wait to continue it in front of me. They pulled their chairs into opposite corners of the room, arms crossed (note the body language!), glaring at each other. We started with **Ear Mirrors** to slow the pace. At this point, neither was listening to the other at all. Here's how it went:*

Belinda: "It's not fair. You are so mean. You had no right to go into my room and tear down my posters. That was my allowance money and now it's wasted forever. That one poster is not even mine and I'll have to pay for it. You shouldn't even go in my room, it's none of your business."

As an outsider, perhaps you'd think, "That's no fair. Poor Belinda." But there really are two sides to every story . . .

Mother: (Notice, <u>not</u> being an **Ear Mirror**.) "That's not true. I've been telling you for six months to fix those raggedy old things. Half of them were hanging off the wall by one thumbtack and it made your whole room look trashy. In fact, your room is always a mess. I don't know how you stand it."

*What's your guess? Would this make Belinda say "You know Mom, you're right. I never thought about it that way. My room is a mess. I think I'll clean it up." HA! It was like throwing gasoline on the fire. One of them soon stomped out of my room (which always makes the therapist look sharp) to cool off. After that, we were able to regroup. With considerable refereeing on my part, they used the **Ear Mirror** technique to get past their own stubborn viewpoints and shift over to focus on a solution.*

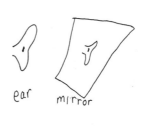

Ned and his mom learned to do **Ear Mirrors** together.
That is a special way to talk and listen to each other.

❧ The Talking Stick

Sometimes it is hard to wait patiently listening when you know what you really want to say! That leads to interrupting and then raised voices to be heard. That's a good time to try the "**Talking Stick**." Actually this is a version of an old Indian technique used when the great chiefs met in council. Whoever held the special stick would **speak and be listened to.** No interruptions.

Hey, if you ain't got me, baby, keep your mouth CLOSED and your ears OPEN!

The **Talking Stick** can be anything from a handy pencil to a specially decorated wand. It can be combined with the **Ear Mirror** technique so that whoever holds the pencil gets to talk and the other person listens and is the **Ear Mirror**. By slowing down, reflecting back, and seeing the other person's side, you can more easily shift to a negotiation or compromise attitude. The **Talking Stick** is especially helpful with young children or impulsive individuals. **Remember, when people listen with their minds already made up, they are not hearing with their hearts.**

"Trust in your heart . . . Never deny it a hearing. It is the kind of house oracle that often foretells the most important."

— Baltasar Gracián

Darlene, Age 6

❧ Feedback

It is hard work to really listen to a child. To keep things on track, you can use "**Feedback.**" That is, find out if you truly understand what has been said. Ask a question about **what you thought you heard** the child say. Counselors call this "perception checking." From time to time, ask "Did you mean . . . ?" or "Are you saying . . . ?" and then use your own words. This simple technique is invaluable for avoiding misunderstandings and hurt feelings. It saves time and lets the child know you really care.

"A torn jacket is soon mended; but hard words bruise the heart of a child."

— Henry Wadsworth Longfellow   Jessie, Age 7

❧ Put It Into Words

There is a special type of feedback I call "**Put It Into Words.**" Teaching this feedback model to young people does them a great favor. They can learn how to get the point across without seeming insulting or rude. It is especially handy when correctly used at school or with adults.

Start with an "I message" and end with a statement of what you **want** to do. Throw in a "when" or "because" if it helps. The point is you can **say the feeling** makes you want to do something (scream or run away) **without really doing it.** Children can learn to **express their intensity without having to act it out.**

PUT IT INTO WORDS

I feel _____
when _____
It makes me want to _____.

---

*TIP: Use a cue card until the **Feedback** comes more naturally. Once it is fairly automatic, the order can be changed around or a part or two can be omitted. Don't forget to model, model, model instead of just expect the child to use it. In fact, sometimes, you may have to jump-start the process by saying the cue words.*

*For young or impulsive children you will probably want to stick with the four basic feeling words: **happy, sad, mad, and scared.***

*EXAMPLE 1: **I feel** so frustrated **when** I see the food in the living room because that's breaking a family rule. **It makes me want to** just turn off the TV and make you all go to bed right now.*

*EXAMPLE 2: **I feel** so delighted **because** you studied so hard for your spelling test. **It makes me want to** give you a big pat on the back.*

Dr. Greene (1998) reminds us that not all children are ready or willing to hear other people's feelings. In this case, he suggests we start slowly with comments such as "**I have feelings too you know.**" After a while, the child may reply "Oh, yeah, like what?" Or even "What do you want me to do about it?" Thus, we are again gradually **shaping** the behavior.

*TIP: By the way, you can use the **Put It Into Words** technique in your adult life. Let's take a situation of a supervisor talking to an employee. Notice the **Feedback** can be positive or negative.*

*EXAMPLE 1: **I feel** so frustrated **when** my phone messages are incomplete or inaccurate, **because** I can't get back to people. **It really makes me want to** scream (or fire you or whatever).*

*EXAMPLE 2: **I feel** so honored **when** you go to so much trouble to get the phone messages just right. **It makes me want to** say a special thank you (or celebrate Secretary's Day early or whatever).*

If that's the worst thing
That ever happens to you,
YOU'LL BE LUCKY!

I feel so sad when you cry.
It makes me want to just
hold you for a while.

Which would YOU rather hear?

REAL LIFE: I once had a teenage boy in my office who had a quick temper and volatile reactions. Nathan was not at all pleased about coming to see me, and as he became more and more agitated, he jumped up, stomped to the wall, and punched it with his fist. Not a very smart move, as the wall was concrete. He broke several bones in his hand and required a cast.

*Apparently this behavior had been more successful at home, where he had put holes in his bedroom wall, which was made of plasterboard. It was a painful but wonderful lesson. Our first task — after seeking medical attention — was to help Nathan learn to **Put It Into Words**. In this case, something like "I feel so ticked off, I want to punch the wall and get out of here" would work.*

❥ Recognition

Finally, remember to **praise** or **encourage**. Even when we've had a difficult conversation, we can thank a child for talking or for trying to come up with a solution. Because children often have short attention spans, they can be complimented for listening and not being distracted. Indeed, children should be guided in the listening techniques we have discussed, and they should be given credit for using them. There is nothing wrong with an occasional unexpected treat. A valuable memory could grow from saying "What a great talk. Now let's go out for a hot fudge sundae."

REAL LIFE: A profoundly difficult episode erupted with my brother when I was about 10 or 11. Screaming and shrieking, I slammed the door of my bedroom and lay on the bed crying. It wasn't fair. Why did we have to have someone like that in our family? Why couldn't we just send him away somewhere or lock him up forever?

After a while my father knocked on the door. When I opened it, he stood there with a whole watermelon and a big knife. I let him in. I don't remember the words, but I do remember he just listened. He heard my anger and resentment and bitterness and shared his own. He'd always wanted a son and didn't understand why we were burdened this way either, but he felt committed to standing by "my own flesh and blood." Otherwise, I don't remember much of the conversation, but I do remember the sweet watermelon juice running down our faces, helping dilute our pain.

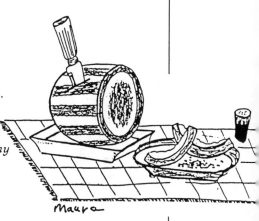

Maura

FINAL NOTE

My experience with many different caregivers has convinced me that poor listening is one of the greatest blocks to children's success in life. Most people ignore, misunderstand or simply forget 75 percent of what they hear! But with effort and practice, listening skills can be greatly improved. Children who are listened to, learn to listen. By giving the gift of listening, we are going a long way toward enhancing feelings of self-esteem and confidence. By actively listening to a child, we are sending a message that "You are worth my time."

L.W.

"The smallest gestures are the most potent."

Author Unknown

OVERVIEW ~ Step 3:
LIMITS

OUT OF CONTROL CHILDREN

CLEAR EXPECTATIONS
- Pick Your Battles
- Pathway to Peace
- Slot Machines
- <u>This</u> but not <u>That</u>
- Umbrella Rules

ENFORCING THE LIMITS
- 10 Words or Less
- Warnings Teach Self-Control
- Pay the Price
- Prepare Ahead
- Mean It

PAYING THE PRICE
- The Black Hole
- Time-Out
- Loss of Privileges
- Consequences vs. Punishment
- Spanking: Pros & Cons
- The Dreaded "C" Word

A PIGGY PORTION OF LIMITS SECRETS
- What to Expect
- Special Cautions
- Motivators
- Picture Charting
- Lucky Lottery
- Making the Most of a Motivator

FINAL NOTE

Secrets of the Third Little Pig

Step 3

It doesn't hurt to pig out once in a while, but don't be a hog!

LIMITS

Spoiled Brat.

They're afraid to tell me "No."
They always will say "yes."
I get everything I want
And never anything less.

It's candy for breakfast,
Popcorn for lunch.
I never drink the healthy stuff,
I drink my soda and punch.

I got what I wanted,
Ever since my birth.
Do you know what I think?
I should rule the earth.

Larie' Age 11

LW.

Trevor, Age 6

"Sometimes I don't know the difference between right and wrong, but there's always some grown-up around to tell me."

— Dennis the Menace
(Hank Ketcham)

As children grow and make strides toward independence, the world can sometimes seem an overwhelming place, no matter how much they want us to believe they are in control. When caregivers set **limits** — that is, give clear rules and make sure they are enforced — they are providing the stability against which children can test their actions. The boundaries or limits help children develop a sense of security. They know they can count on someone to guide and protect them, even if at the time they are angry and resistant. Limits help build self-discipline and improve impulse control.

OUT OF CONTROL CHILDREN

We have all heard about (and most likely experienced) children who are out of control. They seem to be in constant power struggles with adults. Even less ruly children sometimes get into power plays. For example, a two-year-old tantrums in order to hold a breakable object, a six-year-old demands an expensive toy, or an adolescent insists on wearing heavy makeup. Many times the real issue is not whether the child gets to do a particular behavior but rather "Who is in control?"

REAL LIFE: One of the most dramatic examples of a youngster clearly out of control was three-and-a-half-year-old Matthew. He was a beautiful child — clever, attractive and healthy. The problem was he'd been allowed to "run the show" in his home since infancy.

An interview with his parents revealed they had both been physically abused in their own childhoods. In an effort not to repeat the pattern, they had erred in the other direction. They had set no limits at all for their son lest he get "hurt." Whatever this boy wanted, he got — or he became obnoxious. At their wits' end, Matthew's parents came to my office exhausted and confused. They really thought they'd been doing a good job as parents. They were loving and kind and gave Matthew exorbitant amounts of attention. Why wouldn't he just "be good" in return?

*Within a few minutes in my office, this three-year-old dumped out all the puzzles, threw every puppet on the floor and ruined a roll of postage stamps by dropping them in a glass of water on my desk. His parents just sat there pleading with him to "Please be good. We'll get you an ice-cream when we leave if you just be good." No response. I kneeled down to Matthew's level and said, clearly but without meanness, "You're not going to act like this anymore. You are going to **obey** your parents. You are going to do what you're told." At this point, he glared at me a moment, spat at my face and ran off giggling.*

*To make a long story short, we set up **strict limits** in a behavior management plan. These are the rules (1, 2, 3); this is what happens if he breaks a rule; this is what happens if he cooperates. For the first several days, the plan worked beautifully. Matthew was forced to cooperate and comply or **he** was sorry . . . not his parents. His old tricks didn't work anymore. His mother called me in tears to express her gratitude.*

*As is common with this dramatic a change, Matthew did not let go of his old patterns so easily. Matthew tried one last-ditch effort to make our plan fail. He went to the garage, picked up a heavy rake, snuck up behind his mother sitting in an easy chair and banged her severely over the head. Matthew's mother called me again — this time on the emergency beeper, terrorized, unsure what to do. I assured her she already had the tools and knew what to do. We reviewed the steps. More important, I told her she should be **happy** — this is a good sign! The plan is working, and Matthew is just showing his fury about your new clear authority. My* *unspoken reaction was "Thank goodness we're dealing with this at age 3, not age 13." (P.S. — Matthew's doing fine now. He is still strong-willed but accepts discipline. He just successfully completed Kindergarten.)*

Setting limits is absolutely critical. Children need restraints as they develop into fully competent adults. They will test caregivers to see just what those restraints are — how far they can go and what will happen "if."

Hersh (1998) believes the lack of limits in today's society has made it harder than ever for teenagers to cope with the complex mix of challenges they face (drugs, violence, sexuality, alcohol). She compares the current difficulties with the previous generation: "At least when we challenged boundaries, we knew where they were. We knew what our parents thought about things."

Chill out, Mom! I just had to get my flying saucer.

Chicago psychologist, Dr. Barbara Lerner (1999) goes so far as to point to **lack of limits** as the basis for the "senseless spiral of schoolhouse slaughter" after the Colombine High School shootings. She emphasizes that the Colorado shootings made the eighth in two years, and contends the root problem with the killers is **overindulgence rather than abuse.**

Thus, the teenage gunmen had "a moral hole" that resulted from few demands and soft discipline. Because they were allowed to be so self-absorbed, they never learned to truly love or value others. Lerner insists parents need to "make it clear to their kids early on that there are limits to what can be accepted" and that some actions are so wrong that "they cannot and will not be tolerated."

So what if I don't have any money... I want some candy NOW!

Setting limits means being very explicit with children about the expectations and rules. Boundaries are clear. Appropriate penalties are understood. The child definitely knows what is allowed and what isn't.

When there are no limits or the limits are constantly changed or not enforced, children will flagrantly disobey in order to force the adults to do something. Worse, children who never learn the meaning of the word "no" expect instant gratification. They expect to have whatever they want on demand! Unfortunately, this means they also fail to develop critical traits such as patience and self-discipline. They do not learn to say no themselves when later presented with outside temptations, such as drugs or shoplifting.

Bobby, Age 7

"Children actually like discipline — even enjoy it, because they feel more secure and protected."

— Dr. Lee Salk

CLEAR EXPECTATIONS

The key to setting effective limits is to clearly know and state your position. If you are uncertain, you may end up giving in. The tricky part is to "say what you mean and mean what you say." **Don't** say "no" when it really means "maybe" if the child becomes too difficult. This will only ensure that the child will be even more difficult next time.

❧ Pick Your Battles

Stop and take the time to examine your own values and attitudes. **Decide what is important and what isn't.** There are some areas where caregivers feel very strongly and must simply "put their foot down," and there are other areas where they can be more flexible. It is likely to be very important to you that children not drink alcohol or smoke cigarettes; it is probably much less critical if they wear unconventional clothing, no matter how unattractive it seems to you.

Dr. Ross Greene (1998) uses a wonderful metaphor of **Baskets** to help adults sort through which battles to pick. He asks us to "picture three baskets in a row." Basket A holds those **very few** "things your child has to do just because you've said so . . . those things that could be **harmful** to your child, other people, animals or property are not negotiable." Basket B is the most important because it holds behaviors that are important or undesirable but which are still negotiable. Dr. Greene calls this the "wheelchair-ramp" basket because you are **helping** your child think, communicate, negotiate and problem-solve. Basket C holds behaviors that are not important or undesirable enough to say anything about for the time being. That helps reduce your child's overall frustration so you can focus your energy on Basket B. Over time, Basket C behaviors may move to Basket B.

❧ Pathway to Peace

For older children and adolescents, caregivers frequently complain "Their room is a mess, I can't stand it." This is a great issue with which to explore your own priorities. How important really is it that the child's room be as neat as the rest of the house (as long as you can close the door)? Whose problem is it if the child can't find their waist pouch or favorite jeans in the mess? By deciding what is important and what isn't, you may make up rules such as:

① There has to be a clear path from the door to the bed.
② No wet articles in the room.
③ No leftover food, plates, glasses, etc. in the room.
④ Keep the door shut when there's company.

Clean your room.
Trevor, Age 6

Usually, this set-up is a relief. Adults don't have to be constantly nagging. A few, however, simply cannot live with it. For them, neatness in every room is a priority. If that's the case, they have to pick this as a battle and list more rigid rules.

REAL LIFE: A principal at one of the schools where I worked said **this** **tip alone cut down on 50% of the arguments in her house.** *Imagine. She was in charge of a whole faculty of teachers who were in charge of a whole school building of children, yet she had been having daily battles with her teenage daughter about her room! By picking her battles they got along much better.*

❥ The Slot Machine

A wonderful analogy is the gambling mentality that goes along with playing "**The Slot Machine**." If you've ever watched people at slot machines, you notice an intensity that grows with each pull of the handle. The thinking is, "Maybe this time will be the big win." When it isn't, they drop in one more coin, because **this** could be the one, and so on, one after another. It's a perfect "randomized reinforcement schedule." People continue because they **never know when the big payoff will be** . . . and once in a while they do win. This usually just reinforces or strengthens the behavior so they keep doing it more.

BASICS OF BEHAVIOR

Children engage in behavior
because there is a payoff.

(OR)

Kids do things for a reason.

Children whose caregivers inadvertently have them on a "randomized reinforcement schedule" are very much the same. They work **The Slot Machine**. Let's just pick the example of a toddler who wants candy at the check-out counter. Initial requests are met with a mild "No" by mom. But then the toddler becomes more intense, begging, whining, pleading (more and more "coins" put in), while the parent continues to deny the demands (no payoff). With persistence, however, Mom may finally say "OK, just stop it, you can have it!" WHAAAA-LA! The **Big Payoff!** Mom gets a temporary reprieve (her own reinforcement), but the next time this child wants something, similar tactics will be used with even **MORE** persistence. Why? Because they "work," albeit with considerable "investment" of effort.

"Having it all doesn't necessarily mean having it all at once."

— Stephanie Luetkehans

Jon, Age 6

*TIP: Good news! The **Slot Machine** works both ways. You can randomly reinforce appropriate behaviors. This way, children never know when they'll get an **unexpected surprise for cooperating**. To continue our previous example, "You know, Joanie, you've been so patient standing in line without whining, I think you should pick out a package of sugarless gum." (P.S. -- I know this sounds idealistic, but it works! You must change YOUR behavior first in order for the child to change. Just keep thinking of the **Slot Machine**.)*

❧ This but not That

Sometimes you'll have to make on-the-spot decisions about limits. For our previous examples, you might clearly tell the two-year-old that he cannot hold the object himself, but it would be acceptable if you held it or put it on the bed so he could look at it or maybe even touch it. The limit is he can do **"This but not That."** With the teenager and makeup, you may decide that lipstick is acceptable but eye shadow is not. In the case of demanding a toy, the adult will have to decide the limits in that situation — a firm "no," an agreement to consider it for a birthday, an offer to use allowance money to save up for it, a substitution of a more affordable treat or activity together, or so on. Remember, it's your job to communicate the limit: **This** is OK, **That** is not.

❧ Umbrella Rules

Grouping similar unacceptable behaviors under one **"Umbrella Rule"** is very effective. Usually just 2 or 3 **Umbrella Rules** are sufficient. NO BOTHERING covers a lot of ground — poking, interrupting, whining, name-calling for starters. A typical list of rules in a family may be: No Bothering ~ No Rudeness ~ No Interrupting.

Example: NO BOTHERING

I can't push, tickle, annoy, tease, insult, mouth off, get smart, poke, or whine.

I might as well go out and play.

TIP: Look for the behaviors that stand out the most and try to group them under a generic term. A behavior that is frequent may need it's own label.

*REAL LIFE: Once, I sneaked a peek at a family in my waiting room several minutes before their first session. The parents were each reading as their 6-year-old daughter began playing with the toys. First, Megan banged the metal trucks, and one parent yelled "STOP THAT." She did stop **that**, but she then discovered to her delight that the trains could make a loud whistle. This time both parents yelled "STOP THAT!" and again she did stop **that**. Next, Megan found some blocks and a wooden mallet and began hammering away. That did it! The parents flew into a rage, told her how bad she was and made her simply sit in a chair with no toys. Not surprisingly, she began crying and fuming.*

*Later when I talked to Megan she was truly confused. In her mind, she **had stopped** each time they told her. She couldn't understand the problem. The problem wasn't **labeled** with an **Umbrella Rule**. If her parents had said "That's **NOISY**, stop it," Megan would have been in a much better position to decide if she wanted to cooperate or not.*

"A child cannot read your mind."

— Linda Johnston

Glen, Age 5

Many limits, such as curfew, need to be set in advance. Decide what is reasonable for you (even negotiate it with the child if you want), make it very clear, then stick by it. Children must not be able to say later that they did not really understand the rule. Keep in mind you should set limits only on what you can enforce. There are some things you can prohibit but not prevent. Caregivers can prohibit marking the walls with crayons or drinking alcohol but cannot absolutely prevent these activities in that children still have the free will to decide. With limits, however, violations will have specific consequences.

ENFORCING THE LIMITS

So now that we've set rules and regulations, how do we enforce them? Many times, especially with younger children, a clear calm, but authoritative, command is sufficient. They simply need to hear that the parent is in control. Sometimes a brief explanation is helpful. You may tell the child why you have set that particular boundary or rule but do not allow yourself to get into a lengthy defense of your position. Bright children are especially good at trying to get their parents in long discussions of "why."

Once a brief explanation has been given (if you decide to give one at all), that's the end of it. Further complaints or grievances by the child can be **labeled** with an **Umbrella Rule**. You might say, "That's BACK TALK," and deal with it as a misbehavior if continued. You can always talk about it later, such as during your special **listening** time.

HINT 📖: Refer to Step 2 - LISTENING.

❯ 10 Words or Less

In general, I recommend caregivers try to discipline in "**10 Words or Less.**" Talk about it later. Just as with praise, you can "relive the experience" with details **later.** When you discipline, you want to get in, make your point and get out. That leaves it up to the child to make a decision to cooperate or not. Notice that Stop means **STOP**, not pause and start again.

> "You can't talk your way out of problems you behave yourself into."
>
> — Stephen R. Covey

Laura, Age 9

❥ Warnings Teach Self-Control

Warnings are a method of teaching **self-control**. If a child violates an **Umbrella Rule** such as "**No Bothering**," the behavior is **labeled with a choice** to stop or continue and have a consequence. Think of the benefits! A warning . . .

- ✦ Teaches a child what **you** think is inappropriate (although he or she may not agree)

- ✦ Confronts the issue early before frustration sets in and tempers flare

- ✦ Gives the child the **choice** of compliance or not (self-control)

HINT 📖: For more details on **self-control**, see Step 5 - TIME.

❥ Pay the Price

In the past, I used the words "Time-Out" (for young children) or "Loss of Privileges" (for older children) as part of the warning. Now, I simply use the phrase "**Pay the Price**." This has a number of advantages. First, it avoids previous negative associations children may have with Time-Out, such as at school. Second, the warning remains constant over time, even as the child ages. Third, it is compatible with children of different ages in one family. Finally, and most important, it **implies a conscious decision**. An analogy is adults who choose to speed while driving and get caught. They **Pay the Price** (a speeding fine).

KEY WARNING (Notice 10 WORDS OR LESS):

That's ____ *(Label Behavior with an **Umbrella Rule**).*
Stop it now or **Pay the Price**.

The "Price" that is "Paid" is divided loosely into two age groups. Usually, for "younger" children, the cost is boring time alone. For older children, the fine is a loss of a favorite privilege for that day. The cutoff is around age 10, although it can vary. Consider each situation unique and look at factors such as the child's mental age and family constellation.

*REAL LIFE: Jennifer, an extremely intelligent but manipulative 10-year-old, had to **Pay the Price** using Time-Out because I thought she needed something obvious and concrete to set the limit. On the other hand, with 9-year-old Jacob, I recommended **Loss of Privilege** as the consequence because he had two older siblings, and this would fit better with the overall family pattern.*

❥ Prepare Ahead

Obviously, you would not spring a new discipline system on a child unexpectedly. Sit down and go over the rules and consequences when things are relatively calm. Family meetings are great for this.

For a younger child, practice and pretend the warnings and the time-out procedure. Role playing can be really fun. For example, have the child pretend to be the parent. You be a grumpy child who is rude or whiny. Kids love it! They have to give you the warning. If you do not stop (show self-control), they put YOU in time-out.

For older children, make a list of the privileges they will lose in order of most favorite to least favorite. Usually, it is not a good idea to ask them what privileges should be taken away. You might hear that they want to "suffer the consequence" of not changing the kitty litter. Instead, just notice how they usually spend their time. What do they like to do given free choice or free time? That's a powerful privilege and it should be at the top of your list.

EXAMPLE LIST

Computer
Television
Playing Outside
Phone
Toys/Games

For each offense that is continued after an explicit warning, a child loses a privilege for that day (or the next day if it is already bedtime). Major point: A child is not "grounded" for extended periods (weeks, months). Your focus here is to **develop compliance** and **teach self-control**, not to punish the child.

❥ Mean It!

Often children will deliberately push the limits — that is, deliberately do something they know you will disapprove. In this way, children are seeing if you "really mean it." By backing up your one warning with a consequence, you show that you really do. On the other hand, ignoring the disobedience once you've labeled it is as bad or worse than never setting the limit in the first place.

Decisions ... Decisions

When children err, they are not belittled or grounded forever. They simply have a boring thing happen which is no fun. This teaches them that when you say it, you mean it. Remember, **don't say it if you don't meant it!** If you label a behavior as "bothering," you'll have to back it up. Of course you can still **Pick Your Battles**. If you know your child is irritable and ready for bed, you may choose to not label it but deal with it some other way such as distraction or sense of humor. That's fine.

HINT 📖:   For more about how to **Pick Your Battles**, refer to the CLEAR EXPECTATIONS section earlier in this chapter.

Now I mean it, Junior! I'm not telling you again. You BETTER do what I say or you'll BE SORRY!!

*REAL LIFE: When my daughter was about 5, we were at a fast-food restaurant with a playground full of preschoolers. Soon, one little boy caught my eye as his mother repeatedly begged him to get ready to leave. First she pleaded. No response. Then she yelled. No response. Then she yelled **louder** (as if that would make any difference at all). No response.*

By that time, many parents and a few children were watching the scene, and this mother was obviously furious. Then she started counting! In our house, counting is serious. It's not used much, but if you get to three, you'll be very sorry. This mother slowly called out each number: 1 . . . (oh no) . . . 2 . . . (louder) . . . 3 . . . (the audience was getting scared now) . . . 4 . . . (oh wow, now what???) . . . 5! Then nothing. No back-up. No consequence. No regret. My daughter looked at me dumbfounded.

This mother finally climbed up into the playground apparatus and hauled her child down as he alternately screamed and laughed. She grabbed his shoes and socks and carried him to the car on the verge of tears herself. Now, if you were this little boy, would you believe your mom the next time she threatened to discipline you? Just think how much POWER this boy wielded! He could manipulate his mother and have an audience to boot!

PAYING THE PRICE

❥ The Black Hole

Be careful of "**The Black Hole.**" This phenomenon happens when children somehow get so far "in debt" with their consequences, they can never see the light at the end of the tunnel. Here, caregivers have erred by "adding up" blocks of Time-Out or days and days of lost privileges. In this situation, children have no reason to improve. They perceive that it won't make any difference anyway.

REAL LIFE: One set of parents came in to tell me 6- year-old Alisa "owes us three hours of Time-Out." Out of frustration, they kept "adding time." It reminded me of that a judicial sentence: "99 years to life, whichever comes first." If you were Alisa, would that make you shape up?

♪ Time-Out

For younger children (generally up to age 9, but remember it varies for the child's maturity level and the parent's style), here is a good rule of thumb: 1 MINUTE IN TIME-OUT FOR EACH YEAR OF AGE.

TIP: Buy a real cooking timer that you can hold and carry around. They run about $5 to $7 in most discount or department stores. Do not try to use your kitchen timer. The timer is a prop. It is part of the drama. It means something when you have to walk away with it or reset it. You don't want to be running back and forth to the kitchen to use the timer on your microwave or stove.

Mom's Timer

THE TIMER STARTS ONLY IF THE CHILD IS **CALM** AND **QUIET**. If the child gets noisy or yells out, you make a **brief** comment (remember 10 words or less!) such as "You're not ready yet," "You blew it" or "I'll be back when you're ready." Then you must reset the timer to the **beginning** after the child becomes quiet. **DO NOT** start pleading with the child to "Be good, so I can start the timer." (Please! You'll know if this is you when you read it.)

DOUBLE the Time-Out only if you have to **wait** and take the Time-Out later. You may have to wait if you are in the car on a busy highway or just leaving out the door in the morning. **NEVER** triple, quadruple, etc. . . . you're just creating a **Black Hole!** The WARNING is similar:

That's _____ (Umbrella Rule).
Stop it or **Pay a DOUBLE Price when we get home.**

OK, I admit 13 words not 10, but it's important! I've had many parents tell me what a real godsend this particular technique is out in public.

*REAL LIFE: One mom told me all she had to do when they were out was go over to David and whisper "**Double Time-Out**" in his ear. All the neighbors were shocked at his compliance and wanted to know the secret.*

"When you are definitely challenged, win decisively. When the child asks, 'Who's in charge?' tell him."

— Dr. James Dobson

Amy, Age 10

➤ Loss of Privileges

Withholding privileges is usually an effective consequence for pre-teens and adolescents. For noncompliance after a warning, loss of a **daily** privilege is adequate, while "complete grounding" with no allowance for one week may be appropriate for a very serious offense (again, something dangerous). Remember, it is wise to have a preset list of consequences. It is very much like a speeding ticket for an adult wherein the penalty varies according to how far off you were from the established limit. It's a "fine" that's set up ahead of time and applies to everyone no matter who you are or what you drive.

REAL LIFE: Julio's mother came in my office one day furious. Although his behavior at home had greatly improved since our sessions (and let's not overlook the power of praise!), his school grades remained poor. She had consequently "grounded him for the whole semester till his grades came up."

GUS

That's like saying "you can have some water at the end of this 10-mile run in the blistering heat if you keep running without stopping." The reality is that you do need to stop and get a drink along the way, just like children need reinforcement along the way. Set up short-term expectations and rewards/consequences. In this case, we set up a weekly progress report that was to be rated and initialed by each teacher on Fridays. Julio would bring it home, and his parents administered the rewards or consequences for the week, not the grading period.

With middle/junior high and high schoolers, it's best to work with reasonable chunks of time rather than **Black Holes**. For a "minor offense," do the **clear labeling** and **warning**, then specify the consequence.

That's _____ (Umbrella Rule).
Stop it or **Pay the Price**.

In this case the **Price** is no TV tonight. Of course, the first response will be "But I wasn't being rude" or "You didn't hear it right." Being the clever parent you are, you do not fall for the bait. You do not negotiate or explain yourself. You apply the consequence: "OK, that's no TV tonight." The next protest (most likely, "You're so mean" or "That's not fair") yields a new warning, for example:

That's BOTHERING (or whatever your label).
Stop it or there will be another **Price**.

It's been my experience that the first night or two, children will keep pushing, pushing, pushing and lose everything. Very quickly however, they learn to just stop, because the **KEY** is that by continuing they are making it more painful for THEMSELVES than for you! You are not suffering, THEY ARE.

This works only if **every day is a new beginning**. A terrible day before does not imply you are doomed to a horrible next day or week. You start with a clean slate and try to shape up. (The exception is if they lose the privilege right before bed. Then it's obviously ineffective to say "No TV tonight." That loss of privilege would carry over to the next day.)

Make a list ahead of time of what the consequences will be. Most likely this will vary for each child unless there are too many children in one family to individualize. In my practice, the following might be typical lists:

Joseph	Sandra
Outside Time	Telephone
Video Games	Television
Guitar	Computer
Television	½ Hr. Early to Bed

TIP: Don't forget to have a "back-up." If a child gets through all the consequences, there should be an aversive chore such as pulling weeds for ½ hour or scrubbing the bathroom tile. I don't mean to be negative here. I'm just saying you have to plan ahead so you're disciplining out of reasoning, not out of anger. You must have a plan, just in case.

"Children have a finely tuned way of quickly evaluating adults."

Justin, Age 6

— Violet Oaklander

➤ Consequences vs. Punishment

It is important to understand that **consequences are very different from threats or punishments.** There are a number of problems with threats. First of all, they tend to be effective only in the short run and quickly lose their power. Also, they usually mean the parent feels out of control so is resorting to threats. Sometimes, adequate threats are hard to think of and even harder to enforce, so that they lose their effectiveness in this way too. For example, a caregiver may threaten to not let a child have a birthday party for misbehavior. Then when the time comes, that seems too drastic. The consequence is revoked. What did the child learn? Next time you threaten, you probably won't mean it either. Just as you pick your **battles** pick your **consequences.**

➤ Spanking: Pros & Cons

Punishment, such as a spanking reaction, also has its drawbacks. On occasion, it may be necessary, but usually it does more to make the punisher feel better than it does to help the child learn self-control. Punishment also tends to lose effectiveness over time. Generally, people who spank **must spank harder and more often to have the same impact.** Also, severe punishment tends to teach compliance for fear of getting caught rather than help the child develop inner controls. Finally, some people fear corporate punishment teaches aggression.

A recent study holds the most shocking news of all. Spanking and other forms of corporal punishment may have a negative impact on cognitive development. Among almost 1000 preschoolers, those who were rarely or never spanked by their parents did better on intelligence tests (Straus & Paschall 1999). Researchers speculate that chronic spanking may damage both motivation to learn and brain development (hitting replaces talking).

Having said all those admonitions about **NOT** spanking, I will tell you the only two times I **do** recommend spanking. One is when a young child has done something clearly **dangerous.** Because the child is never spanked otherwise, to receive a spanking for something such as running into the street would be dramatic and unexpected. It would make an impression about the seriousness of the offense.

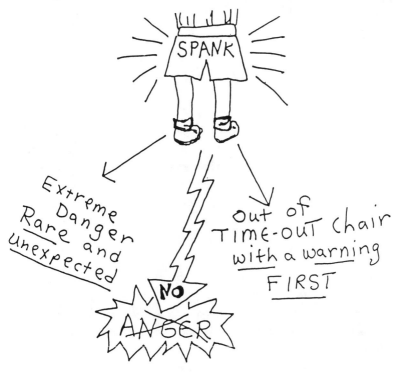

The other time I recommend spanking is to establish the authority of the Time-Out chair. If your consequence is Time-Out, and the child is up and running around, you're back to where you started — frustrated and probably yelling. Even so, don't forget you are also trying to teach SELF-CONTROL and GOOD DECISION-MAKING, so the system must include an **opportunity for the child to self-correct before spanking.**

TIP: The following is a procedure adapted from Dr. Barkley's excellent work titled The Defiant Child *(Barkley 1987). Often at first, children will test you and refuse to stay in the chair. When your child leaves the chair, you firmly put him or her back with a stern look and loudly say something such as:*

"If you get out of that chair again,
I'm going to **SPANK** your bottom."
    or
". . . I'm gong to **SLAP** your behind."

or whatever words are comfortable for you. Exactly on the word "spank" or "slap," LOUDLY clap your hands right in front of the child's face.

Then it's their choice. Chances are they'll get the message. If they do get up again, you have to follow through. With your **hand only,** *give two (count them) swift smacks on the buttocks. Then place the child back in the chair. If the child leaves the chair, do not give a new warning, but go right to the spanking (two smacks). Most children respond immediately to the warning with the clap. Almost all children "get it" after only one or two incidents of spankings. Note these points:*

✦ *Use only your hand, not any other object. (I have had several pediatricians disagree with me, saying a hand is for hugging, and a paddle should be used for spanking. I see it differently. I believe you need to feel how hard you're spanking. If your hand hurts; so does their bottom.)*

- *Do not take their pants down.*
- *Spank **only** for leaving the chair, not for any other misbehavior (except the aforementioned explicit danger.) If they fuss, yell or have a tantrum in the chair, pretend it doesn't bother you. Turn up the stereo or put on your headphones.*
- *If it is not effective after 4 spankings (i.e., the child continues to leave the chair), seek help from a professional therapist.*

"Without limits, children
just keep racing until they are
over the edge."

— Mark Barnes, Ph.D.

Mark, Age 11

● The Dreaded "C" Word

Pick up almost any parenting book and you'll see the emphasis on consistency, Consistency, CONSISTENCY. Most people assume this means that if there are two caregivers they both have to do the same discipline all the time. For me, consistency means they have to have the **same general plan (rules, consequences, motivators), but they don't have to pick the same battles**. As long as misbehaviors are labeled and warned, the child knows what to expect.

"A good parent remembers what
it was like to be a child."

— Ann Quindlen

Patrick, Age 7

REAL LIFE: Haley is a 7-year-old being raised by her grandparents after being abandoned by her mother at age 4. They suspect her father is in jail, but who knows? Haley was a pistol even with me — a trained, experienced child therapist. I knew these two wonderful but elderly people had their hands full.

"Setting consistent limits and coping with problems of discipline tend to be the most difficult areas of parenting, under even normal circumstances."

— Cynthia Monahon

James, Age 7

Moreover, their parenting styles were completely opposite. Grandfather was an abrupt, no-nonsense authority. Grandmother was a sweet and loving marshmallow. Haley obeyed her grandfather out of fear and mostly walked all over her grandmother. When we set up a discipline plan for Haley, both adults were worried about their opposing styles. Remember temperament? We weren't going to change either adult's personality, and that was not the point anyway! But both could fit their style within the framework of our plan.

For example, let's say Haley was cranky and complaining one night. If Grandfather was there, he might label it as "bothering," give a warning, and back it up if necessary. Grandmother, on the other hand, may choose not to pick this battle. She might choose to walk out of the room or engage Haley in an activity. The consistency comes in that if Haley does hear a label from either one, she knows what's expected of her and what's going to happen next.

Setting limits means **being strong not rigid.** Certainly, consistency is critical, but we need a balance between the child's needs for independence and for limits. Caregivers need to constantly reevaluate what is appropriate for a child's particular stage of development.

Also, once limits are clear and consequences are consistent, there may be a few occasions when caregivers will want to reconsider and change something. By seeing adults change their minds under the right circumstances, children can learn a great deal. There must be careful thought and negotiation — **not impulsive reactions.** This way children can learn that they are separate people who can be effective and influential in their world.

A PIGGY PORTION OF LIMITS SECRETS

Now that you have the general game plan of setting limits, here are some additional **SECRETS** to help you out . . .

❥ What to Expect

Be prepared for some resistance from the child. Children are not going to celebrate — at least not out loud — when they are told certain things are prohibited. In fact, remember **children often become worse before they get better.** This is for two reasons. One is to see how strong you are, and the other is to protest your new approach. Our case of Matthew at the beginning of this chapter beautifully illustrates this phenomenon.

> "A parent must like his children, but he must not have an urgent need to be liked by them every minute of the day."
>
> —Haim Ginott, Ph.D., Psychologist

Caregivers must be prepared to be unpopular in the short term for long-term payoffs. In fact, by facing a negative reaction calmly and firmly, we are setting an excellent example of how children can learn to deal with frustration.

Some caregivers feel guilty about imposing rules or "being negative" with their children. This feeling may be particularly strong with dual-working parents, caregiving grandparents, or single parents who already worry about insufficient family time. Stepparents and divorced or separated parents may feel pangs of guilt as well. Some adults are afraid of losing a child's affection. It is definitely a difficult task, and sometimes all we can do is choose the least negative approach. We have to keep in mind our own values and priorities and what is best in the long run.

"If you have never been hated by your child, you have never been a parent."

Cindy, Age 7

— Bette Davis

Giving in now may seem easy, but we have to have confidence in our own beliefs over time. Most children come to appreciate sensible boundaries with clear consequences. They may even use the caregiver's rules as an "excuse" when they feel peer pressure to misbehave. As much as they protest outwardly, deep down they come to recognize that **we care enough to risk a conflict.** For example, when tempted to shoplift, they may fall back on your "strictness" in order to back out: "My parents would kill me."

> "Parents can't feel right towards
> their children in the long run
> unless they make them behave
> reasonably, and children can't
> be very happy unless they are
> behaving reasonably."

— Benjamin Spock, M.D.   Brandy, Age 12

It is easiest to get into the family pattern of setting and respecting
limits when it starts early. It is hard, but not impossible, to make up
for lost time. With older children especially, there may be resentment
for not being allowed to make their own decisions. The wisest
approach is sincerity. Acknowledge their feelings and admit that you
have not been careful in setting or enforcing home rules but intend to
change. For example, "I'm sorry I haven't been as consistent as I think
I should have been, but I'm going to change. I worry and care about
you. I'm not trying to take away your freedom. I just want to let you
know what is not acceptable."

❥ Special Cautions

✦ **Do not overdo it.** Too many rules can be overwhelming, and too
  many restrictions can inhibit a child. That is why it is critical to
  pick which things are truly important. Generally about 3 simple
  rules are sufficient if they are generic enough to cover a number of
  behaviors. For example, do not have a list of rules such as, NO
  Yelling, NO Cussing, NO Whining, NO Back Talk, if you can
  group them all under one **Umbrella Rule**: NO RUDENESS.

+ **Make sure your consequences are adequate but fair.** In the case of pre-schoolers in particular, mild consequences of a few minutes of "time-out" paired with an expression of adult disapproval can be quite effective. Try not to overuse the technique of anger which should be saved for only the most serious instances. (Yes, anger can be a "technique," not an automatic reaction.)

+ **Aggression gets no warning.** I found this out the hard way. Several times, bright youngsters figured out that if there was a warning against hitting, for example, they could get in one good punch "for free," knowing they could then stop and have an OK-day. So, any aggression (hitting, biting, kicking, hurting) is an "automatic offense."

+ **No tattling allowed.** If you buy into what one child says another did, you'll cause new problems. In general, the adult must see or hear the incident. Sometimes the warning can be given to both children ("That's bothering. You both stop it or the next one goes to time-out."), then you stay close enough to see who pushes it one more time. When children complain this approach is "not fair," tell them to get smart. If someone is bothering you, go into a room near an adult so the misbehavior can be seen. (Surprise! Leaving the bothering situation resolves the problem immediately anyway!)

"If the child does not get a clear message, he/she cannot make an appropriate response . . . Leave nothing to chance."

— Grad Flick, Ph.D.

Sally, Age 5

❧ Motivators

Many caregivers worry that they might be "bribing" their children if they use a reward for appropriate behavior. Yet take a different perspective. Would you get up, drive to work and stay there laboring all day if you weren't getting "a reward" . . . your paycheck?

Please do **NOT** hear me saying you will have to follow these young people around until they are 21 giving out concrete and tangible rewards! What I **am** saying is that when everyone is in the process of change — particularly one as dramatic as setting up and following rules — it helps to have a positive alternative during the transition.

Frequently when children are really mad, it might seem "worth it" to go ahead, misbehave and face the consequence. But when there is a reward in play as well, they often stop, think and make the more positive choice.

Over the years, I have worked with all kinds of behavioral management approaches including star charts and point systems. There is nothing wrong with them — if you have a method that's working, stay with it. Personally I have been disappointed with star or point charts for two reasons: the novelty usually wears off within a few weeks, and keeping track of multiple behaviors or tasks is so complicated the charts become a source of hassle rather than help.

I am going to propose two alternate motivation systems you can **use in conjunction with the warnings and consequences system** we have just discussed. They also work quite nicely with the system of **compliance and obeying commands**. The only adjustment necessary is to use your creativity so that the motivator fits the child's age!

HINT 📖: For more details on **compliance and obeying commands**, see Step 6 - RESPONSIBILITY.

❥ Picture Charting

The beauty of this system is its simplicity. Either the child had an **OK-Day** (no Time-Out or no privileges revoked) or **not**. You may have had to give a warning, but if it never escalated to a negative consequence, that counts as an OK-Day. That means the child charts it. A young child can color in a balloon or circle or whatever the picture is. An older child can date the block in his graph. The goal is to get an entire picture or graph filled to receive the **pre-agreed-upon motivator**. The name of the motivator is usually written at the top of the chart. Examples follow:

Day at the BEACH

6-year-old Alex is working on getting a trip to the beach for his whole family. If he has to go to Time-Out one day, the chart does not have to start all over again; he simply loses an opportunity to color in a balloon and thus get closer to his goal.

TIP: Sometimes very young or impulsive children have trouble keeping up good behavior for the whole day. If you see this is the case, you may have to break down the time units into smaller chunks. For example, there may be three units per day (breakfast to lunch, lunch to dinner, dinner to bed). More balloons will probably need to be drawn, but this allows the child to see each success and keep from getting too discouraged by a mistake early in the day.

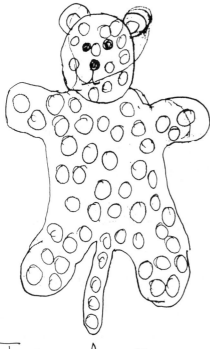

8-year-old Teresa made up her own picture chart with this jaguar. Notice the number of spots! This will take a while to fill, so will likely be a bigger "payoff."

Teresa, Age 8

13-year-old Will always wants the latest CD, so his mom (single parent) had a built-in motivator (Lucky Person!). When all his squares are dated, he has "earned" a CD. Notice that a 3 X 5 index card divided into squares works beautifully for this. Of course, the number of squares required for completion depends on your financial status.

6/15	6/16	6/17	6/20	6/21
6/23				

"One of the secrets of a happy life is continuous small treats."
— Iris Murdoch

Adam, Age 7

❥ Lucky Lottery

Years ago a presenter at a convention I attended suggested the following unique approach to motivate difficult children. Although I have been unable to locate his name, he deserves all the credit for this fun idea.

Basically, you take a mystery surprise and put it in a special envelope. The surprise might be something great or it might be a "zonk." The child gets to choose an envelope that night before bed only if it has been an OK-Day. I usually like to make a set of envelopes and use numbers, colors, or shapes to distinguish each envelope. The child is not allowed to feel the envelope but just has to decide "#3" or "the orange circle."

The technique is so fun because **you never know if you'll hit the jackpot!** It's another "random reinforcement schedule." This just might be the big payoff. A child may open the envelope and find . . . a dollar! . . . or a penny. A coupon to rent a movie and make popcorn! . . . or a Band-Aid®. The possibilities are limited only by your imagination.

Surprises inside might be:

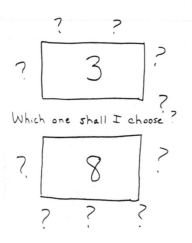

Which one shall I choose?

A piece of gum
A coupon to bake cookies together
Extra spending money
A rubber band
A coupon for a hug from dad
Stickers
A paper clip
A ticket to go skating
A coupon to go for a walk at
night with flashlights
A tiny toy
A balloon
The chance to put up the tent
and camp in the back yard

A neat twist on the **Lucky Lottery** is that you intentionally put only one piece of a puzzle in an envelope. Take an index card, write or draw the motivator on it, cut it into however many number of pieces is fair, and spread the pieces around into different envelopes. The child has to collect the entire set to complete the motivator. In the meantime, a lot of zonks or other bits and pieces may come up.

REAL LIFE: This strategy worked especially well for 10-year-old Jade, who collected expensive porcelain dolls. She found the first five pieces of her puzzle fairly quickly. The sixth piece seemed to take forever to find (smart parents), but she was highly motivated!

TIP: For an older child, you can use a pre-cut puzzle such as the 50 states of America. A child can draw a piece out of a bag each night (if earned of course) until the puzzle is complete and the reward is earned.

"Bringing up a family should be an adventure, not an anxious discipline in which everybody is constantly graded for performance."

—Milton R. Sapirstein

Mike, Age 5

♪ Making the Most of a Motivator

For either **Picture Charting** or **Lucky Lottery**, try these ideas . . .

+ **Gradually increase the expectancy to earn a motivator.** For example, the first month, every OK-Day could earn a payoff. The next month, it may be **two** OK-Days in a row, gradually building up until the reward is entirely phased out. Another approach is to roll the dice on an OK-Day. An even number (perhaps a 6?) means a payoff. Otherwise, "You had a chance, better luck next time."

+ **Make sure that charts match the payoff.** For example, 5 filled-in circles may be fine for a trip to get an ice-cream cone. A trip to a park or going on a picnic may take 15 or 20. An amusement park may take 50 or 100.

+ **Do not get into the habit of spending a lot of money for the motivators.** Time together doing a special activity is fine.

Herb,
Age 7

+ **It is the child's responsibility to mark the chart, not yours.** If the child forgets, "Oh well, too bad." It is your responsibility, however, to double-check the accuracy of the mark (for example, that an extra one is not "accidentally" colored).

✦ **It is your responsibility to provide the motivator as soon as possible once it is earned.** You would not believe the number of kids who have had their enthusiasm dampened because the adult "never got around" to giving them what they had agreed on.

FINAL NOTE

The job of setting limits is one of the hardest for caregivers. Because it often brings a negative reaction from children, especially at first, it is not immediately rewarding for us. However, when young people know that we are in charge, that limits are not excessive and that there is consideration for their feelings, they come to **accept** and even **appreciate** the structure. In this way, we are helping children toward the goals of self-responsibility and self-discipline — on the path to resilience.

"Self-reverence,
self-knowledge,
self-control,
these three alone
lead life to
sovereign power."

Ben, Age 5

— Alfred, Lord Tennyson

OVERVIEW ~ Step 4:
LOVE

STRINGS ATTACHED

BONDING

BONDING PROBLEMS
- ❥ Attachment Disorder
- ❥ Emotional Abuse
- ❥ Insecure Attachment

IMPROVING ATTACHMENT
- ❥ Attunement
- ❥ Teenagers
- ❥ Letting Go

RELEASING RESENTMENT
- ❥ Forgiveness
- ❥ Marital Conflicts

PIGGY PORTION OF LOVE SECRETS
- ❥ Affection/Tenderness
- ❥ Dignity
- ❥ Prompt Attention
- ❥ Availability
- ❥ Time Together
- ❥ Responsibility
- ❥ Reading Together
- ❥ Surprises
- ❥ Not Interrupting
- ❥ Role Modeling

FINAL NOTE

Secrets of the
Third Little Pig

Step 4

LOVE

Love

I Love my lizzard.
I Love my frog.
I even Love my
Haggish-dog.

My cats are cool.
My fish are neat.
I really love my
Parakeet

I love my snails.
Up in a tree.
I love snakes,
and they love me.

Mom and Dad
Are my favorite, yet
Even though
They're not a pet.

Pets Mom
&
Dad &
Me

Larié
Age 11

"So hear my words with faith and passion
For what I say to you is true.
And when you find the one
you might become,
Remember part of me
is you."

— Lyle Lovett

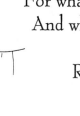

Sally, Age 7

Because it seems so obvious, the importance of demonstrating our love to children can be easily overlooked. Yet it is the routine messages of love, often in indirect ways, which lead to a **close attachment** to caregivers. Children with this strong bond have a distinct advantage. They have increased self-esteem, greater enthusiasm in life and persistence in the face of adversity. They get along better with others, and they are more sensitive to others' feelings.

The term attachment refers to the **emotional bonding** between children and significant adults. It starts at birth and continues throughout life with constant, gradual changes. Research over and over again has shown how critical love and attachment are to children's developing personalities. **Relationships with others as adults are greatly affected by the kind of attachments people form during childhood.**

Some people can be considered "securely attached" because they get along easily with others and have few problems in their personal relationships. As adults, these people have particularly happy, trusting love relationships and are least likely to end up divorced. Guess what? **Childhood memories** of these adults recall their caregivers as especially **warm, caring and responsive.**

Less securely attached adults have problems such as trouble trusting and understanding others. Some are very insecure or too dependent. Guess again? These adults remember their primary caregivers as **harsh, rejecting or uncaring.** There was a general pattern of dysfunctional communication during their early formative years. Often as children, these people felt as if they had to constantly "meet approval." The message was that love needed to be **earned.** If they did not meet approval, they felt unloved and unwanted.

Daddy, I'm glad we don't have to wait for THE END to live happily ever after!

STRINGS ATTACHED

I have been repeatedly surprised at how many highly successful adults still carry scars of early rejection or **conditional love.** That means love **with strings attached.** Children only receive attention and recognition if they have done something "good enough." Otherwise, they don't "deserve it." While my focus of therapy is usually brief, solution-focused and child-oriented, I have had a number of cases with adults where the root of their poor self-image (even if others saw them as fine) was conditional love in childhood.

REAL LIFE: One case involved Dr. S., a well-known and well-respected professional. Within her community she wielded both power and wealth. Within the confines of my office, however, she was a little girl again. She was terrified of her family's opinions. She constantly questioned herself . . . what if? what if? She was even afraid I would "fire" her from therapy for not being a "good enough" client. These fears stemmed from her inability to obtain unconditional love from her parents. She was never "good enough" for them just as she was. She had to constantly prove herself. It took a phenomenal amount of work in counseling to get past the blocks of self-doubt.

> "Most people see the problem of love primarily as that of *being loved*, rather than that of *loving*, of one's capacity to love. Hence the problem to them is how to be loved, how to be loveable."
>
> — Erich Fromm

Children know intuitively when they are loved, and if it is genuine, "no strings attached." Research shows what we really teach is what is in our hearts — our unexpressed feelings. This carries much more weight than what we say or even do. A child "learns to think and feel what **we** think and feel, what we do on the **inside**" (Jenkins 1992).

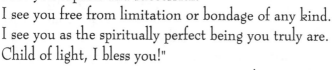

"I see you as a child of light.
I see you guided and directed
　　by an inward Spirit
　　　　that leads you unerringly
　　　　　　into the path that is right for you.
I see you strong and whole;
I see you blessed and prosperous;
I see you courageous and confident;
I see you capable and successful.
I see you free from limitation or bondage of any kind.
I see you as the spiritually perfect being you truly are.
Child of light, I bless you!"

— Anonymous

BONDING

Recall from previous chapters that **the number one external factor to help a child rise above adversity and become strong and resilient is bonding with at least one significant adult.** While we know the bonding can happen anywhere along the life path, and we have reviewed examples where it took place in childhood or adolescence, **infancy** appears to be the most critical period.

Believe it or not, we even have to return here to **biological factors** — hormones! Scientists have actually found that a secure mother-infant bond keeps a baby's hormones in balance. What's more, "bonding produces in the mother an outpouring of the hormones prolactin and oxytocin" (Sears 1998). These are "biological helpers" that give moms maternal feelings and perhaps even mother's intuition.

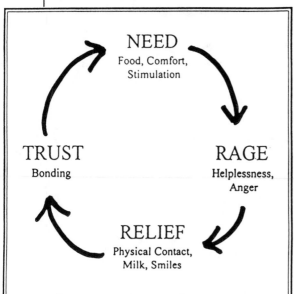

Bonding Cycle

Of course, the environment is critical as well. Cline (1992) diagrams the first year of life as a cycle of bonding and attachment. The chart depicts an adaptation of this cycle.

When babies do not get their needs met, their rage is expressed by loud, agitated crying. These needs are real. They need to survive, and crying is their only method to do so. When a caregiver picks up and soothes the baby, that is a normal and healthy response. The child gets gratification (warm fluid, touch, a smile) and becomes satisfied. Out of this satisfaction, then, grows trust.

TIP: It is not possible to spoil an infant in the first year of life. During that first critical year, anything that provides nurturing and relieves distress is fine. You cannot overdo cuddling and stimulation unless you impede a child's sleep or need for a bit of quiet time. You simply cannot provide "too much" bonding for newborns. So relish your baby, fall in love, enjoy each new day as much as you can.

It is only during the second year of life that we need to start imposing limits and teach children to delay gratification. But by then, they are developing their mobility and their language skills. They are getting around and starting to communicate. Consequently, they have much more control and influence in their world.

BONDING PROBLEMS

When normal attachment fails to take place, the cycle leading to trust is broken. Lack of attachment has profoundly destructive influences on a child's personality development and relationship with others.

❥ Attachment Disorder

In extreme cases, a child who does not bond with at least one significant adult during infancy — or has an established bond broken — can suffer Reactive Attachment Disorder. This is a severe disturbance characterized by "inappropriate social relatedness in most contexts, beginning before age 5 years" (DSM-IV 1994). The disturbance is attributed not solely to developmental delay but to pathogenic ("disease producing") behaviors of the child's caregivers. Pathogenic care may include persistent disregard of the child's basic emotional needs (comfort, stimulation and affection) or basic physical needs (food, shelter and clothing).

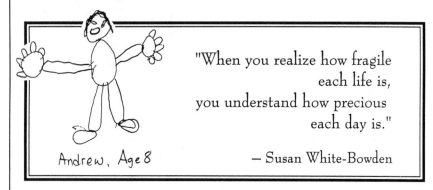

"When you realize how fragile
each life is,
you understand how precious
each day is."

Andrew, Age 8

— Susan White-Bowden

Generally, the more severe the break in attachment, the more disturbed the child. Severe breaks often involve babies and young children who were abandoned or given up for adoption and went through a series of foster homes, sometimes abused, before finding a placement with stable caregivers.

Sometimes, severely impaired and aggressive behaviors are seen. Masten and O'Connor (1989) report the case of a young girl who experienced "the abrupt loss of primary caregivers at age 15 months." By the time she was admitted to a psychiatric hospital at age 30 months, she was in the custody of a state welfare department, living in a foster home. Behaviors at the time of admission were very bizarre: odd postures, hand wringing, head banging, screaming, moodiness and (not surprisingly) "intense fearfulness around strangers."

Happily, in this case the bonding break was able to be repaired. The child was placed in a "prescriptive" home after two months of hospitalization. This home is described as very stable with "consistent, responsive caregiving" by "mature, experienced parents" who were "loving, patient and self-confident." Follow-up documentation 3½ years later showed dramatic recovery. Intellectual level was average, and personality tests were generally appropriate, although her responses did show a theme of sadness. By second grade, she was reported as doing well in all areas, and her separation fears had stopped.

Attachment Disorder behaviors may vary from somewhat inappropriate to severely aggressive. More disturbed children are destructive to themselves, others or materials. Cruelty to animals is often evident. I do not refer here to pulling wings off flies, which is not an uncommon method of exploration to see "what happens if . . ." I refer to children who deliberately inflict pain and receive pleasure from it. One first-grader I met used to catch turtles to throw them against trees or buildings to crack their shells. Another boy would lock his dog in a tiny box and several times tried to set the dog on fire. Indeed, preoccupation with fire is another "red flag" of Attachment Disorder.

REAL LIFE:

This drawing depicts a new client with this fire preoccupation. He was so angry about coming to see me, one of his first drawings showed him standing on a stool smiling as he sets me on fire, and "two other people are outside putting fire on the building to burn you up."

Less extreme but equally disturbed behaviors are often seen. These children appear superficially charming and even indiscriminately affectionate with strangers, yet they lack eye contact and are not affectionate with caregivers. They lie about the obvious and are offended when they are not believed. They are often demanding and clingy, ask repeated nonsense questions and show abnormal eating patterns. These children inevitably require intensive psychotherapy and even then, prognosis is not good. It is as if the lack of bonding led these children to become filled with rage.

REAL LIFE: Having worked in both a juvenile detention center and a self-contained special education center for the emotionally handicapped, I have seen a number of children with Attachment Disorder. They do things which defy our logic: wipe their feces on the bathroom wall or put a live toad in a jar full of red ants. One of my students, 9-year-old Kevin, had a face like a cherub and a disposition that was superficially sweet. He was several times featured on a local news telecast that attempted to place children in adoptive homes. Because he presented so well, he had several opportunities for a new life. But each time, he would sabotage himself. The third potential adoptive family had half their house burn down after he set a shower curtain on fire.

Children's attempts to explain their feeling of rage often eludes words but comes through in the artwork. Volcanoes are a particularly predominant theme, as shown by two examples below.

Sylvia, Age 10
"What it feels like inside sometimes."

Steve, Age 9
(Painting)

"It's a rainbow on the outside, but underneath it's fire. It's a volcano blowing up!"

REAL LIFE: Probably the scariest youngster I ever worked with was Jason, age 5 when I first saw him. His birth and infancy history were horrid. He was born 2 weeks prematurely to a 16-year-old unwed mother. She was initially unaware of the pregnancy and tried to spontaneously abort when she was 4 months along. Infant bonding was inhibited by Jason's medical condition at birth, as he had to be in intensive care for over a month. Then he was placed in a series of questionable foster placements for 3 months. Data available suggests these placements were hardly nurturing, and one was investigated for possible abuse. Jason was finally adopted by a gentle, loving couple who ran their own business.

Despite this excellent placement, Jason did not respond to his new parents' nurturing. It was as if the potential bonding mechanism was damaged beyond repair. As an infant, Jason went rigid when held. As a preschooler, he became increasingly violent, not only to classmates but to adults as well. By kindergarten, he had been suspended for kicking his pregnant teacher in the stomach! A psychiatrist placed him on several medications to stabilize his mood, then referred him to me for counseling.

Although our first session started out pleasantly with art therapy, the more I pushed Jason for conformity (wait your turn, share the paints, etc.), the more hostile he became. At our second session, he picked up the scissors and came at me, cursing, kicking and spitting. I was able to grab him and get him in a passive hold. This involves "sitting" on the child as he lies prone on the floor, his arms crossed in front and held in my hands. In this hold, the most damage he can do is bang his head, possibly causing a bloody nose. Otherwise, he cannot hurt me or himself.

All I asked of Jason during this hold was to calm down and stop yelling while I counted to 30. He screamed, thrashed, cried and cursed. He yelled out he was dying because he couldn't breathe and that the devil and the police were going to get me. Interestingly, when he would finally stop in exhaustion, he would always start screaming again by the time I got to 29. He simply would not let me win the battle. We did that for almost 1 1/2 hours. (Pity my poor following client, who waited and waited in the reception area hearing the screaming!) Every muscle in my body ached the next day.

Jason, Age 9

Ultimately, I "won." Jason finally stayed quiet until I reached 30. Very simply, Jason learned that if I said it, I meant it, and his violence would not work with me. Unfortunately, his psyche had long ago been severely damaged. He made some, but marginal, progress in therapy before the family moved. In one of his more cooperative moods when he was older, he did the above drawing trying to depict the demons he felt within. Notice the lock and chain on his heart.

I was able to keep in touch with the family over time. Jason regressed after the move. He became more violent and defiant. He started fires and lit firecrackers stuck in frogs' mouths. He even killed his own pet hamsters *"accidentally." Jason was sent to a special treatment facility for unattached children. He reportedly "failed" the program and was made to repeat it (at $5,000 a shot). He was finally placed in a secure residential facility at age 12.*

I survived
Attachment
Disorder
Therapy...
and lived to
tell about it.

Obviously, this is an extreme case, and the influences of genetics and pregnancy trauma cannot be downplayed. On the other hand, this is a classic example of a child who never formed a secure attachment. Therapists who work with these types of children deserve a medal.

A part of me wonders, though, what will happen when Jason is out in the real world as an adult. At this point, society cannot incarcerate him for something he "might" do, yet all the flashing signals are right there: the boy is going to seriously hurt someone someday, and the victim's grief-stricken family is going to cry out, "Why? Why didn't someone prevent this?"

❧ Emotional Abuse

Sometimes it is very hard to differentiate between caretakers who abuse children and those who use "harsh discipline." This is particularly true when we get into the issue of **emotional abuse**. By definition, emotional abuse is "failure to provide warmth, attention, supervision, and normal living experiences" (Florida Department of HRS, 1986, Page 1). Let's see how it plays out in real life.

REAL LIFE: When I worked at a middle school (grades 6, 7 and 8), most of the referrals involved students who were disruptive, defiant or failing. The referral about 12-year old Kim struck me not only because it was so different but because the teacher who wrote it was so astute and compassionate. "Kim seems different somehow since the beginning of the year. He is more quiet and withdrawn. Maybe he's depressed? He is an excellent student, and I didn't get anything new from a parent conference. I'm worried about him. When I ask, he says 'Everything's OK' and won't talk more."

When I met Kim, he was a delightful young man of Asian descent. He was attractive, alert and extremely diligent. He cooperated with all the tasks but never spoke a word except to answer my questions. The academic tests verified what his teacher said — he had excellent skills. His drawings, however, hinted at deeper, underlying problems. His self-portrait was barely an inch high. Any drawing less than two inches for a child this age can be a "red flag" of extreme insecurity and self-doubt. Family drawings suggested he felt isolated and rejected in his family, though he refused to comment on this.

"Sometimes even music cannot substitute for tears."

— Paul Simon

I made a point to see Kim for a 15- to 20-minute visit every Tuesday when I was at that school. Gradually, he seemed to trust me and the barriers came down. One day Kim said he was very afraid — terrified — of not doing well in school. That didn't make sense! Kim's last report card was all As and Bs. When I told him that, tears welled up. Finally, it came out . . .

Steve, Age 15
"Not good enough"

His parents were extremely disappointed in his report card. They believed he should be a straight-A student as he had been all the way through elementary school. Consequently, Kim was going to be "punished" for nine weeks until the next report card, when he should have all As.

*His punishment? Every evening, **for two hours**, Kim had to kneel in a corner with his knees on a pile of grains of raw rice. Imagine it. Imagine how your knees would hurt after just a few minutes of this! Imagine 15 minutes, ½ an hour, an hour, 2 hours! It was unfathomable to me.*

Clearly, this was a case of emotional abuse. Let me tell you, this is a spot most therapists hate to be in. After much agony, a child finally comes to trust the therapist enough with a secret, and then the therapist is ethically and legally bound to report it. Sometimes things improve, but sometimes they don't. Sometimes, it just gets harder on the child because he "told."

I wrestled with these issues as I dialed the Abuse Hotline. The first HRS case worker was confused. She'd never had a case like this. I ended up telling the story to another more experienced worker who also had the same trouble. Finally, I was connected with a supervisor.

*After hearing my report, he concluded that kneeling for 2 hours a night on grains of rice for over 2 months was **NOT** emotional abuse! He declared it "harsh discipline," and the case was closed. You be the judge. If that's not emotional abuse, what is?*

I even reviewed the case with my own supervisor to no avail. My only recourse seemed to be working with his teachers to understand Kim's plight and to ensure his report card would not be "disappointing" to his parents in the future. Also, the teacher who had first noted Kim's problem agreed to be a mentor for him . . . to establish a bond as much as possible.

It has been over 15 years since that incident. Kim still crosses my mind on occasion. How did the adult within him turn out? He's most likely a father himself now . . . is he continuing or breaking the patterns from his own childhood? Was the teacher who became his mentor enough to help him "rise above it"?

"Challenges make you discover things about yourself that you never really knew. They're what make the instrument stretch — what make you go beyond the norm."

— Cicely Tyson

In a case like this, whether you want to call it emotional abuse or harsh discipline, we must ask "WHY?" Why do some people hurt their children? Actually, very few are "criminal" or "mentally unbalanced" — most are "normal" but are **reacting** to past or present stresses which make them feel overwhelmed. Financial, employment or legal problems can cause an adult to **take it out** on a child. Many adults who were mistreated themselves have **no model** of how to raise a successful family.

Some parents, like Kim's, have **unrealistic expectations**. They expect a child to behave like an adult while he or she is still developing, or they expect perfection. Some caregivers are **isolated** from other adults, and they find caretaking too demanding. Some may expect the child to satisfy their own need for protection and self-esteem.

Here's the key: Look for a **pattern**. Every parent makes mistakes. We all make errors in our reasoning and action at times. When these errors are repeated and become a pattern, it is time for more serious help.

❧ Insecure Attachment

In the previous cases of Jason and Kevin, I was specifically pointing out the most extreme examples of **unattached children**. There are in reality many more **insecurely attached children**. They manage to "keep their heads above water," usually showing **despair** more than rage.

"Lost loves can never be
forgotten or replaced,
But if we allow it
the heart grows bigger
to make room for
new loves."

Brent, Age 7

— Susan White-Bowden

I believe that attachment is like most other features of human personality: it runs on a continuum. Children can be **securely** attached, **mildly** attached, **insecurely** attached or **unattached**.

Researchers have studied the level of attachment between parents and their children at one year of age. **Children who are MOST securely attached at age one have been found to have a lot going for them when they are older** (Sroufe 1983). At preschool age, they are popular and able to get along well with their peers. At kindergarten age, they are flexible and self-reliant when faced with problems.

Laura, Age 9

One day Laura went to school with her friend Katlyn she did all her assements then it was Math time her wrust subject she finish almost all her work exsept 5 problems she went to daycare she tried to do it but ther was to much noise. so when she got home here mothe got mad at her and told her that she was sick of her and said she was going back in the 3rd grade

AUTOBIOGRAPHICAL STORY
Note this child perceives her mother modeling
anger and frustration about her schoolwork, rather than patience and a
spirit of cooperation.
Notice too that this youngster is expressing the second strongest fear of
American children today.
After the #1 fear of losing a parent is the fear of
failing and repeating a grade.

"Memories of shame, guilt, rejection, hatred, resentment, and other unloving feelings cannot be converted to love."

Jack, Age 10

— Deepak Chopra

On the other hand, children who do not show that secure attachment to their parents at age one do not do as well later. Studies repeatedly show insecurely attached children to be more clingy with adults, less self-directive and often less happy and more aggressive. **Children who are not securely attached have more behavior problems when they reach school age and these behavior problems often last into adolescence.** As infants, they are more drowsy, squirming and irritable. As preschoolers, they are somewhat isolated from peers, and as young children they grow poorly and underachieve in school. Not only do they have more accidents and behavior problems, they score lower on ability and achievement tests (Zuckerman & Beardslee 1987).

How do these children develop such a sad pattern? Frequently, insecurely attached youngsters start off in the world by having a depressed mother. Some 12 to 20 percent of American mothers with children under age 5 suffer from **depression** (Garrison & Earls 1986). The mothers display symptoms such as listlessness, sadness, dissatisfaction with their own lives, trouble concentrating and frequently eating and/or sleep disorders. In reference to parenting, these mothers tend to perceive their children as "bothersome" and "hard to care for." As far as discipline, they tend to be quite punitive and in fact view their own lives as "out of control" (Field, et al. 1985; Whiffin & Gotlib 1989).

Usually the pattern starts early, with insufficient bonding during infancy. Rather than anticipate and respond to a baby's emotional signals, depressed mothers are **consistently unresponsive**. The babies try to let it be known they have needs (by crying) but when their moms don't respond (repeated failure), they feel powerless. Often they will try to comfort themselves by sucking or rocking. What are they learning about the world? (Pause here and guess . . .) They learn that other people are unreliable and that the world is not safe or trustworthy.

REAL LIFE: Jeremy's parents sat before me, a loving couple full of care and nurturing for their two adopted children. Their younger daughter was adopted a few days after birth. While she had her ups and downs, most of it could be considered as "normal" growth stages.

Doing something fun: Playing a Game

Notice that although Jeremy is portraying a happy family situation, he is somehow separated from the rest of his family members.
In this case, it is a board game between them, and Jeremy's eyes are even facing the opposite direction.

Jeremy, however, showed more emotional problems. He was exceedingly anxious in general. Specifically, he worried about being separated from significant others. At school, he had to always know where his teacher was. At home, he sought constant reassurance that his mother or father were close by. For example, he would be watching TV and yell out "Mom?" If she answered "I'm here," from the next room, he'd be fine. If not, he'd jump up, panicky, running until he found her. Even at age 7, he was preoccupied as to whether he would ever find a girl to marry him!

"When there is something big
and uncertain to face, a
comforting, reassuring hand
can help us overcome the
anxiety we feel, allowing us
to accomplish what we could
never do alone."
— Susan White-Bowden

John, Age 9

Even though Jeremy is too young to remember it consciously, his early
infancy experiences had a dramatic impact on his later lack of security.
Before his adoption at age 6 months, he was often left alone in his crib or
strapped to a baby carrier in an empty room. His incompetent biological
mother either ignored him or, more often, was out of the house. Instead of
learning the normal cycle of getting needs met by communicating them (by
crying), Jeremy learned that the world was not a caring and predictable
place. He learned he was an ineffective being and that nurturing was
arbitrary.

Although Jeremy is gradually becoming stronger and more self-confident,
those early emotional scars will most likely be carried for a long time,
manifested in this burden of anxiety. He is blessed to have warm,
supportive parents to help him through it.

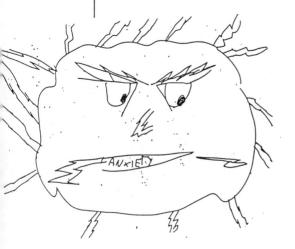

TIP: With children, I use specific
words to help them label their feelings.
Just appropriately naming the
nebulous, uncomfortable feeling within
as "Anxiety" gives them a start to get
a handle on it.

IMPROVING ATTACHMENT

Knowing the research about bonding is powerful information! This is
not to say that securely loved children will be perfect. Rather, they
have more assets to draw from, particularly in handling their feelings
and getting along with others. Keep in mind that children's
development is a **continuous process.** They need love and nurturing
when they grow older just as they did as babies.

The good news is that caregivers who have been less than nurturing can
change. This change, in turn, can significantly impact some insecurely
attached children. (Keep in mind I am not referring here to severely
disturbed unattached children.) Caregivers can be taught specific
behaviors to become more **warm, supporting** and **loving.** In turn,
the children become more affectionate, cooperative and able to handle
challenge (Field, Widmayer 1982). Think of it! By changing what
you do, you can help a child become more competent and happy!

❥ Attunement

Bonding through displays of love starts very early in life, in fact
immediately after birth. A caring mother shows her love to her infant
by being sensitive and responding to his signals. She is quick to pick
up the baby when he is distressed and will readily comfort him if he is
fussy. A responsive mother also reacts to her infant's desire to play by
sharing the play time, using age-appropriate toys and activities.

"Love is like a mirror. When
you love another you become his
mirror and he becomes yours . . .
And reflecting each other's love
you see infinity."

— Leo Buscaglia

George, Age 9

As the baby becomes older, the mother will enmesh herself in her child's emotional state. For example, when a baby puts a ring on a peg and looks up excited, the mother may laugh and clap for him. Thus, even though the baby is not talking verbally, the mother is understanding and responding to his signals, in this case, excitement. Psychologists use the term "attunement" to describe this participation in the baby's experience — sharing his emotions and feelings. It is my belief that caregivers can "attune" to children no matter what their age. It takes a commitment to invest time and energy to display your love.

As far as older children, they are certainly more complex in their abilities and emotions. Even so, they too require much sensitivity from caregivers. A sad child may be worried about a school test, thinking about a problem with a friend or just feeling tired. A responsive caregiver shows love by reading the cues, showing support, and offering — not forcing — the opportunity to talk.

Larie, Age 11

Turn this page upside down to see the child's reflection in the lake.
This is a poignant portrayal of how children
may not show their true feelings
on the outside.

❥ Teenagers

Adolescence is a tumultuous age. It is easy for children to feel neglected — and they deliberately do things which may trigger alienation! Even with adolescents whose development has been fine, the typical struggle with independence at this stage can sometimes lead to frustration and anger. This in turn makes the youth more vulnerable to problems such as drug abuse, delinquency or sexual promiscuity. This is a time when caregivers need to clearly show their interest in and respect for their children. A word of warning: at this late stage, if attachment has not been strong all along, be prepared to put in a lot of work to improve the situation.

"If you love something, set it free.
If it returns to you, it's yours.
If it never does return, it never was."

— Anonymous

Val,
Age 7

❥ Letting Go

Now, you're probably thinking that my reference to "letting go" means just the opposite of bonding. In reality, it is all part of the continuum of children's development from helpless infants to responsible adults. Somewhere along the line, our love includes stepping back, trusting and being there when they fall down. This is the most **unselfish** kind of love.

Erich Fromm (1956) regarded the separation of child from parents as a difficult but necessary task. He wrote that the adult caregivers must not only tolerate but "must wish and support the child's separation . . . it requires unselfishness, the ability to give everything and to want nothing but the happiness of the loved one."

More recent writers have expanded on this. It seems that children who are nourished too long and too excessively, regardless of what they do, never progress beyond the self-love of infancy. They become narcissists. They never learn "through love, to view others as separate persons with a worth and value equal to their own" (Lerner 1999).

Consequently, gradually during childhood, and especially in adolescence, "**unconditional love must become conditional upon certain expected behaviors**" (Parker 1999). Otherwise, we are creating narcissistic children who believe their interests and rights are most important. When thwarted, they become rage-filled and seek revenge, often dramatically, as seen in the increasing incidents of tragic, callous violence.

RELEASING RESENTMENT

When we feel we have been wronged, it is easy to carry our resentment like a burden. Feelings of anger, injustice and hurt can seethe inside us. Releasing resentment is **not a favor** we do for others. It is **a key to our own well-being**. It frees us from being stuck in the past with old pain. Remember wounds of the heart in the section titled Good Intentions: STICKS AND STRAW?

"People who have been injured can find themselves with a double burden: there's the original injury and then there's a choking hatred and disillusionment to digest. That's often a meal we are forced to eat by ourselves."

Kate,
Age 4

— Dr. Molly Layton

❥ Forgiveness

Forgiveness is not easy. Our instincts tend to lead us to hostility and revenge instead. What we need to teach our children — more from example than from words — is that it's OK to be angry if you've been hurt. It is NOT OK to hurt someone back.

If we say we forgive, then go on to hold a grudge, what are we really teaching? This goes for all aspects of life from "the silent treatment" after a spat with a loved one to cussing out a stranger for poor driving. Similarly, we can usually force a child to mouth the words, "I'm sorry," but we cannot make a child truly feel sorry.

"Forgiveness is a process that begins with apology and continues with a show of repentance."

— Wes Crenshaw & Greg Tangari

Will, Age 9

The best we can do is **model forgiveness** and **teach empathy**. We, as caregivers, are not always right. It's a humbling but powerful message to tell your children you are sorry and ask forgiveness. Your children come to see that you are human and make mistakes. Even more important, they see you can **make amends.**

Empathy comes from understanding that people who lash out and hurt us are often hurting in their own way. When people do something deliberately mean, it does not imply they hate us. They could be going through a tough time themselves. Children who are experiencing a divorce in their family are a good example. Engelhardt and Sontag (1998) offer the following memory trigger to help teach us to . . .

Find ways to praise your child's empathy

  Open your own heart to those who have hurt you

    Refrain from joining in your children's fights

      Give your child the tools to handle anger

        Invite your child to walk in another's shoes

          Value and model forgiveness

            Experience together your Higher Power

Age levels are important. Young children (4 - 7 years old) tend to be self-centered, but they are beginning to be aware of others' feelings. Open the path to empathy with questions such as, "What can you do to help the other person feel better?" or "What would you be feeling right now if that happened to you?"

Older children (8 - 12 years old) experience more hurt feelings by being bullied, teased and rejected. Try to teach the child to avoid bad mouthing or getting revenge. Fall back, if possible, on some of the many tools in this book: problem-solving, feedback, self-control, optimism, ear mirrors. Adolescents can learn this and more because of their increased ability with abstract thinking. They can see even more clearly that something else might be going on "under the surface" of a person's unkind behavior.

Smile your on

candid camera

Cindy, Age 7

❥ Marital Conflicts

Adults who constantly argue in front of children probably have no idea how devastating this can be. Children do not need to hear that Dad is lazy or Mom nags too much, especially if there is a lot of yelling and insulting going on. While parents may think that they're solving a problem or just blowing off steam, the children can become anxious and fearful. Their hopelessness to change the situation can lead to guilt, self-blame and childhood depression. Some children try to be the referee — an awesome task for a psychotherapist, much less a child. Some children believe they have to take sides.

REAL LIFE: Notice the sense of guilt and blame in Angie's drawing of her parents fighting. In fact, the child and her sibling are hiding to stay out of it directly, but they're staying close enough to hear everything.

Angie, Age 8

Please do not misunderstand me to say adults should distance themselves and hide all possible problems. On the contrary, if there is respect and maturity, children can learn some good things. They can see that differences of opinion exist and that open communication can contribute to resolution or at least honesty and understanding.

"You cannot shake hands
with a clenched fist."

— Indira Gandhi

Ben, Age 11

REAL LIFE: Now see the difference in Angie's drawing after her parents participated in counseling. Problems will crop up in any marriage. These parents learned techniques to handle them, and everyone was happier.

Angie, Age 8

James, Age 11

"There is no difficulty that enough love will not conquer; no disease that enough love will not heal; no door that enough love will not open; no gulf that enough love will not bridge; no wall that enough love will not throw down; no sin that enough love will not redeem . . .

It makes no difference how deeply seated may be the trouble; how hopeless the outlook; how muddled the tangle; how great the mistake. A sufficient realization of love will dissolve it all. If only you could love enough you would be the happiest and most powerful being in the world . . ."

— Emmet Fox, *The Sermon on the Mount*

A PIGGY PORTION OF LOVE SECRETS

Regardless of a child's age, intentionally send messages of love to build a secure attachment. To help build a stronger bond, here are some specific **SECRETS** . . .

❧ Affection/Tenderness

A smile, a hug, or a simple "I love you" can go a long way in fostering self-esteem — especially if it's given for no special reason other than "because you're my kid." Counselors and psychotherapists use a big term called **unconditional positive regard**. While this sounds verbose, if you go back and read each word carefully, you will see exactly what it means: showing support and good feelings for the other person regardless of the circumstances (that is, whether the person "earned" it or not).

REAL LIFE: One of the saddest interactions I ever saw had nothing to do directly with the case on which I had been working. The case itself involved a rebellious teenage boy named José. He had repeatedly been disciplined at school for issues such as insubordination and defiance. School personnel had requested a parent conference to discuss their next step. Not only did both parents show up, they brought with them their infant, strapped in a baby carrier placed on the floor.

*The baby was restless and cranky, but as adults we rose to the occasion and conducted the meeting. I observed the most astounding thing as time went on: **not once** in the course of more than an hour did either parent ever actually **touch** the baby! They did a number of other behaviors — pushing in a pacifier, attempting a bottle, holding up a rattle, even rocking the carrier with a foot — but neither ever actually made physical contact!*

Though the focus of our conference was obviously the older brother's behavior problem, I could not help but wonder if the roots of it had started long ago with poor bonding during infancy. I would also love to know how this baby, who is probably a teenager herself now, is developing.

"The most any human can
ever hope for is to be loved.
This is all that really matters."

— Gloria Estefan

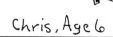

Chris, Age 6

➤ Dignity

While we may be disappointed or frustrated with the **child's actions**, we need to be clear that this is an unacceptable **behavior**, not that the child is mean or despicable. Criticism that says "you are a bad kid" can be damaging to a child's self-concept and can cause resentment. In contrast, feedback which says "pulling up the neighbor's flowers was not a fair or kind thing to do" leaves open the possibility that there is room for improvement. In one way we are condemning the child; in the other way we are encouraging change and allowing improvement. Of course, as part of this latter philosophy, the child would be required to **make amends** too.

*REAL LIFE: In my office I often ask children to tell me about themselves by using **Sentence Seeds**. Eight-year-old Janet's replies were heart-breaking. Sample responses were:*

The best thing about me ... "I don't know anything for that."
The worst thing about me ... "I'm bad."
The teachers think ... "I'm dumb."
If I could wish for anything I'd wish ... "I could be good."

HINT 📖: For more details on **Sentence Seeds**, see Step 1 -
PRAISE, Step 2 - Listening Times.

*As it turned out, evaluation showed that Janet was in fact Gifted!
Unfortunately, she also had a strong profile of Attention Deficit
Hyperactivity Disorder (ADHD).*

*Because of her restlessness, impulsivity and
distractibility (hallmarks of ADHD), she was
always being told how "bad" or "dumb" or "lazy"
she was. Although her treatment was of course
multi-faceted, one key piece was to allow the
child to keep her dignity. No negative names
were allowed. **Specific inappropriate
behaviors were labeled and given a
warning.***

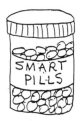

HINT 📖: For more details on **labeling behaviors**,
see Step 3 - LIMITS.

*Similarly, positive features were highlighted and pointed out. Several
months later, Janet walked proudly into my office and proclaimed she had
become "smart." Obviously her IQ didn't change, but her view of the world
sure did!*

HINT 📖: For more details on **positive features**,
see Step 1 - PRAISE.

Timmy, Age 5

"Children are our life blood,
the essence of our future.
What we put forth to a child,
be it positive or negative,
will be incorporated into
that child's persona."

— Maureen Garth

❧ Prompt Attention

As difficult as it is in our busy schedules, we need to respond quickly to our children's cues. Having confidence that a caregiver will **be there** when needed leads children to feel secure. This sense of security makes children more comfortable in tackling tough situations and coping with problems.

Maawm! Would you get me the remote????

TIP: The line between prompt attention and manipulation can become fuzzy. Keep in mind that we need to respond as soon as possible when a child is truly needy. We must not cater to a child's every beck and call, however. If this happens, "bonding feels more like bondage" (Sears 1998). Remember, overindulged children can become narcissistic and incapable of being sensitive to others' needs and feelings.

❧ Availability

Being accessible does not mean always being **physically** available, but we must be **psychologically** available. Ideally, we should be willing and able to take a call from our children at any time, with the understanding that this privilege will not be abused. Children should know how to reach their caregivers (or designated substitutes) at all times. Availability in a child's life is one of the strongest predictors of overall academic success. A major study involving over 1,000 schools across the nation showed that parents of students who do the best are involved with them and show interest in their grades and homework (NCES 1985).

Adolescents least likely to get in trouble with the law or drop out of school are those whose caregivers provide supervision after school — even if it is not "on site." This may mean telephone contact, an agreed-upon schedule of chores and homework and a familiar environment (Steinberg 1986). On the other hand, teens who spend their time unsupervised (especially if caregivers do not know exactly where they are) are much more likely to be swayed by negative peer influences.

"As a child, my family's menu consisted of two choices --
take it or leave it."

— Buddy Hackett

Ron, Age 7

TIP: Make arrangements for children to call a substitute (relative or reliable neighbor) if you are not available. When a child comes home to an empty house, a special note on the counter or a phone call from you (ideally at the same time every day) can instill feelings of security.

Dear Larry,
    Hope you had a good day at school. There's left-over pizza in the fridge if you get hungry.
    Your chores today are:
① unload dishwasher
② water outside plants
③ call grandma and see if she's feeling better.
✱ Don't forget your homework
    Love, Mom

*REAL LIFE: One afternoon my beeper went off in the middle of a session. This was mind-boggling, as all clients and colleagues know the beeper number is strictly for emergencies and crises **after** office hours. With apologies to my client and growing irritation, I checked the beeper for the incoming number. My stomach sank as my own home phone stared me in the face!*

Immediately calling back, I became increasing agitated, thinking "this better be important!" It was. One of our cats had gotten hit by a car. Misty was bleeding and lethargic, causing my daughter to become hysterical. I could not to leave the office immediately, but I was able to reach a neighbor. We made arrangements to get the cat and my daughter to the vet, where I would meet them shortly.

"Misty with arm in cast."

Larie, Age 11

*Of all the memories of that awful day, I hope the one that stays with Larié will be that I was **psychologically available** when she needed me. Her concern was urgent, and she received immediate help. (P.S. After 2 days in "intensive care" and several months of follow-up treatment, Misty survived and now has only a limp to show for the trauma.)*

❧ Time Together

Studies have shown that spending time together is critical to a child's healthy development. Of course we would expect that, since we already know that bonding is a major protective factor which shows up in resilient children. And how will the bond grow unless some time is invested?

"Only one security cannot be taken way, and it resides within. Security based on our own belief in ourselves, in our ability not only to cope and survive, but to celebrate life is the only security that lasts."

— Earnie Larsen & Carol Larsen Hegarty

Shared time helps people communicate, show positive feelings and solve problems. Happy, healthy families make an effort to devote time to activities everyone can enjoy. There is no question, however, that finding time to do things together is a big problem.

HINT 📖: **Time Together** is addressed in detail in Step 5 - TIME.

The importance of spending time with a parent is reflected here in Sally's drawings for her father. He had good intentions but was often called back to work unexpectedly.

Thank you for ..

Being my dad and always being there
doing things with us maybe we could
do more camping trips .... Stuff like that

I feel disappointed when ...
you say something/promise. and
you don't do it.

There are 1440 minutes in each day. How many do you allot just to be with your child?

"*There's a time for all things.*"

— *William Shakespeare*

Lee, Age 12

❥ Responsibility

Recall that Responsibility is another one of the big protective factors leading to resilience. Like time together, this issue is so critical it deserves its own chapter.

At this time, I mainly want to point out that children need to see that **everyone** has responsibilities. Caregivers do not need to feel guilty or apologetic for their careers. Young people can learn that adults have work responsibilities that demand time and energy.

Children should, however, feel that they are just as important as their caregivers' careers — not competing with them. A family can be viewed as a **team** where each member has important roles and jobs.

HINT 📖: For more details on **Responsibility**, see
        Step 6 - RESPONSIBILITY.

John, Age 9

"It's my job to walk the dog."

"The willingness to accept responsibility for one's own life is the source from which self-respect springs."

"I'm helping Mommy. We water the flowers."

Kathy, Age 7   — Joan Didion

TIP: Toddlers can be expected to put their toys away. Preschoolers might set the table. Six-year-olds might help load the dishwasher. Adolescents can take out the garbage or help cook dinner. All children can contribute to pet care in some way. It does not really matter what the task is, so long as the child is involved. Some adults even deliberately create tasks (such as watering the plants, even though it just rained) in order to give the child the feeling of contributing an important service.

➤ Reading Together

Because adequate reading level is another key protective factor, reading to children is clearly a message of love. Read to children a little every day if you can. Bedtime is great, but it can be any time of the day. Even older children and teens can enjoy special reading time. Caregivers can read more complex books to children than they would be able to read themselves (we recently finished *The Hobbit* at our house). It sets up a beautiful family tradition.

Not only that, reading together has a tremendous influence on a child's academic success. The major factor influencing a child's school achievement is NOT socioeconomic status — income, occupation and education (White 1982). The major influence is **a home atmosphere where reading is valued** — reading material is available at home, caregivers support education, and they talk to the children.

TIP: Reading in unison has been found to be a highly effective way of improving oral reading. This involves the adult and child reading aloud together. If the child becomes "stumped" on a word, the adult simply says it aloud, and the two continue reading together. This technique seems to be much less frustrating for children than alternating reading sections.

> **Surprises**

To give children happy memories of their childhood is one of the greatest of all gifts. Happy early memories become treasures that can trigger stability and reassurance in tougher later years. A child's life can be one of exploration and wonder — don't forget to join in. **For no reason at all** dare to listen to some music together, go for a walk in the woods, or have an indoor picnic. Instead of waiting for the child to "earn" a treat by good grades or whatever, suggest a spur-of-the-moment trip to get an ice-cream cone.

"Humanity takes itself too seriously. It's the world's original sin."
— Oscar Wilde

Joe, Age 8

Feel the joy in this child's drawing about "a happy day." Her parents had followed counseling advice and had an unscheduled chunk of family fun time. The child announced, "I wasn't even expecting it!"

Tara, Age 6

TIP: Kasl (1994) suggests we replace our knee-jerk reactions of "No, not now" with a simple "Why not?" She asks questions such as,

"**Why not** blow up the new balloons right now, in bed?"
"**Why not** run around the store and look at things?"
"**Why not** go out to the airport just to ride the tram back and
        forth?"
"**Why not** have a friend over to spend the night?"

*We can simply ask ourselves, what could really happen? If it feels like "no" for some reason, figure out why. **Use limits** if you need to. For example, tell the child, "It's OK to have your friend sleep over, but I am very tired. You'll have to have lights out by 10:00, and you'll have to make your own breakfast."*

> "Life is a series of surprises,
> and would not be worth
> taking or keeping
> if it were not."
>
> — Ralph Waldo Emerson

Mike, Age 5

REAL LIFE: Eleven-year-old Marcie came to see me recently while going through a grief process after losing her father to cancer. One of her biggest concerns was that whenever she tried to remember her father, she could only see him sickly, bald and lethargic in bed. Using relaxation and visualization techniques, we were able to prompt some happy memories which we put into a homemade booklet. Notice that what Marcie remembered was not a big gift like a video system, but unexpected happy times together.

Marcie remembers her dad had a sense of humor. Some people did not understand. He did things like sway the car back and forth going up a mountain. One time he put a stink bomb on an elevator! One time he put fake poop on someone's couch! Marcie's dad made lots of people laugh.

Ask yourself right now what are some of your happiest memories from your own childhood? Were they big events or simple shared times? Ask yourself too what kind of deposits you're making in your child's memory banks?

❥ Not Interrupting

Many caregivers with behavior-problem children complain that they are unable to do things, such as talk on the phone, cook dinner, or visit with a neighbor, without the child interrupting what they are doing.

"Having children is like having a bowling alley installed in your brain."

— *Martin Mull*

The following steps help children be more independent when you are busy. These ideas are adapted from Barkley's (1987) excellent work. The procedure requires that we pay attention and praise a child for staying away and not interrupting us. It sounds like a paradox — if the child is not interrupting us, **we have to interrupt ourselves**! It gets back to changing OUR behavior in order for children to change THEIR behavior. Many caregivers provide a lot of attention to a child who is interrupting them but almost no attention to a child who plays independently and does not interrupt. No wonder youngsters interrupt adults so much!

To teach a child to give you time and space when you are busy, try the following. (Before starting this, make sure you have plenty of "chips in the bank!" That means you spend sufficient time interacting with your child other times.)

♦ **Give firm instructions in two parts.** The first part tells the child what to do while you are busy. It should be something pleasant (coloring, cutting, doing a puzzle), **not** a chore. The second part specifically says not to interrupt or bother you. For instance, you can say "I have to talk on the telephone, so I want you to stay in this room and read your book. Do not bother me." Remember, give the child both parts.

♦ **Stop in the middle of your activity.** Go to the child and give praise for staying away and not interrupting. Remind the child to stay with the assigned task, and return to what you were doing. Wait a few moments longer before returning to the child and again praising. Return to your activity, wait a little longer, and so on.

♦ **Gradually reduce how often you praise.** At first, you will have to interrupt what you are doing and go praise the child very frequently. For very young children, it may be 30 seconds to 2 minutes. After a few times like this, wait 3 minutes, then wait 5 minutes, slowly increasing the period of time before going back to praise the child. Eventually, you can complete your activity without interruption or stop just briefly now and then if it's a long activity.

♦ **Keep listening.** If it sounds like the child is about to leave the activity to bother you, immediately stop what you are doing. Go praise and redirect the child to the same or a different task.

LW

♦ **Provide special praise as soon as you are finished.** You may even periodically give the child a small, unexpected privilege or reward for having left you alone while you worked on your project.

♦ **Practice beforehand.** If you choose talking on the phone, you might want to have your spouse or a friend call you once or twice a day simply as a time to practice this method. That way, when important calls do come in, you have already trained the child to begin to stay away for a while so you can handle these calls without interruption.

♦ Here are some activities that caregivers normally do, during which you can try this method.

Preparing a meal	Accomplishing any special project
Talking to an adult	Using the telephone or computer
Writing a letter	Reading or watching television
Doing paperwork	Visiting others' homes
Talking at the dinner table	Housecleaning

☀ Role Modeling

In the last 15 years or so, it seems that behaviors of "rudeness" have increased dramatically. I used to consider it a developmental stepping stone of adolescence. I now constantly see it in 8- to 10-year-olds. Sadly, this rude attitude has become so ingrained that children themselves often do not recognize it as negative or unusual. One high-school student was very aware, however, writing, "Maybe rude comes with age, experience and a cell phone, or maybe it's a college class, Pushy and Rude 101. Wherever they learned it, [they] are everywhere" (Longster 1997).

> "True politeness is perfect ease in freedom. It simply consists of treating others just as you love to be treated yourself."
> — Earl of Chesterfield

"The Big Mouth"
"Stop and Think = Steve, Age 7

Often it is not **what** is said but **how** it is said. For example, if someone asks, "Do you want to go to the mall?," you could reply with the words "Of course, I want to go to the mall." On the one hand, these words could be said in an impudent, sullen manner while rolling the eyes, which implies "Are you too stupid to realize that?" On the other hand, the same words could be said with excitement and anticipation suggesting gratitude for the invitation.

It's not what you said that got you in trouble, it's how you said it!

*REAL LIFE: Fourth-grader Sandra is a perfect example of "oblivious rudeness." During a session including her mother, Sandra was constantly throwing out little barbs of sarcasm and insults toward her mother and me. When she was confronted, she adamantly denied any rudeness because she could not **recognize** it. With their permission, I then tape-recorded about 15 minutes of conversation. We replayed the tape aloud, pausing frequently to let Sandra listen to herself. At first she didn't "get it," saying "everybody I know talks like that." Maybe so. Regardless, this was not OK behavior (remember LIMITS and **Picking Your Battles**).*

How could you be so stupid? I'm smarter and better than you obviously.

You are just as important as I am. I am no better than you.

THE {POWER} OF VOICE

This drawing is one Sandra and I made together during one of her therapy sessions to help her tell the difference in different tones of voice.

*We spent an entire session just focusing on **tone**, the **way** something is said. In this case, Sandra learned to monitor her own responses and correct herself if she slipped into "Queen of the World" thinking. Monitoring by her mother was also part of the plan. For example, no more sarcastic sitcoms were allowed at home. If she did watch them with her friends, that was something we could not control.*

"Queen of the World Thinking"

Susan, Age 10

"My big mouth got me in trouble again."

Pat, Age 11

"Life is not so short
but that there
is always
room for courtesy."

— *Ralph Waldo Emerson*

FINAL NOTE

My work with caregivers throughout the years has convinced me that inevitably, they "love" their children. The challenge is sending that message of love so their children recognize it and grow from it. These messages can include displays of affection and prompt attention. They can be as simple as being available and as difficult as teaching respect.

"To cheat oneself out of love
is the most terrible deception;
it is an eternal loss for which
there is no reparation,
either in time or in eternity."

— Kierkegaard

Marsha, Age 7

By being aware of the importance of "secure attachment," we can take the first steps toward changing our behavior to become warmer, more supportive and more available. It is very encouraging to know that when caregivers change their behavior in this way, children respond by being more capable human beings. In this way, our messages of love help children become more competent, self-confident and resilient.

"*Love is a fruit
in season at all times,
and within the reach
of every hand.*"

— *Mother Teresa*

Andy, Age 9

OVERVIEW ~ Step 5:
TIME

STATISTICS ABOUT TIME
- Average Americans
- Television

CONFRONTING THE TIME MONSTERS
- Response Cost System
- Self-Control
- Brain Open, Mouth Shut
- Technology: Screens
- Changing Patterns
- Budgeting Time
- A Perfect Day
- No is OK
- Family Calendar

A PIGGY PORTION OF TIME SECRETS
- Transition Time
- Everyday Events
- Time is Not Always Money
- Daily News
- Meal Time
- Bed Time
- Car Time
- Shared Projects
- No Second Guessing

FINAL NOTE

Secrets of the Third Little Pig

Step 5

Pigs that wallow together
live in Hog Heaven.

TIME

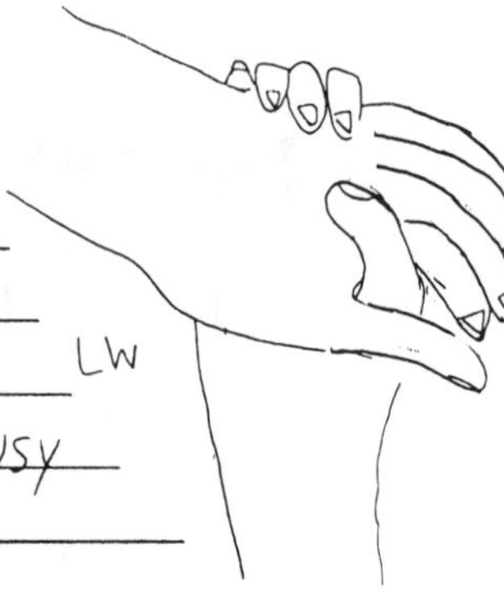

Me And You.

Come on Mommy,
You never want to play.   LW
Your always much to busy
Every single day.

Come on, Daddy,
Throw me a ball.
You all way say "Tomarrow"
We never play at all.

Mommy, Daddy,
Don't you have time for me
I kind of miss you
I get lonely you see.

Take me to a movie,
Take me for a walk.
Lets go out for dinner,
Or Lets just sitt and talk.

I dont care what we do.
I just want to be with you.

Carié '97 11yrs.

"Few people actually waste time, they just don't use it properly."

— Edwin Bliss

Jesse, Age 8

With all the things that demand our attention in everyday life, it is easy to consider time with children as a "luxury." Nothing could be further from the truth. The opportunity for children to spend time interacting with their caregivers contributes a great deal to their emotional development. For one thing, they learn things directly from more experienced adults. They also indirectly pick up many higher values. Most importantly, they have an opportunity to bond with their significant caregivers, something we know is critical for resilient children.

STATISTICS ABOUT TIME

Some of the statistics about shared time with children are startling. The findings below are based on research by a number of different investigators (Hart 1987; Jenkins 1992; Robinson 1977; Schaefer & DiGeronimo 1994).

♪ Average Americans

♦ The average working couple spends only **thirty seconds a day** talking with their children.

♦ The average father spends **less than five minutes a week** giving individual attention to each child in the family.

♦ The average five-year-old spends only **twenty-five minutes a week** interacting closely with his/her father; **twenty-five hours a week** are spent by the same child interacting closely with the television!

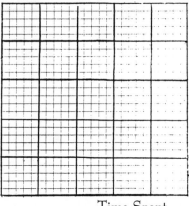

Time Spent in
Parent Interaction

Time Spent
Watching TV

We know that children are like sponges. They actively absorb that to which they are exposed. If they are not spending time with us, then who or what are they spending it with? If we as caregivers are not instilling our values in them, where are children picking up their virtues?

Often children spend as much or more time with substitutes as they do with their main caregivers. The list of substitutes is endless — babysitters, teachers, television, computer (especially "the Net"), video games, peers, even "the street." Some of these are excellent stand-ins when we cannot be available. Others, of course, are hardly desirable. My point is we need to be **aware** of how our young people are spending their time and if that's what we want for them.

❥ Television

On the positive side, television gives us access to information unheard of in previous generations. We can watch news in the making, see astronauts live in space, and find out about other cultures around the world. There are entire stations devoted to educational and fun programs for the family, and it is commonplace to tape a movie or show to watch later at our convenience. We can hear about the joys and pains of others and feel comforted or motivated for change.

*REAL LIFE: I admit that I am a rare television-viewer, but there are times when the image on the screen portrays a message with power unmatched by other means. When I taught a college course in Human Development, I had my students watch an episode of Oprah Winfrey. The guest that day talked about her severe childhood abuse and how she had escaped the pain by escaping her reality. She still carried the wounds. She developed multiple personalities so that "other people" could take her abuse and she could survive. Of course, I know about MPD (Multiple Personality Disorder), but here was a lady in flesh and blood **daring to tell her anguish so others could be healed.***

"There are shows on the airwaves right now that model kindness, compassion and generosity . . . Make an effort to **find** them and encourage your children to watch them."

— Charles E. Schaefer &
Theresa Foy DiGeronimo

Joe, Age 8

All of us watching were touched. Many cried. Was there any other way I could have made the same impact on these young adults? Probably not. A lecture may have gotten the information across, but actually seeing this woman on television as she courageously shared her story was powerful. In fact, very unexpectedly, several of the students opened up to me, when writing their essays, about their own abuse.

On the negative side, television can become an electronic hypnosis machine, with children dully absorbing whatever is on the screen. Look at these additional statistics (Hart 1987; Jenkins 1992; Robinson 1977; Schaefer & DiGeronimo 1994).

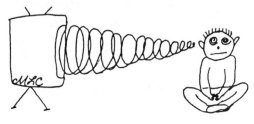

♦ The average American family watches more than six hours of television every day. The average American child watched 6,000 hours of television before entering kindergarten at age 5.

♦ The average American father spends **10 to 20 hours** a week engaged in television watching. He spends less than **10 minutes** a week engaged in quality time with his child.

♦ Children witness an estimated 20 acts of violence during each hour of TV viewing.

"It is only with the heart that one can see rightly;
what is essential
is invisible to the eye."

— Antoine de Saint-Exupéry

Ted, Age 12

Unfortunately, a lot of routine television viewing gives children **adult-created images** that may not have the values we would intend for them.

REAL LIFE: I also shared with my college class a show randomly selected from Saturday morning cartoons. We were treated to the tantalizing plot of one of the characters having a collection of boogers (yes, you read right, from picking his nose) which he kept in a special clear jar. Is this TV at its finest or what?

Lee, Age 10

Rudeness is a value that appears regularly as the basis for humor on some sitcoms. Insults and sarcasm are shown to be funny. Dyer (1985) concludes that "continuous watching of television programs and commercials reinforces smart-alecky behavior."

Violence also becomes a form of entertainment on television. Jenkins (1992) notes a study by the American Academy of Pediatricians which concludes "repeated exposure to TV violence can make children violent and accepting of real-life violence." Reducing TV time by ½-hour a day will reduce a child's violence intake by seventy incidents per week!

The T.V. Monster

A huge concern for me about television is that when children are simply watching, they are not interacting with other people. If this is frequent, it can **prevent the development of healthy human relationships.** Passive television viewing interferes with "the talks, the games, the family festivals, and the arguments through which the character is formed" (Brofenbrenner 1986).

> "Television is the most serious competitor for our children's minds and values — followed closely by computer and video games. Stand firm. When your boys say, 'But other kids can watch as much as they want,' be prepared to say, 'These are the rules in our family.'"
>
> —T. Berry Brazelton, M.D.

Ron, Age 11

CONFRONTING THE TIME MONSTERS

Lack of time is a problem for all of us. Many of us feel conflicted about how we spend time. Should we pay the bills and return phone calls or spend a day with the kids? Then there are the unexpected "TIME MONSTERS" that catch us — a traffic jam, morning meltdowns, ill family members, an overflowing commode, a trip to the vet (or dentist or orthodontist). Emergencies happen. On top of that, we need to have time for ourselves, whether it is quiet time for relaxation or active time for exercise. Let's see what we can do to have more time and make that time as pleasant as possible with children.

> "We are frantically busy 'providing' for our kids: food, clothing, education. We rarely have time to 'provide' them with **ourselves**."
>
> — Jonathan and Wendy Lazear

Michael, Age 11

❥ Response Cost

If backtalk and rude attitude are a problem at your house, you probably don't enjoy the time you **do** spend with your children. You might consider a "**Response Cost**" system. Don't worry that you'll have to do this system forever. It's simply a strategy to break old habits and establish more respect and communication in the family. Gradually, you will want to shift to social reinforcement (praise, unexpected surprises, etc.) in place of money. Even so, some caregivers have told me this system works so well, they are reluctant to give it up!

To start, simply agree to pay the child the week's spending money in coins. Make a big deal of it. Say, "We're giving you a raise -- a hefty increase in salary! What do you have to do for it? Just breathe! Imagine all that money! What will you do with it?" Get the child to buy into this. Spend a few minutes fantasizing about how the extra funds will be handled.

Then clarify a bit. "By the way, you will be getting paid in COINS." (Nickels, dimes or quarters and how much per week are individual family decisions). "Oh, and you will be FINED for any specific behavior I consider rude. Whatever is left at the end of the week you get to keep!"

As an example, let's say your child received $1 per day for the week. On Sunday (or whatever day you decide), you put $7 worth of quarters in a clear cup, possibly on top of the refrigerator. Every time your child talks back or is rude, LABEL it (remember you are TEACHING here), fine quickly and let it go. Any argument, such as "You can't fine me just for rolling my eyes, you cannot tell what I'm thinking" is met with a clear, calm, neutral response such as "I'm sorry you feel that way." Walk in another room if you can. Let the **teaching** sink in. Fine again only if you really have to, if the child won't let up.

"Me and my big
mouth"
Sally, Age 7

REAL LIFE: We implemented this technique with 13-year-old Kendra. She was thrilled because she was to be given a roll of quarters a week! That's $10 more than she'd ever had before! She envisioned all the things she would buy with her $40 at the end of the month, mostly CD's and posters for her room. She was sure she could overcome her backtalk habit. Guess what? After the first week, she had only 50 cents left! (Happily, this improved dramatically after that.)

❥ Self-Control

Some parents have told me they worry that if children are not allowed to "vent" their anger, they will hold it in and be worse off. wrong, Wrong, WRONG! Contrary to popular belief, "venting" is futile and often makes things worse. People who yell, curse, throw things, stomp their feet, hit the wall and so on are **more likely to remain just as upset** for hours afterward! (Bushman 1999). What's worse, if they keep it up it can lead to major health problems such as heart disease or other illness (Williams 1994). Remember too that exploding with anger is an impulse, and poor impulse control is a major risk factor.

"The first person who gets mad loses."
– Dr. Wanda Eppes

❧ Brain Open, Mouth Shut

By now you know that visual examples are a great way for all of us to learn new concepts. And who wants to just listen to another lecture anyway? Below is a drawing I have done with innumerable children of all ages over the years. It works for various issues: stopping rude remarks or blurting out anger at someone.

This is invariably a fun activity. The children laugh about putting a Band-Aid® over the figure's mouth, but the analogy hits home. BE SMART. Talk about it later, not when you're mad and can get yourself in more trouble. Usually this is a full-page picture — with a real Band-Aid® of course! It gets posted on the refrigerator or some other prominent place. That way EVERYONE (even caregivers) get to see it often and be reminded!

IT'S OK TO BE MAD.
THINK IT IN YOUR BRAIN. BE CAREFUL! Do not let it
come out of your mouth until you are calmer and
ready to problem-solve.

What to do? BACK OFF! CHILL! STEP BACK! Angry people tend to move forward, **toward** the source of the conflict. Teach your child (and yourself!) to take a step back if you're standing. Lean back in your chair if you are sitting. For young children, I will often trace their shoe print with a marker as a reminder:

MAD

SUPER MAD

STEP BACK

Then you FREEZE! (Remember that old game? Have some fun and practice it.)

FREEZE

SPO+

Yell STOP in your head.

Jake, Age 8 with Dyslexia.

Now, take some deep breaths . . .
slowly,
deeply
through
your
nose.

Many times, I will ask a child to blow up a **real** balloon to see how much air can be held inside. Then we imagine the child has a balloon inside. The deep, slow breaths fill up the balloon.

~231~

Slow down and count your breaths. I usually have children either spell out their name with slow breaths or they may want to count up or down from 10.

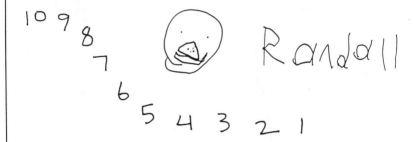

10 9 8 7 6 5 4 3 2 1   Randall

Finally, so the trigger that started the anger doesn't flare up again, ask yourself, "Is the anger justified?" Can you change anything? How important is this issue? For children, think of other substitute behaviors — like going outside to ride your bike or taking a shower to cool off. Below is a list of alternate activities done with a fifth-grade boy.

CONTROLLING THE  MAD

1. Think of a treat
2. Go away
3. Act like statue
4. Funny picture in the mind
5. Ear phones - music
6. Repeat something "This will stop soon."
7. Draw or write something secret

—— Brian, Age 10

❥ Technology: Screens

Just as people invest funds in the stock market, we allow children to invest their time in "Screens" — television, video games, and computer. The issue is not **if** children should spend their time with screens, but **how** and **how much**. If we are going to have technology in our homes, we must not use it blindly. Instead, we can foster **active learning** and expand awareness. Appropriate use of technology can enhance children's cognitive and language skills, improve reasoning and logical thinking skills, allow access to a wide array of information, allow fun practice and drill, and stimulate curiosity and creativity.

"If I study and watch TV at the same time, I end up studying the TV."
— Charlie, Age 16

Zach, Age 5

Too much exposure, however, can have a negative effect. Screens, with their vibrant colors, fast action and audio effects can cause children to expect a fast pace and high level of entertainment. They want **input, input, input.** And when they do something — move the mouse or switch the station — they get **immediate feedback.**

Real life is not that way. In school, children are typically expected to **sit still, listen, and follow along** the printed page. It is my opinion that the phenomenal number of children identified as having attention span problems in this country today is in part due to this very issue. Granted, research shows a number of factors, most predominately heredity, correlate with a diagnosis of Attention Deficit Disorder (ADD), with or without Hyperactivity (ADHD). However, my work with children over the years has led me to conclude that excessive TV watching and video game playing leads to distractibility, impatience, poor listening and impaired concentration to printed material.

There have also been recent cases where excessive computer-use has been linked to depression and even suicide. Depression is not caused by the computer, but it may allow children to become socially isolated. They substitute online chats, computer activities and video games for true social contact.

> "Answer as honestly as you can — Your community is preparing a time capsule which will be opened fifty years from now. Your class has been asked to select one television show that realistically reflects the current times. Which show would you select? Give reasons for your choice."
>
> — Center for Applied Research in Education

Duane, Age 8

*TIP: Watch TV **with** your children and use it as a springboard for communication. Mute the commercials and use the time to focus on your own **values**. If something is portrayed that seems inappropriate, say it out loud. What would you want them to learn instead? Also, ask comprehension questions—which has a great carry-over to reading comprehension. Ask your child "who, what, where, when, why" questions. ("What made Alex lie about that?" "What do you think will happen next?")*

Be a wise consumer of technology and the time it takes from other interactions. There is an incredible amount of educational software available on the market. When selecting software, try to build a well-rounded library. Software should be easy to use and teach specific skills. Keep in mind that developmental levels also affect your choices. Pfohl and Ferstl (1996) divide children's developmental levels into three different age groups to consider software:

✦ Preschoolers (Approximately ages 3 to 5)

Important developmental tasks are language skills, organization (classifying and sorting) and eye-hand coordination. Suitable software for this age would include memory skills, classification, alphabet and numeral recognition and simple visual-motor skills. Software should be active, colorful and easy to use.

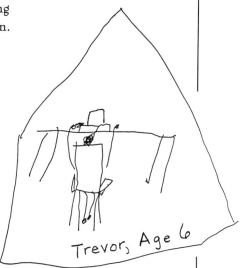

Trevor, Age 6

✦ Early Elementary (Approximately ages 6 to 8)

Developmental tasks at this level are reading, writing and editing skills, problem solving, use of logic, ready recall (memory) and reasoning. Software should be engaging, require the child to manipulate information and be challenging without being frustrating. Tasks should emphasize reasoning and language skills.

✦ **Older Elementary** (Approximately ages 9 to 12)

At this stage, children are beginning higher level thinking skills, synthesizing information, utilizing abstract concepts, and solving advanced problems. Software that includes sound, high resolution graphics, action and challenging activities are most enticing for this age.

TIP: You might want to particularly emphasize a good typing program. It has been found that children as young as kindergarten can learn correct placement of their fingers on the keyboard and practice speed and accuracy. By the time they are in 5th to 6th grade, they make tremendous strides, not only in their work production, but the benefits transfer to real-life paper-and-pencil writing, including spelling, punctuation, and grammar!

Be aware of violent software. Some of the graphics are quite gory. (Is this OK with you?) Also keep in mind on-line services should be closely supervised. The Internet may be exciting but it can make inappropriate material available to children. Also teach children never to give out personal information about themselves to **anyone** on-line.

*TIP: Video games can make excellent **motivators** to get other things accomplished. You might want to make "FUN" video games time **contingent** upon "PRACTICE" computer time. For example, for every 20 minutes of typing time or math facts, the child can spend 20 minutes on a chosen game.*

❥ Changing Patterns

Beyond respect and technology, then, let's explore other issues of time together. Is it really that important? If so, how do we go about changing the patterns that have already been established?

There is powerful evidence that family members benefit from positive time together (Hart 1987). In a family where time is shared together, members . . .

☆ HAVE THE ABILITY TO COMMUNICATE BETTER
☆ SHOW APPRECIATION FOR EACH OTHER
☆ RESOLVE CONFLICTS & PERSONAL PROBLEMS

Good news! People can change. We can learn to adapt to everyday stressors better. We can learn to have more fun when we are with the people we care about.

Troy, Age 6

Dear Mom, I feel sad when you don't spend enough time with me.

Don't make the mistake of assuming that a busy family is a joyful family. There are many outside activities — sports, scouts, music lessons, self-improvement classes, workouts, community/church functions — which can rob a family's time together. While each of these activities is great, too many together can make a whirlwind. Everyone feels busy, but there are underlying feelings of frustration and tension.

REAL LIFE: One of my favorite families to work with was also one of the most chaotic. Both Kelly and Kim were good parents and well-respected professionals. Their two elementary-school-age boys were excellent students and highly regarded by their teachers and peers. When they all got together, though, their world was spinning!

They were inevitably late for their appointments. They often arrived winded and hungry. Sometimes they even brought snacks they'd bought on the way from a convenience store or fast-food drive-through and munched during our sessions! They seemed to be in a constant whirlwind, interrupting and talking over each other, not hearing what the other was saying. And always, they'd need to rush out to their next activities, for which they were already doomed to be late.

A CHAOTIC FAMILY

Sally, Age 10

Closer exploration revealed both parents resented the children because they never had any adult time together, and they felt the children didn't appreciate all the "sacrifices" they were making in time and money. This family had every night of the week scheduled with at least one, usually two, activities. Everyone was taking karate (but not all at the same time), and both boys were on different Little Leagues and soccer teams (which of course had different practice and game schedules).

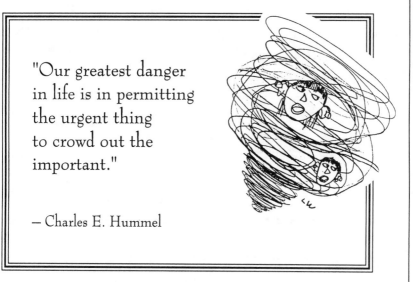

"Our greatest danger in life is in permitting the urgent thing to crowd out the important."

— Charles E. Hummel

*At the risk of being too simplistic — because certainly there were various issues we worked on in therapy — one of the greatest breakthroughs for that family was just **one night a week of no outside activity!** Some family members had to change/drop their activities but the rule was: **No going out, no watching TV, nothing but each other on Wednesdays.** It was the one night they would actually sit down and eat together! Then they had to **do something** together: cards, board game, write letters to relatives, make something in the kitchen, whatever. That was also the one night of the week everyone got to bed at a reasonable hour, so better sleep contributed to better moods.*

❧ Budgeting Time

Caregivers need to control and budget family time much as they would the family finances. Just as certain amounts of money can be designated for bills, groceries, savings or entertainment, time can be designated for certain activities. Just as we are careful not to spend excessively on extravagant things, we must be careful not to spend time on unnecessary commitments.

"The work will wait while you show the child the rainbow, but the rainbow won't wait while you do the work."

— Anonymous

It is important to examine our values and see if we are really spending our time on what we think is important. Take a look at the chart on the next page. Note that "Playing with Kids" and "Talking/Reading to Kids" both fall in the top 10 of activities we say we like to do. (Sadly, they rank below going to a bar or lounge.) Even so, neither places at all in the top 10 activities we really **do**! Notice, too, that Americans spend more time watching television than any other activity besides sleeping and working.

Rating 1 to 10	WHAT WE LIKE **Activity**	Minutes Per Day
9.3	Sex	1
9.2	Playing Sports	8
9.1	Fishing	6
9	Enjoying Art or Music	2
8.9	Going to a Bar or Lounge	5
8.8	Playing with Kids / Hugging, Kissing (Tie)	4/1
8.6	Talking or Reading to Kids	1
8.5	At Church / At Movies / Sleeping (Tie)	7/3/468

Rating 1 to 10	WHAT WE DO **Activity**	Minutes Per Day
8.5	Sleeping	468
7.0	Working	193
7.8	Watching TV	137
7.8	Eating at Home	53
6.1	Getting Dressed	38
6.6	Cooking	33
8.2	Visiting	26
6.3	Commuting to Work	23
8.2	Eating Out	20
7.0	Bathing	18
6.6	Shopping	17

(SOURCE: *American Demographics*, 1993)

"Most people say
their families are
important . . . . but
they don't live
that way."

— Anonymous

Cindy, Age 7

*TIP: As a first step, try a **family meeting**. Set aside a calm time (make "an appointment") for everyone to get together. Share how you are feeling rushed and bothered about lack of time together and would like to change that. Don't wait until you "get around to it." Block out a family time for the following week or two. Be prepared for a few complaints till people get used to it. Start out simple, perhaps only an hour together. Make sure you have a specific activity — a family walk, drive to the park, board game, making/baking something, etc.*

Just for fun, I often hand out a small white paper plate with the word "TUIT" on it. It's a reminder for those who feel so pressed for time they "never get around to it." No more excuses — you now have "A Round Tuit."

Healthy families view time as a "controllable commodity." They value their time together and allow it to be spent only on quality activities. We simply cannot do everything we would like to do. How would you like your children to remember shared time together?

When asked to "draw a picture of your family doing something together."

Greg, Age 10

"While everything else in our lives has gotten simpler, speedier, more microwavable and user-friendly, child-raising seems to have expanded to fill the time no longer available for it."

— Barbara Ehrenreich

Mark, Age 5

❥ A Perfect Day

Now, let's thrill to the excitement of living a "perfect day." Consider the amount of time experts say we should spend on various activities. If we all did everything various specialists say we should, we would need 42-hour days!. "Take a minute" (pun intended!) to check it out.

JUST HOW MUCH DO YOU FIT INTO A DAY? Maybe half as many activities as the experts say you should? Never as many as you want to? Get your running shoes ready — and compare your day to the chock-full one put together below from experts' advice (Peterson 1989):

	Experts Suggest	Your Time
Exercise	30 Min.	_____
Personal Grooming	45 Min.	_____
Time with Children	4 Hrs.	_____
Reading Newspapers	45 Min.	_____
Pets	50 Min.	_____
Housekeeping / Chores	1-2 Hrs.	_____
Work	7-10 Hrs.	_____
Commuting	1 ½ Hrs.	_____
Errands	Up to 2 Hrs.	_____
Grocery Shopping (Men)	17.88 Min.	_____
Grocery Shopping (Women)	22.25 Min	_____
Cooking, Eating Dinner	1 Hr.	_____
Entertaining	1 Hr.	_____
Dental Care	18 Min.	_____
Sex / Intimacy	50 Min.	_____
General Time with Spouse	6 Hrs.	_____
Volunteering	30 Min.	_____
Time with Plants	10 Min.	_____
Time for You	1 Hr.	_____
Reading a Book	15 Min.	_____
Spiritual Development	15 Min.	_____
Sleep	7.5 Hrs.	_____

Total: About 42 Hours
Now you know why you're so exhausted at the end of the day!

"It takes all the running you can do, just to keep in the same place."

— Lewis Carroll

➤ No is OK

If we are perplexed about just how much we can fit into a day, a big step will be to free up time where we can. Time management experts repeatedly advise: JUST SAY NO. You are an adult. You are in charge of your priorities. If you don't look out for the best interest of yourself and your family, who will?

REAL LIFE: Dr. & Mrs. M were popular with their colleagues, neighbors and friends. So were their children. Their lives were not as hectic as Kelly and Kim's, but they found their time together was always crowded out by their commitments. The problem was solved when they marked "BUSY" on their calendars for Sunday afternoons/evenings. When other invitations came up, they could honestly say they "already had plans."

I'm sorry — I'd like to, but I just can't. I'm all wrapped up at the present.

✦ Family Calendar

Purchase or make a large calendar that displays the entire month with plenty of space for each day. If you make one, use a poster board and have your kids help measure off spaces and label days and dates.

Mark off at least one day (maybe one per week?) for a family time. Also, **any** notes from school are immediately put on the calendar — field trips, supplies due, practice dates. Even major projects and tests can be put on the calendar. Try using a different color marker for each child. Put your adult appointments on there as well — business meetings or dental appointments — so the children can see.

TIP: Teach children to budget their time. For example, when a big exam is coming up (say Friday), mark it on the calendar in that child's color. Then count backwards three days (Tuesday) and mark "begin studying for test." For major projects, count backwards and mark when it is half-way till the project is due. Record accomplishments too! Mark on the calendar the day your child moved up a belt in karate or finished reading a challenging book.

FAMILY CALENDAR

SUNDAY	MONDAY	TUESDAY	WEDNESDAY	THURSDAY	FRIDAY	SATURDAY
1	TOM — A on Math Test! 2	SOCCER 3	4	SPELLING TEST TOMORROW 5	got a B+ Jim! 6	7
8	JIM: START TERM PAPER 9	SOCCER 10	11	SPLG TEST 12	13.	JEAN SPENDS NITE JIM WASH DOG 14
DAD: GOLFING 15	16	SOCCER 17	18	MOM'S NITE OUT. FIX OWN DINNER SPLG TEST 19	20	FAMILY DAY — CLEAN THE GARAGE 21
22	TOM: START STUDYING 23	SOCCER 24	TOM: 1/2 WAY DONE? 25	SPELLING TEST 26	TOM'S BIG EXAM 27	TOM WASH DOG 28

> "Of all the time-saving techniques ever developed, perhaps the most effective is frequent use of the word **NO**. Learn to decline tactfully but firmly, every request that does not contribute to your goals . . . Remember many people who worry about offending others wind up living according to other people's priorities."
>
> — Edwin Bliss

Sam, Age 10

A PIGGY PORTION OF TIME SECRETS

Now that we know some ways to catch a little more time during the day and how to spend that time more pleasantly, here are some extra **SECRETS** for you . . .

❥ Transition Time

It is hard to enjoy time with children when we are not in a good mood ourselves. One study of teenagers showed one of their main complaints was parents who are in a bad mood at the end of the workday (Dornbusch et al. 1987). Granted it is not easy to shift gears from a stressful day on the job to automatically give comfort and attention to demanding youngsters. Let's keep in mind that the child may also have had a bad day and may need our support. We don't want to lose a valuable opportunity for developing attachment.

Mommy! Come sit down and make a lap for me.

Give yourself a little time to unwind when you first get home. Call it "**Transition Time.**" Even young children can be taught to wait "until the big hand gets on the six" or "until the timer goes off" to enjoy the adult's company. About 20 minutes of "adult time" would be fair. By then, you will have had time to engage in some specific activity — a shower, a snack, exercise or reading the mail — to defuse your "job feelings" and get ready to focus on your "home feelings." If you allow this transition, you will be surprised at the comfort you yourself can derive from the bonding time that follows with your child.

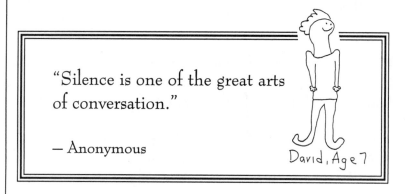

"Silence is one of the great arts of conversation."

— Anonymous

David, Age 7

❧ Everyday Events

While children are not capable of understanding (nor should they be burdened with) adult worries, they should be kept informed of important matters and allowed to discuss their ideas and feelings. Be willing to take the child's concerns seriously and spend time to listen and respond. Of course in the end, you are the adult, leader and guide.

Even young children, and especially adolescents, have things they are worried about, although they may not seem like complex problems to us. They may also have trouble expressing themselves, which is where our active listening (from Step 2) comes in.

"The family riding our boat together."

Donnie, Age 10

❥ Time is Not Always Money

Leisure time does not have to cost money. It can mean a trip to a library, beach or picnic. Perhaps on special occasions, caregivers may spend money for bowling, skating, miniature golfing or a sports event. Whatever everyone finds enjoyable, try to block out a routine time, such as once a week, every other week, or the third Saturday of the month. (Use your calendar!) Certainly vacations are a good way to relax together, but there are plenty of ways to share time around the house, with little or no cost. Baking cookies, riding bikes, gardening, putting photos in albums or painting with watercolors are a few ideas.

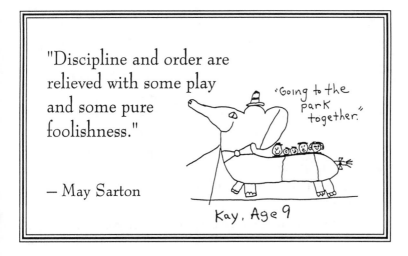

"Discipline and order are relieved with some play and some pure foolishness."

— May Sarton

"Going to the park together."

Kay, Age 9

✸ Daily News

Watching the news on TV or reviewing the newspaper together may be appropriate. This depends upon the child's age and social maturity. The more children are made aware of events happening in the world around them, the better they will be able to understand and interpret the things they learn in school and from their general environment. Use commercial breaks to discuss what might happen next, what you would do if you could, or what this event is related to in the past. You might be surprised at the positive response you will get from a child.

"We like to go for a walk around the apartments and talk about things."

My Dad   Me   Corey, Age 6

✸ Meal Time

Having a meal together can be a way to enjoy each other's company. For some families, a breakfast ritual together is a good start to the day. Even if this is not feasible in your family, don't allow the morning to be so hectic that people are unkind to each other. Get up a few minutes earlier if you have to in order to keep things calm. A good day can start off with a hug or word of encouragement. Try not to allow hurried schedules to threaten dinnertime together either. This is the one guaranteed opportunity to interact and share the day's events. If necessary, block out certain nights of the week for dinner together.

"Life is all memory except for the one
present moment that goes by you
so quick you hardly
catch it going."
— Tennessee Williams

Angie, Age 8

Let's be careful about TV during dinner — people passively
watching television are not communicating with one another.
Some topics to increase communication during dinner may be an
interesting experience from the day, a new joke or story, or what
each person is reading or working on at present.

HINT 📖: For more details on ways to increase
communication, see **Sentence Seeds** in
Step 1 -PRAISE.

Other suggestions are to allow children to invite friends to dinner
— perhaps on a rotating basis. Try playing a word game after
dinner before clearing the dishes. Look for opportunities to honor
a family member for a notable event or accomplishment by using a
special place setting, candles or flowers.

Meal preparation and cleanup are excellent times to teach and
interact with young people. Keep it fun and involve everyone.
Even small tots can set place-mats and napkins or tear lettuce for
the salad. Older children can follow recipes and learn invaluable
skills such as measuring and following directions.

~251~

❥ Bed Time

Getting ready for bed is a great time for displays of affection. Reading a book, playing puppets, or telling a joke are all ways to share ourselves. Try to establish a routine of some kind that is comfortable for everyone. If there are two caregivers, you might alternate nights of one reading a story while the other tucks the children in bed. Maybe you will want to read or do a puzzle with everyone, then the next night spend special time individually.

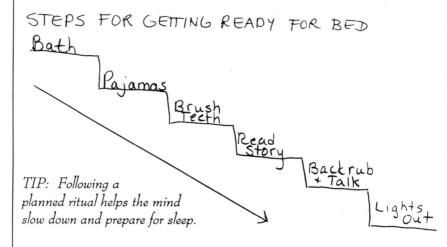

STEPS FOR GETTING READY FOR BED

Bath

Pajamas

Brush Teeth

Read Story

Backrub + Talk

Lights Out

TIP: Following a planned ritual helps the mind slow down and prepare for sleep.

Whatever your bedtime ritual, start it when children are young and **do not abandon it** when they reach adolescence. If they are used to you sitting on the edge of the bed a few minutes every night to chat, it will seem perfectly normal at a time other adults are complaining their teens "never talk."

❥ Car Time

Transportation adds up to a big chunk of time. Just total all the minutes spent in the car traveling to and from places. Consider it a perfect sharing time. There will be no interruptions such as the doorbell or phone, the TV will not distract, the radio can be turned off, and no one can leave the room. Use your active listening skills (while keeping your eyes on the road, of course) to allow children to share their inner selves — wishes, secrets, fears or worries.

For younger children, you might want to sing together, practice the alphabet or share general information such as the days of the week, months of the year or money concepts. Older children can practice school skills aloud, such as foreign language terms or math facts. · I notice some children prefer to spill their deeper issues when the caregiver is driving because there is less discomfort of eye contact.

"The car trip can draw the family together, as it was in the days before television, when parents and children actually talked to each other."

— Andrew H. Malcolm

Edgar, Age 7

❧ Shared Projects

Working and creating together helps people communicate and accomplish things. It also sets the scene for cooperation for those times down the road when emergencies arise. Shared projects can include planting and maintaining a garden or cleaning out the garage or attic. Almost all children enjoy making things, and so crafts are a good choice. Because of the time-crunch, there are more and more pre-assembled craft kits on the market. They allow easy access to fabric, clay and wood at the same time they encourage creativity.

Use your imagination or consult one of the many excellent books available at the library or local book stores. You may want to get involved in a specific craft (T-shirt painting, macrame, etc.) or simply go for simple projects that involve household items (buttons, aluminum foil, etc.). Enjoy yourselves!

"Building with your hands builds self-esteem."

— Susan Magsamen

Paul, Age 6

REAL LIFE: While I was giving a friend a lift recently, I apologized for the grimy appearance of my car. I knew it was long overdue for a bath. Jennifer tried to be helpful by asking, "Why don't you just go to one of those stations with the drive-through car washes? That's what I always do." My reply: "Because that wouldn't be fun!" My daughter and I like to put on our swim suits, make bubbles and splash each other with the hose when we wash the car.

Remember to enjoy each moment of today... it is a precious gift.

Is that why they call today the present, grandma?

❧ No Second Guessing

Worrying is a huge time waster. Make the best decisions you can and follow through the best you can. Learn from your mistakes, then move on. Give yourself credit for your efforts as well as your accomplishments.

FINAL NOTE

Children need to spend time with their primary caregivers.
Surprisingly enough, even teenagers **want** more time with their
caregivers. Hersh (1998) chronicled the lives of teens and found
that they described their mothers and fathers in less-than-
flattering terms: oblivious, uninterested, and "forgotten bit players
in the drama of their children's lives." And yet there was one
thing all the adolescents had in common! "They all said they'd
like to see more of the grown-ups. They all said that in one form
or another."

Considering the stressors and demands of everyday life, it is no
easy task. But as adults we can set priorities and budget time in a
positive way. With a little creativity, we can come up with many
ideas to involve and enjoy our children during the daily routine.
Time together improves communication, shows love and helps
resolve problems. With our time, we are helping children on their
life journey.

"One of the most tragic things I know about human
nature is that all of us tend to put off living. We
are all dreaming of some magical rose garden
over the horizon — instead of enjoying
the roses that are blooming outside
our windows today."

— Dale Carnegie

OVERVIEW ~ Step 6:
RESPONSIBILITY

DEVELOPING COMPETENCY
- ❥ Responsibility Robbing
- ❥ Getting an Early Start
- ❥ No Dumping
- ❥ The Work Force

OBEYING
- ❥ Team Work
- ❥ Odd/Even Days
- ❥ Natural Consequences
- ❥ Lying
- ❥ Sorry Sack
- ❥ Choices
- ❥ Commands

ARRANGING FOR SUCCESS
- ❥ Learning Days
- ❥ New Opportunities
- ❥ Acknowledge Effort
- ❥ Coping Tools
- ❥ Hand-ling Problems
- ❥ Provide the Means
- ❥ Role Models
- ❥ School Issues

A PIGGY PORTION OF
RESPONSIBILITY SECRETS
- ❥ Nurturing
- ❥ Risk-Taking
- ❥ Pets
- ❥ Teens Who Work
- ❥ Tackling Bad Habits
- ❥ Making Amends

FINAL NOTE

Secrets of the
Third Little Pig

Step 6

RESPONSIBILITY

Responsability

Me and Daddy watch T.V.
Our favorite show is on.
Then Whoops, I spill my soda!
the lecture has begun.

"My little girl, Rebecca,
You musn't spill your drink.
Life is full of choices   and you
must stop and think."

Before it all sunk in,
I heard my mother say,
"You didn't take the trash out John,
The trash men came today."

Larry Apil

"The surest way to make it hard for children
is to make it easy for them."
— Eleanor Roosevelt

At birth, children are completely dependent on their caregivers for meeting their every need. Approximately two decades later, we expect them to be caring, self-sufficient adults. What is the magic potion we use to accomplish this? Unfortunately, it is not magic. It is not even pleasant much of the time. It is, however, unmistakably necessary — teaching our children to carry responsibility. Children must first learn to care about themselves and others to see themselves as capable of accomplishing things. Feeling responsible for oneself and others helps develop an attitude of rising above adversity.

I came across something by an anonymous writer which gives "Directions to Prepare for a Life of Grief." It states that you should "begin from infancy to give the child everything he wants. In this way, he will grow up to believe that the world owes him a living. Pick up anything he leaves lying around — books, shoes, clothing. Do everything for him so he will be experienced in throwing the responsibility onto others."

Of course, this is not the way we would plan for our children to turn out. Yet sometimes it really does seem easier in the short run to "just do it ourselves" in order to avoid conflict.

DEVELOPING COMPETENCY

Part of the problem with developing responsibility in the family has to do with the nature of families in current times. In the past, family survival often depended on the contribution of each family member (such as on a farm or a family-owned business). Now, in the typical family, parents "go off to work." Thus, the way the family earns its living is separate from the time they spend together.

As a consequence, there may be less opportunity for direct parental guidance and fewer guidelines for family responsibility. Parents should not feel guilty about their careers, however. They just need to show how each member contributes to the family through work, school and chores.

❧ Responsibility Robbing

No question about it. Teaching responsibility can at times be painful for us and our children. Sometimes it seems easier to just pick up the toys than engage in a battle of wills with a preschooler. It may be harder to watch a child struggle with the vacuum cleaner than do our own vacuuming quickly and efficiently. It may even be close to heartbreaking to see the kitchen when a teenager is in the midst of preparing a meal.

> "It seems to me that we are doing things we do not want to do for kids who do not want to have them done."
>
> — Robert Paul Smith

Alex, Age 8

Unfortunately, giving in to the simple solution now is often what causes much bigger problems later. Every time we do something for children which they are capable of doing themselves, we take away the opportunity to develop competency. We are "Responsibility Robbing." Children need to see themselves as capable of action and able to accomplish things to develop a strong sense of self-esteem. Let children do what they are capable of doing. **Do not pamper them** by performing tasks they can do for themselves.

REAL LIFE: A classic study by Rodkin and Langer (1977) clearly shows how important it is to take control and have responsibility. Elderly patients in an institution were given a simple plant for their room. One half of the patients were told not to worry about the plant. They could enjoy it, but the nurses and aides would tend to it for them.

The other half were given **responsibility.** *They, not someone else, had to take care of the plant. They had to water and feed it regularly. They had to move it around the room to get sunlight part of the day. The life of the plant depended on them!*

Guess what? There was a dramatic difference in the **attitude** *of the care-taker patients — they were happier and more energetic. What's more, they were healthier. They had less physical complaints and problems!*

The difference is in the people,
not the plants.

Relate this to children . . . Is it possible we could actually be
hurting them by trying to **help** them too much?

"We've indulged ourselves and our children with
unprecedented materialism. We've pursued
interests and careers with unparalleled zeal . . .
we've replaced traditional values of hard work and
discipline with artificial self-esteem.

Current psychological research confirms . . .
violence [as in the horrific school shootings] may
be caused by overinflated self-esteem . . . The
challenge is to get tough with ourselves."

—Kathleen Parker

"My weapons." Ryan, Age 11

❥ Getting an Early Start

So far, we know responsibility helps people feel better about
themselves. It also helps children get a bigger sense of their world
and their impact on it. For example, picking up toys now may
translate to not littering the environment later. As you might
suspect, it is always easier to start when children are young.

By beginning with small tasks and building up, children gradually
learn how to handle responsibility. In this way, taking
responsibility becomes a "habit." So much of what we do is based

on habits — sometimes habits passed down from generation to generation. Some family habits are unpleasant (such as fighting at the dinner table), yet others are wonderful habits (such as politeness and respect for elders).

*REAL LIFE: Imagine a family habit where being given chores and responsibility is considered an honor! The Henning family had pulled this off. A "mixed family" (two of "her kids," three of "his kids" and a baby on the way) meant that there had to be considerable structure and cooperation for things to run smoothly. Their system was admirable. Responsibility was considered a **privilege**.*

On each child's birthday, he or she was "allowed" to earn one more chore. Seven-year-old David seemed more excited about "getting to wash the dishes" when he turned eight than about having a party. Older children were "allowed" to add chores on their birthday such as washing the car or using the weed-eater. You can see the analogy of this family system to a corporate system. In many businesses, employees are rewarded with increased responsibility as well as financial incentives.

"I take out the trash."

Jason, Age 8

➤ No Dumping

It is truly hard when we suddenly "**Dump Responsibility**" on an adolescent. This is already an age for struggling with issues of independence and rebelliousness. A young person with no previous experience handling responsibility will feel overwhelmed. I see this problem repeatedly with middle-school-age students. Their parents complain about how irresponsible the kids are — about homework, money, curfew, chores.

Yet when we go back and review their history, the children have had very few demands ever made on them. We simply cannot expect an adolescent to accept responsibility overnight. We have to introduce it gradually but at a steady pace.

"Encourage the quest; don't solve it."

Jonathan & Wendy Lazear

Used to Responsibility   Overwhelmed

REAL LIFE: Dawn and Kim were two very complaining teenagers. A single mother, Tammy became increasingly frustrated with their insults about whatever meals she fixed.

In counseling, we finally agreed that the girls would take turns. One would help prepare the entrée and the other would make the salad. Instead of waiting to be called to dinner (and having to interrupt their TV!), the girls were involved in the kitchen. After some initial grumbling, they started to take pride in the meal. Their appetites and attitudes both improved.

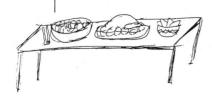

➤ The Work Force

Children should be encouraged to carry a level of responsibility in accordance with their maturity. Start very young with simple tasks. Children vary tremendously in their development, and caregivers can look at their strengths and weaknesses to help select age-appropriate chores.

*TIP: Have children join the **Work Force** by allowing them to contribute to the family and thus develop personal competency. Consider the following chart to see what "opportunities" might be available for different-age children.*

scott, Age 9

Age 2
Put pajamas away.
Pick up toys.
Undress self.
Throw out waste paper.
Wipe up spill.

Age 3
Comb hair.
Wash face and hands.
Dress self.
Clear place at table.
Tear lettuce for salad.
Help water plants.

Age 4
Set table.
Put groceries away.
Polish shoes.
Help do yard work.
Dust furniture.
Get mail.
Put dirty clothes in hamper.

Age 5
Pour own drink.
Clean mirrors and windows.
Fold clothes and put them away.
Clean out car.
Feed pet and clean its living area.
Make own sandwich.
Make bed.

Age 6
Choose clothing for day.
Shake rugs.
Water plants.
Peel vegetables.
Hang up clothes.
Tie own shoes.

Age 7
Cook simple food (hot dogs, boiled egg, toast).
Prepare own school lunch.
Rake leaves and weeds.
Take pet for walk.
Responsible for own minor injuries.

Age 8
Run carpet sweeper.
Organize magazines and mail.
Take out trash.
Empty dishwasher.
Clean·out silverware drawer.
Help prepare meals.
Fold and put away family laundry.

Ages 9 to 11
Wash counter tops.
Keep bathroom tidy.
Help plan grocery lists.
Do dishes independently.
Wash car with supervision.
Help do laundry.
Total care of pet.

Ages 12 and Up
Do laundry independently.
Do yard work.
Prepare family meals independently.
Clean living area and own room.
Supervise young children (if sufficiently mature).

OBEYING

Accepting responsibility is not the same as blind obedience. An obedient child does strictly as told — no more, no less. While there is certainly a place for obedience, we generally want a child to see the bigger picture. A resilient child is resourceful and independent in judgment when necessary.

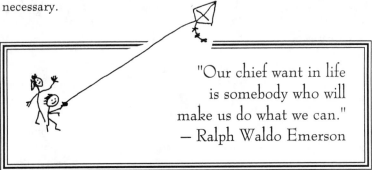

"Our chief want in life
is somebody who will
make us do what we can."
— Ralph Waldo Emerson

❥ Team Work

Let's foster a spirit of cooperation! Fousing on the family as a "TEAM" **where each person's contribution is important** helps children feel they are providing a helpful service. This works out especially well in terms of allowance. Rather than people earning money for each "job," everyone is given a certain amount of spending money just for being part of the family. (The amount, of course, would depend on issues such as each child's age and what they are required to buy on their own.) Similarly each family member is expected to perform some work for the family just for belonging to it. The family team requires work and offers benefits.

❥ Odd/Even Days

Cut down on **squabbling** between siblings. It seems someone is always ready to say, "It's my turn" or "I get that one" or "I had it first." If you have just two children in the family, give one **odd days** and the other **even days**. Use something stable to assign the numbers, not something that changes, like their age. Possibilities are their birth month, i.e. February (2) is even while November (11) is odd, the actual birth date or number of letters in their first name. Then whenever a squabble comes up, you won't feel so pulled into it. You calmly ask, "Whose day is it?" and that person gets to choose.

This works great for tasks as well as privileges. On "your day" you may get to choose the first piece of pizza and sit in the front seat. But you may also have to clean up the unexpected dog mess. "Your day" does not mean you're boss of the family. It's just a way to settle petty arguments. Also, the children learn cooperation and negotiation — "I'll let you watch your show tonight, if I can watch mine tomorrow."

Notice the system can be adapted for more than 2 children. In that case, assign each child a color and color-code your calendar, either randomly or by the week. Then each morning, remind everyone ,whose day it is.

TIP: Watch out for months ending in 31 (or 29 in Leap Year). Since the next day is always 1, you'll have two odd days in a row. Instead, split the extra day or make it a Parent Day.

> "Ultimately, the only power to which man should aspire is that which he exercises over himself." — Elie Wiesel

Laura, Age 7

✦ Natural Consequences

When children do refuse to take assigned responsibility, many times caregivers can simply withdraw from the conflict and allow the "**Natural Consequences**" of irresponsibility to happen, i.e., a toy not picked up will get stepped on and broken. Usually, it is best to agree with children ahead of time on specific consequences for irresponsibility. One family I know sets up a "penalty fund." For each chore neglected, a nickel from their allowance goes into a special change box to be donated to charity.

HINT 📖: For more details on **preset consequences**, see Step 3 - LIMITS.

REAL LIFE: A set of parents recently told me they had grounded 9-year-old Timmy from all athletic events for a month. This was especially upsetting to the boy because he was not a very good student but excelled at sports. He reveled in his karate practice and took pride as a winning pitcher on his baseball team. His crime? He had blatantly lied about making the mess in the kitchen, blaming it instead on his brother and sister.

Certainly, lying cannot be condoned. But how do karate and baseball actually relate to either offense . . . making a mess or lying? A more **Natural Consequence** *would be to do extra clean-up chores and perhaps writing an essay about lying or apology notes to his brother and sister.*

♪ Lying

For older children and teens who lie, a great **Natural Consequence** is writing (or typing on the computer) a good essay on the topic of lying. It must be _____ words long (you pick the length), tell some different reasons why people lie (to cover-up, to exaggerate, etc.), why the lie you told was wrong, what you will do next time instead and so on. This may be a week-end project where no other fun activities are allowed until it is completed satisfactorily.

TIP: Children who are impulsive, especially those with ADD/ADHD, tend to blurt out answers to "cover up" before really thinking about it. I call this a "Pop Out Lie." Then they have to lie again to cover that up. If you know your child tends to blurt out cover-up lies, "PRE-ASK" your questions.

For example, "I'm going to come back in 5 minutes and ask you about this mess. No, do not tell me now, I don't want to hear it. Think about it and I'll be back to get your answer." Or, "I'm going to ask you about your homework as soon as I'm off the phone. No, don't tell me now. Don't say you don't have any or not. Just double check, then I'll ask you in a few minutes." By forcing them to "stop and think," many children will be more truthful.

Herb, Age 7

> "Honesty is something you can't wear out."
> — Waylon Jennings

✦ Sorry Sack

One of the biggest causes of friction at home is people leaving their "stuff" lying around. Somebody (usually Mom) gets sick of it and cleans up but then resents it. Try to make it easier for family members to keep track of their own belongings . . . and make it hard on them if they don't. One idea is to get different colored baskets for each person lined up near the hall or at the bottom of the stairs. Everyone just drops in their "stuff" for the day if they don't feel like carrying it to the bedroom. This means shoes, books and toys. Before bed, everyone has to empty their own basket.

On the other hand, if they don't put it away or in their basket, they'll be sorry. The "**Sorry Sack**" can work wonders. It is a technique developed by a 64-year-old grandmother who raised eight tidy children . . .

REAL LIFE: Mom told the children she was not their maid but would pick up after them if they insisted. Because maids are paid, however, there would be a charge. Whatever Mom picked up went into the "Sorry Sack." At the end of the week, the children had to buy back their items at 50¢ a piece. Clothes had to be purchased back before toys and games.

This mother reported that within two weeks, the "maid" was almost totally without a salary. The children understood the importance of picking up after themselves, and family relationships improved dramatically. Today, all eight of her children are happily married, well-organized and raising fine families of their own.

By the way, some parents have hesitated to use this technique for clothes that are uniforms for private schools. They don't want their children to "get in trouble." But when they have the courage to follow-through, the child learns quickly — usually from detention at school not from your nagging at home!

Of course you have a choice, son. Do you want to brush your teeth BEFORE or AFTER your bed time story?

❧ Choices

Remember locus of control is one of the protective factors. Children need to have some say-so. They need to perceive that they have some control over what happens in their lives. In almost all cases you can give a child some choice. The child can decide — would you rather walk the dog or feed him tonight? Do you want to water the plants or vacuum the carpet? Your children can start with choosing between two sets of clothing, with the choices gradually extended. When giving choices, we need to be careful not to rush a child and not to be critical of the final selection.

❧ Commands

So far, emphasis has been on cooperation and **Team Work**. In reality, there are simply times when a child needs to OBEY. It may be because there is some danger or an urgent time limit. It may simply be that a pattern of constant defiance has built up, and the caregiver needs to establish "who's the boss."

First, have your preset consequences — time-out for younger children, revoking privileges for older children. Next, be sure to **pick your battles**. If you are going to give a command and insist it be obeyed, make sure it's one you feel strongly about, because you will have to be strong in your follow-up.

"The absence of alternatives clears the mind marvelously."

— Henry Kissinger

Chris, Age 10

Having **chips in the bank** here means instilling a sense of compliance all along. Ask for small favors ("Bring me a tissue, please," or "Can you pick up that spoon I dropped?"). Compliment sincerely for a child's cooperation in the little matters. Understand, though, that asking for a favor leaves room for the child to decide whether to follow-through.

REAL LIFE: A father recently expressed how agitated he was at his teenager. He'd asked her "Could you please unload the dishwasher?" She replied, "I can't, I'm busy." Although he thought he was just being polite, the way he worded it did suggest the chore was optional.

Be clear in your own mind between FAVORS and COMMANDS. If you have to give a command, really **mean it.** Remember from our discussion of discipline, try to use as few words as possible. A command to obey has three parts. You must do ALL THREE! 1) Get ATTENTION, 2) Command with a **TIME LIMIT** and 3) Hear it REPEATED. It goes like this:

OBEY COMMAND

1. "Look at me."
2. "I want you to __(action)__ by __(time limit)__ ."
3. "What did I just say?"

C'mon, man! I know what you just said!

Well, tell me anyway!

One of the most common reactions I get when teaching the command component to caregivers is that many have already **intuitively** caught some aspect of it. Some will tell me, "Really! If I don't get his attention first, he acts like he hears me but later says he didn't." Others will say, "I already make her repeat it so I know she understands it." Don't fall for it if a child says, "I know what you just said" instead of answering the question "What did I just say?"

The TIME LIMIT piece is crucial. Otherwise, it becomes too easy for children to say, "Oh, I was going to do it, give me a chance" or some variety of excuse and then accuse **YOU** of nagging. Instead, this way, everything is clear and understood beforehand. Depending on the child's age and concept of time, some typical time limits are listed below. Be careful of using "RIGHT NOW" unless that issue is urgent. We need to be respectful of children's priorities as well.

TIME LIMITS

Right Now	At the Next Commercial
After This Game	When This Show Is Over
By Dinner	When the Big Hand Gets on the 6
Before 2:00	Before I Get Home from Work

APPLIED EXAMPLES

1. "Look at me."
2. "I need you to pick up these toys right now."
3. "What did I just say?"

1. "Look at me."
2. "I want you to take out the garbage at the next commercial."
3. "What did I just say?

---

1. "Look at me."
2. "As soon as this game is over I need you to get your pajamas on and brush your teeth."
3. "What did I just say?"

The tricky part is that children are not used to this system of compliance. Most likely, they already expect several "warnings" and then think you really mean it only when you yell. In this new approach, you are tranquil and reasonable . . . and you calmly give the preset consequence. You are **teaching compliance with a plan rather than reacting out of anger.**

How many times have I told you to clean up this mess?!

OLD METHOD

PARENTAL
BRAIN
TEASER

OK. No more computer the rest of the day. Now clean it up or you'll lose telephone privileges next.

NEW METHOD

However, because a child suddenly gets a time-out or no TV for the rest of the night, just because "I forgot! I was going to do it," be prepared! You will be told you are mean, this whole thing is unfair, I promise I'll be good if we go back to the old way, and so on. Trust that this is yet another example where doing the **right thing** does not equate to doing the **easiest** thing at the time.

On the positive side, I have had families come back after several weeks, and the adults report they are no longer yelling and the children report they no longer feel nagged. It's a win-win situation! Take care not to overuse this technique. Most often we want to utilize less overt strategies. When authority is necessary, however, it's a powerful approach.

ARRANGING FOR SUCCESS

Failure is inherent in growing up, but we must be careful about expecting children to do things they are not capable of doing. A failure at the outset can be so discouraging, a child may not be motivated to even try again. Tasks can be modified so a child will meet success; later the difficulty can gradually be increased.

✦ Learning Days

Time for training should be relaxed. You may even want to mark special "**Learning Days**" on the calendar to anticipate the practice time together. Especially with a new task, demonstrate and work along with the child for a while. It is very hard to train a child when there are definite time limits and everyone is rushed.

✦ New Opportunities

By trying new things and meeting new people, children have more opportunity to stretch their independence. Encourage children to take part in organizations and activities. Be sure to tell them you are proud of their involvement and contributions to the group.

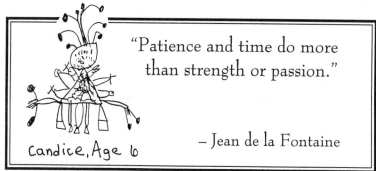

"Patience and time do more than strength or passion."

– Jean de la Fontaine

Candice, Age 6

✦ Acknowledge Effort

Support a child's sincere efforts even if the child doesn't necessarily bring the desired results. Praise the process of doing the job, not just the final product. When there are successful results, get the child to talk about that unbeatable sense of accomplishment. Despite the limitations of any given age, we want children to feel good about what they can do, not upset about what they cannot do.

> "If we do offer praise to our children,
> perhaps it should be for a job or task
> or accomplishment **they** feel particularly
> good about — not one that just happens
> to meet our own standards."
>
> – Jonathan & Wendy Lazear

❧ Coping Tools

We can help children learn to cope with the "downs" in life by gradually allowing them to confront disagreement with others on their own. We can also talk about "what if" situations and "what else could you do" plans. For example, at the dinner table or riding in the car, an adult might ask "What would you do if ...? (a small child hits you, a stranger tried to touch you, you ran out of paint, etc.). When the child answers, keep asking "What else?" and "Then what?" This helps a child see many potential options and increases common-sense judgment in practical situations. Rigid children tend to see only one or two solutions and then get stuck.

Problem solving is an excellent coping strategy that can be taught and role-modeled. Children too often see their parents as successful adults without noting the daily struggles and decisions we have to work through. Show it, teach it, model it.

REAL LIFE: 11-year-old Tony and 9-year-old Tina were in my office with their parents establishing "The Rules" and practicing various consequences. We were emphasizing the point that "you can think it in your head but don't let it come out of your mouth."

HINT 📖:
For more details on **thinking it in your head**, see the section Brain Open, Mouth Shut in Step 5 - TIME

Tony was seething. Finally, he said furiously, "Mom and Dad should have consequences for bad choices, too! What about when Dad loses his temper? He never just thinks it in his mind. He's always yelling, but nothing happens to him!" Dad was dumbfounded. He was a powerful executive in a multi-million-dollar international corporation. At work, he constantly evaluated situations, talked things over, and worked out compromises. He was well respected for his cool head and mastery of negotiations. Yet at home, he simply dictated and exploded. His children never got to see and learn from his problem-solving talents. Think about it: What are your children learning from the way you solve problems at home?

"A child is the only known substance from which a responsible adult can be made."

– Thomas Lickoma

Lori, Age 7

➤ <u>Hand</u>-ling Problems

There are a number of problem-solving models available. Following is a simple version I use called "<u>Hand</u>-ling Problems."

① **Identify the problem.** Be specific. (When you say "No one likes me," what <u>exactly</u> is going on? "Someone called me a name" or "The kids wouldn't let me join the team at recess" are two very different problems.)

② **Ask: "What have I already tried?"** Make a list. Keep asking "What else have I already tried? What else?"

③ **Brainstorm: "What <u>else</u> could I do? What else?"**

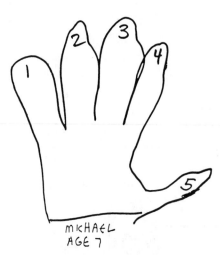

MICHAEL
AGE 7

To make it concrete, hold up your hand and count off one idea or option for each finger. For very young children, trace their hand, then number each finger. Teach them to name one thing for each finger that they could do. For example: hit them, call them names back, laugh and think how funny they look with their underwear on their head, tell the teacher, walk away, get a drink of water, etc. You may even have to use your other hand — or toes!

TIP: I like to get out a stopwatch and give a child three minutes to think of as many options as possible. Even "bad" (silly or outrageous) ideas are OK. Just keep going, for it may lead to another idea. The stopwatch seems to speed things up and helps the ideas flow.

④ **Check it out:** Pick your favorite two or three solutions and try to imagine how they would turn out. How would other people react? What would happen to me?

⑤ **Pick the best answer.**

⑥ **Try it.**

⑦ **Check it again.** How did it go? If you had it to do over again, what would you do different? Do I need to try something else?

Examples of
<u>Hand</u>-ling Problems

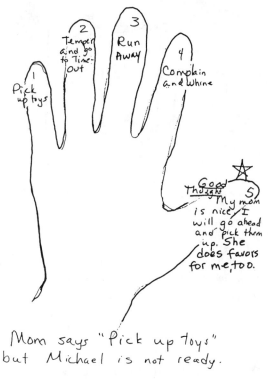

(✷ is step #5 - Pick the best answer)

1. Pick up toys
2. Temper and go to Time-out
3. Run Away
4. Complain and Whine

Good Thought
5) My mom is nice / I will go ahead and pick them up. She does favors for me, too.

Mom says "Pick up Toys" but Michael is not ready.

Michael, Age 7

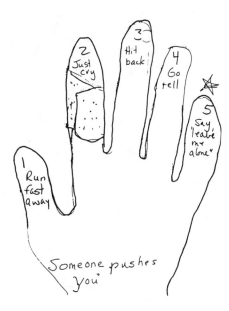

1. Run fast away
2. Just cry
3. Hit back
4. Go tell
5. Say, "leave me alone"

Someone pushes you

Tony, age 6 (with a cut on his index finger that day)

❥ Provide the Means

A chalkboard, message center, chore chart or wall calendar helps establish a system of reminders without the adults having to "nag." An appointment book can be used for homework assignments. An alarm clock can help improve morning responsibility.

HINT 📖:   For details on how to set up a fun and effective family calendar, see Step 5 - TIME.

Shana,
Age 12

TIP: I continue to be amazed at how many caregivers tell me that watching TV in the morning is a constant battle. The question is, "Why is the TV even on in the morning?" The following is a recommended strategy:

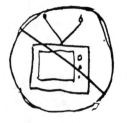

✦   No television until everyone is ready to leave for school or work. The idea is that television becomes the reinforcer to move quickly rather than the issue to delay.

✦ If you have a child who is extremely hard to awaken in the morning, consider carrying him or her to another room and put on the TV for a brief 10 to 15 minutes. Usually, prerecorded tapes with cartoons are excellent for this, so the child does not become involved in a show. Allow the child to have some juice to sip while watching this brief time to help gradually wake up. Then **the TV goes off**, and the routine starts. By then, most children are much more alert and cooperative.

✦ For Attention Deficit Hyperactivity Disorder (ADHD) children, morning routines are especially difficult. Some pediatricians I know who monitor medication for ADHD (especially Ritalin) recommend waking the child up 20 to 30 minutes ahead of the time they have to get out of bed. This way, they can take their dose of medication and drift in and out of sleep until it's time to get up. By then, the medication has started taking effect, and they are more appropriately involved in the morning routine. Ask your doctor if this appears as an appropriate strategy for your child.

"Now I'm in a better mood in the morning!"

Brian, Age 6

"Action always generates inspiration.
Inspiration seldom
generates action."

Natalie, Age 7

— Frank Tibolt

❧ Role Models

Research repeatedly shows that adult behavior is a major factor in influencing children's behavior. What we do in **our daily behavior ultimately effects their attitude about responsibility.** Be conscious of the powerful lessons of responsibility or irresponsibility — you are teaching by example. Remember promises you make to your child and commitments you make to others — take them seriously! You might also look for responsible role models in books or movies. As you read or watch together, comment on how the hero solved the problem, stood up to adversity, or admitted a mistake.

❧ School Issues

Children who come to school with the outlook that school is their job have a strong foundation. Students who are willing to share and cooperate with others will be able to handle learning tasks. Those who expect others to take responsibility for them fall behind.

"The big advantage of a book is it's very easy to rewind. Close it and you're right back at the beginning."
— Jerry Seinfeld

Jimmy, Age 6

✦ **Read, Read, Read**. Remember that reading is a basic protective factor for resilience. Read every day if possible, from the age of 1 until teenage years. Allow the child to see you reading books, magazines and newspapers regularly. Use a variety of materials from fact to fiction, humor to classics, suspense novels and school materials. Read together and separately. Review what you both learned together. Encourage discussion of pictures and ideas.

REAL LIFE: My mother was one of those "Super-Moms" ahead of her time. While most of my friends' mothers stayed at home, my mother worked at least an 8-hour day, often taking her lunch hour to drive home, put in a load of laundry and clean up the house. Evenings were hectic with shopping, cooking, clean-up, homework and so on.

Even so, I clearly remember every night when it was "time to read." Whatever else was going on, the pace slowed and Mom sat on the bed and read a book aloud. Even in adolescence, I would sit on my bed in the room I shared with my sister, acting like I was "busy" but really listening to the story. Reading was important!

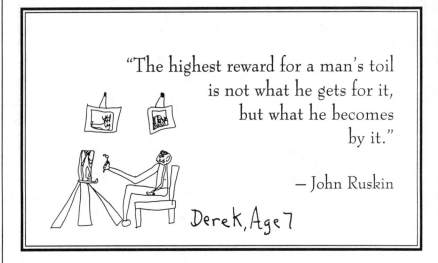

"The highest reward for a man's toil
is not what he gets for it,
but what he becomes
by it."

— John Ruskin

Derek, Age 7

Every child should have much attractive reading material available. Drill on common sight words can be helpful if it is done in a fun-type format. Make flash cards and earn "points." Match cards in games such as Concentration®. A child can be shown how to get words through context, word analysis and later with use of the dictionary.

✦ **Value education.** Visit the child's class often. Talk to the teacher either in person or on the telephone. Always emphasize fun in learning and pride in effort and quality. If you have a disagreement with school personnel, keep it between the adults. Usually it is best if children see a united front, that is, the caregiver and teacher cooperating.

✦ **Engage in "outside" learning activities.** Music, art and cultural offerings, as well as trips to the local library, are beneficial. Visit zoos and museums. Allow your child in the kitchen to help cook and observe. Turn off the TV and engage in games, listening activities and exercises. Activity books are great, from simple dot-to-dots to complex crossword puzzles. Game magazines teach many skills such as logic and visual discrimination.

◆ **Encourage writing.** Have your children write letters or postcards to friends and relatives. A daily writing journal is excellent. Have plenty of crayons, pens, and markers available, as well as the computer if possible.

◆ **Use a computer or typewriter.** Children who use a correct approach to the keyboard not only improve their written assignments on the computer but improve their handwriting and fluency as well. This means the child has to learn the appropriate placement of fingers, not the hunt-and-peck method. There are excellent software programs on the market today which teach typing and reinforce academic skills. Good software programs can allow children entertaining practice and drill in basic skills of reading , writing and math. Other programs stimulate creativity such as designing greeting cards or posters.

HINT 📖: See **cautions about screens** in the section on Technology in Step 5: TIME.

"Children are drawn to computers just as they are to radios, kitchen utensils, hair dryers, etc. Since everything is new to children, they do not come with the built-in fears that adults take to computers. The window for introduction is open."

– High Scope Developmental
   Research Foundation

Maura

♦ **Talk, Talk, Talk.** Encourage conversation. Talk to your child about real life issues. What is happening in the family, on the news, at school. Depending on their age, talk about everything from animals to science fiction. Discuss whatever reading materials family members are involved at the time.

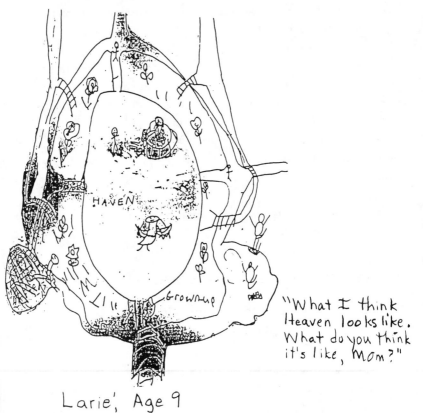

HAVEN

Grownup

"What I think Heaven looks like. What do you think it's like, Mom?"

Larie, Age 9

*TIP: Use "**Sentence Seeds**" to get things going. Compare yourself or the child to other people, places and things. Ask, "If you were an animal, what kind of animal would you be? Why?" or say, "If I was a type of food, I'd probably be _____ because _____." Use family memories, such as "The best vacation we ever had was _____."*
Have fun talking to the child! Interact! Break the passive pattern.

HINT 📖: For more details on **Sentence Seeds**, see Step 1 - PRAISE, Step 2 - Listening Times, and the Dignity section in Step 4 - LOVE.

A PIGGY PORTION OF RESPONSIBILITY SECRETS

Teaching children to carry responsibility with pride and satisfaction must not be ignored or pushed to the back burner of our priorities. Here are a few SECRETS to make this often unpleasant job more agreeable and fulfilling . . .

✦ Nurturing

Although it has been addressed in previous sections, the importance of attachment — availability, warmth, love, affection — cannot be over-emphasized. Those children who feel good about themselves are most likely to help others. In other words, children must first feel loved, cared for and respected before they will be able to reach out, love and respect others. Children's sense of responsibility grows directly in relation to how responsible they perceive others are to them.

✦ Risk-Taking

Perseverance or diligence is a big piece of learning to overcome adversity. The old saying stands: "When the going gets tough, the tough get going." Through the years, I have seen countless children who are extremely bright — often Gifted on IQ tests — who lack diligence. Because success typically comes easily to them, they do not know how to handle a setback. They perceive a **mistake** as a **failure**, when in fact it is an **opportunity to learn**!

Children's Depiction of
STRESS
Trying to do the **Right Thing**

Randy, Age 8

Timmy, Age 5

TIP: Have your child involved in one extracurricular activity. To find a good "match" for your child, consider your child's temperament and past history. For some children, team sports such as basketball or soccer are good choices. For many, however, karate or tae-kwon-do are much more appropriate. They are surprisingly good for children who need to work on self-control and respect for authority (even ADHD and conduct-problem children) as well as visual/motor coordination. Karate is also non-competitive as far as a group. Each child competes against himself to see his own progress up the color-belt chart. Music lessons too have many benefits, although even child development experts (and parents themselves who used to "have to play") disagree on whether a child should be "forced" to play an instrument.

HINT 📖: For details on cautions of having too many outside activities, see Step 5 - TIME.

"He's smirking at himself in the mirror because he doesn't like what he sees. He's afraid he's going to blow it at the tryouts today."

Brian, Age 9

In general, my sense is that a child should **make a commitment** for a certain length of time — say one season, six months or one year. If the child wants to give up the sport or instrument in the very early stages, it makes sense to try to modify the situation and help the child work it out rather than just let him or her drop out. Talk to the instructor or practice with the child alone in order to get through the rough spots. When children stay with something long enough, they can often **make breakthroughs.** This will not only dispel thoughts of quitting but will lead to future characteristics of diligence and perseverance.

Certainly, there may be a legitimate reason for discontinuing a certain activity in an early stage — if there is extreme stress and negativity or a child feels isolated and rejected by peers. If this happens and the child does discontinue the activity, make sure you pick it up in some other area such as a craft class or other sport to maintain the notion of commitment. Remember (and you should by now!) focus always on **effort and pride in trying**, looking for small gains in improvement rather than perfection.

"I'm learning to skateboard."

Amber, Age 9

"That's me with the football."

Brian, Age 7

"Teaching kids to count is fine, but teaching them what counts is best."

— Ralph Waldo Emerson

Matthew, Age 7

❯ Pets

Animals offer excellent means of developing responsibility. Please **do not** buy a pet solely for this purpose though! Visit your local Humane Society or animal shelter and see all the cute little puppies and kitties who are there only because they grew into adult cats and dogs who needed daily care. Reading the "reasons" on the cage card is heartbreaking: "Too big," "needed too much attention" or simply "abandoned." A pet should be brought in the home as an addition to the family, not as a "lesson" which may or may not work out.

"If you don't own a dog, at least one, there is not necessarily anything wrong with you, but there may be something wrong with your life."

— Roger Caras

Sarah, Age 14

Pathetic examples of irresponsibility toward pets abound. A recent issue of our local Humane Society newsletter ran a letter from a widow who adopted a cringing, fearful dog she described as "a lost child." The dog had spent her entire life chained to a backyard stake. "They wanted a watchdog, so her owner beat her, trying to make her mean" (Robb 1997). Another letter in Ann Landers' (1997) column was addressed to "these people who abandon pets" along the side of the road. It reads in part, "your puppy must have been terrified . . . she was starving, weak and covered with mange . . . it's a miracle she hadn't been hit by a car. But that would have been better than being found by the local coyotes." Both of these stories have happy endings. Many do not.

Derek, Age 9

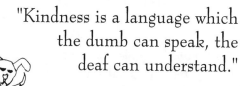

"Kindness is a language which
the dumb can speak, the
deaf can understand."

— Robert Benchley

The sad story of the Dalmatian puppies shows animal abuse and abandonment are not isolated incidents. Around Christmas 1996, Dalmatians were a craze. Disney had recently released *101 Dalmatians*, a movie which portrayed the puppies as cute and cuddly. The fad took off. Unfortunately, these were not toys like most fads — these were real live creatures.

Some people blame unscrupulous breeders who took advantage of the situation. I blame the irresponsible adults who allowed these puppies to be adopted into their homes without making a commitment to them. The puppies did what all young creatures do — they grew up. They turned into adults! Their temperament (remember that issue?) is rambunctious and sometimes moody. They get big and require a lot of exercise. Without it, they get restless and even destructive.

So, across the country, would-be owners turned in hundreds of Dalmatians to animal shelters. Many dogs have been abused and injured. Those that are not adopted are likely to be put to sleep. Dane 1997) reported, "These animals are paying with their lives because people aren't informed about them."

What are kids in these families learning about responsibility? Believe it or not, one of the families that turned in a Dalmatian to a shelter in Los Angeles complained "the pet was nothing like the dogs in the movie."

Pet owners' irresponsibility also causes suffering in a less dramatic way. With best intentions, adults may choose not to get their pet spayed or neutered. Some even want their children to experience the birthing process of the family pet. The dismal truth is that many of these animals never find homes and are put to sleep.

> *TIP: Be responsible!*
> *Have your pet spayed or neutered.*

Well, now that we've gotten through that issue, you can tell what one of my strongest values is. Animals who are loved and nurtured can be such blessings in our lives. People who own animals have consistently been shown to be healthier and happier (Beck & Katcher 1983). Trained animals are increasingly being used as visitors to hospitals and nursing homes because they brighten the patients' day and help them convalesce. Animals can be an unlimited source of "unconditional positive regard."

"You can delegate authority, but not responsibility."

— Stephen Comiskey

Ann, Age 6

❥ Teens Who Work

It is somewhat surprising to find that some experts do not endorse an "adolescent workplace" as a means of fostering independence and responsibility. Some researchers have found that teens who work for pay achieve less in school and develop a negative attitude toward work in general. There have been warnings that "intensive involvement" especially with a stressful job may lead to alcohol or drug abuse. This issue should be interpreted with caution, however. Some experts believe the most important factor is the reason teenagers are working.

In the past, a young person's income usually contributed to the family finances. In contrast, today's teen usually works out of choice to gain "spending money" — for designer clothes, entertainment and music equipment. By working for luxuries instead of necessities, work values become distorted.

If teenagers do have a paying job, caregivers can insist on certain guidelines.

♦ **Limit the number of hours of work.** Typically, when students are overwhelmed with too much homework and too much work time, they let the homework slip. A general guideline is 15 hours or less per week.

♦ **Set grade standards.** If grades drop below a certain level, the student has to either quit the job or drop the number of working hours.

♦ **Insist that a certain portion of money be saved for something meaningful** such as a car, college, marriage, or another goal. In this way, the concept of "working for a living" will retain value.

ONE FAMILY'S EXPECTATION FOR THEIR WORKING TEEN

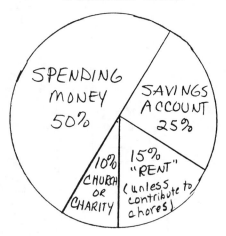

♦ **Clearly decide what expenses will continue to be covered and what will not.** Will you continue to provide basic clothing, but the teen is responsible for extras such as jewelry or movie tickets?

♦ **Consider if part of the earning should be contributed to family finances.** Some parents have children pay a minimal amount of "rent" as they are less likely to be doing chores and contributing with their energy around the house (such as yard work).

♦ **Teach teenagers the meaning of and action to take in case of sexual harassment.** Teenage girls are especially vulnerable. In a recent poll, 20% of 1000 teen girls with full or part-time jobs said they had been victims of sexual harassment in the workplace (*Teen People Magazine* 1999). Make sure your teen is alert to the possibility including how to avoid it and where to turn for help.

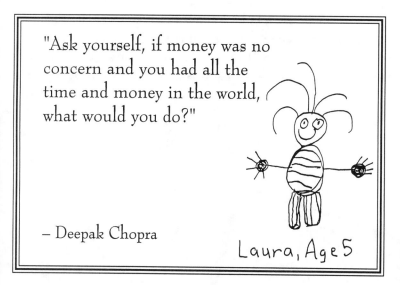

"Ask yourself, if money was no
concern and you had all the
time and money in the world,
what would you do?"

– Deepak Chopra

Laura, Age 5

❥ Tackling Bad Habits

If there is a habit you've been concerned about, take the first step toward
change. Buy a pair of jogging shoes, sign up for Weight Watchers® or
go to an AA meeting.

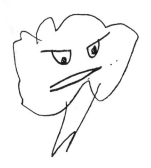

"What cancer
looks like."
Jessica, Age 8

In my practice, I have been surprised
how children have gradually shifted in
the last five years or so to extreme
concern about caregivers who smoke.
Most likely, they have developed these
attitudes from the intense warnings
about the dangers of smoking given
now, both at school and in the media.
Children have directly told me they fear
their parents will die from smoking and
leave them all alone in the world. Some
have even graphically described the
difference between healthy and
polluted lungs.

Caregivers who smoke seem to be sending a message, whether intentional or not. The child **perceives** that they do not respect their own bodies or those who breathe the second-hand smoke. Taking responsibility to quit, by using whatever it takes for success, models responsibility to a child.

SEED THOUGHTS
(Part of VISUALIZATION)

TIP: In regard to smoking, my readings and experience suggest the most effective approach is a combination of nicotine patches, visualization or hypnosis, chewing gum and medication. Specifically bupropion, prescribed by a physician, has a high rate of success!

Douma (1998a) reports that people who try to quit smoking are twice as successful using bupropion (49 percent) as compared to those who do not use any medication (23 percent). Combining medication with a nicotine patch increases the quit rate to 59 percent.

❧ Making Amends

Responsibility means that it is not enough to say "I'm sorry" when we make a major mistake. We must show our remorse and attempt to rectify it. We "**Make Amends.**" We do this both in our modeling and in our expectations. If there has been damage to property, restitution must be made, even if it was "an accident." If feelings have been hurt, an apology is in order.

> "The truth of the matter is that you always know the right thing to do. The hard part is doing it."
>
> — General H. Norman Schwarzkopf

Amy, Age 10

REAL LIFE: Eight-year-old Matthew was filled with rage about the behavioral system and rules his mother and I had set up. At home, he went outside to sit in a tree and stew about it. In a burst of anger, he grabbed a lemon from the tree, aimed it at the house and broke a window. Unfortunately, it was a difficult window to replace, costing $70. While Mother was initially willing to let him get away with a verbal apology, I insisted he Make Amends.

We made a page with 70 squares on it. Each square represented $1, and Matthew had to do chores around the house which Mother paid him for by marking off the boxes. Some of the chores were quite aversive, such as pulling weeds in the hot sun (equal to 4 squares) or cleaning up the bathroom (equal to 3 squares). It took him a great deal of time to "pay off" the window, but he learned his lesson so much more by making amends than if he had merely gotten away with a simple "sorry."

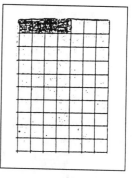

REAL LIFE: Similarly, nine-year-old Tracy was very agitated about having to sit in time-out. Because he had improved so much, he had not had to do this for a long time. Now he was blaming his parents rather than his own behavior. Unfortunately, Tracy had a paper clip in his pocket when he went to the time-out chair, and the chair was unwisely placed near their family heirloom antique table. Only later did his parents find the deep scratches Tracy had made in anger. Although Tracy meant only to irritate his parents as much as he felt irritated, the damage he did was phenomenal. He realized this once he had a page with 200 squares, which took months and months to pay off.

REAL LIFE: Twelve-year-old Sheila thought she was showing off by her use of profanity in front of classmates and a substitute teacher. Her mother called to ask my thinking about having her write sentences over and over that "I will not cuss in class." I questioned Mother, "How will this make amends? How will this affect Sheila and make her want to avoid it in the future?" Most likely it would just cause a negative attitude toward writing.

Instead, we came up with a different formula for making amends. Sheila was required to write a letter of apology to each and every individual whom she may have offended, including each fellow student as well as adults. This took considerable work, as she was also required to proofread, correct and rewrite letters which were messy. In addition, she had to humble herself to present the letter to each of the people, including a letter to the principal. This experience, then, had an entirely different impact from one of "grounding," for example, or having her simply write sentences.

SAMPLE APOLOGY NOTE

Dear Ms. ▬▬▬,
I am sorry about my behavior August
the 18th. I will try better next time.
I won't be rude. I will try to
precipitate next time. I didn't precipita
because I didn't want to come.

Sincerely,
Michael

TIP: In Alcoholics Anonymous, part of the twelve-step program is to make amends to "all persons we had harmed." Let's take a moment to consider if there is anyone in our lives with whom we need to make amends — a child? parent? co-worker? Perhaps the greatest effort would be swallowing our pride.

FINAL NOTE

No matter how uncomfortable or time-consuming it may be, instilling responsibility with children is critical. That means giving them chores, including taking care of their belongings and contributing to the family team. It also means being responsible for yourself and making amends when necessary. The guidelines presented here are only signposts toward our goal of teaching responsibility. As caregivers, we will have to be willing to accept discomfort and even conflict at times, as we help children with this issue. Age-appropriate responsibility will foster resilience.

> *"Give to the world the best you have and the best will come back to you."*
>
> — Madeline Bridges

OVERVIEW ~ Step 7:

HIGHER VALUES

OTHER WRITERS' OPINIONS

MY CHOICES:

1. COMPASSION
   - Help Others
   - Avoid Prejudice and Criticism
   - Look for New Perspectives

2. OPTIMISM
   - Teach Up-Talk
   - Fish Picture
   - Be Realistic
   - Set an Example
   - Teach the $2 = 1$ Equation
   - Label Down-Talk
   - Learn from Mistakes
   - Create Fun & Relive Happy Times
   - Find Your Sense of Humor

3. BELIEF IN SELF
   - Visualization and Seed Thoughts
   - Problem Solving
   - Integrity

YOUR TURN
   - Forced Choice
   - Deep Thinking
   - Lifestyle Check-up
   - Set an Example
   - Examine Spiritual Values

FINAL WORD

Secrets of the
Third Little Pig

Step 7

Those who are pig-headed and boorish
end up alone in the mud.

HIGHER VALUES

She Hears Our Wishes

This is an angel.
She lives in the sky.
She hears our wishes
From way way up high...

She hears our wishes
from every wishing star,
She tries her very best.
An angel from afar.

She tries her very best.
To make true our dream
From every falling star,
From the stars that stream.

Though some dreams take planning,
Though some wishes take time,
She hear the voices of children,
As sweet as a chime.

So just keep your faith.
It will turn out allright
Because she hears our wishes,
In the darkness of night.

Larie '97 Ilya.

~302~

"Our problem is not to find better values
but to be faithful to those we profess."

— Unknown

Haley, Age 11

To this point, we've emphasized developing resilience by using specific
tools and strategies. Now we come to the more subtle aspect of instilling
positive virtues. We know we need to teach children basic life skills such
as appropriate hygiene and good table manners. The hardest lessons,
though, have to do with building character.

Values are passed on from one generation to the next, either deliberately
or not. Through words, but most of all by actions, we transmit lessons
about what we care about. Why not make a conscious decision to teach
a child higher-level values? By helping children focus on caring about
themselves, their family and those around them, we help them feel
happier and more satisfied with their lives.

Today's society is so full of storms and turmoil, sometimes it seems we
are bombarded with stories of violence, crime, sex, abuse, war and
corruption. Many who were once heros have fallen. Technology is
consuming ever more of our time. Families are busier and more mobile
than ever. Penalties for mistakes are more severe too. Risky behavior
now may lead not only to unwanted pregnancy but to death. Illegal
drugs are more potent and dangerous than in previous generations. In
the midst of all this emotional litter, it is more important than ever that
we as caregivers make a commitment to develop not only children's
minds and bodies but their souls and spirits as well.

To start, it is critical to remind ourselves of the balance between
personality and **environment**. Do not overlook the impact of
temperament! It is one of the critical protective factors. Notice the
range of personalities depicted in the "self-portraits" on the next page.

Brandy, Ag 8
"A mouse because
I'm shy to
people."

Sean, Age 11.
"Angry, but trying to
chill out."

Elisa, Age 12
"I'm like a bear. I'm
sometimes sweet like
a teddy bear, but
sometimes I growl
like a cave bear."

Such awareness is powerful. As caregivers, we can reflect — not force — our values for children, and we can do it with the best possible match to their temperament. We are finding more and more that we can use a child's learning style and temperament to help make a "best fit" for him or her in the world. Regardless, the best attempts to mold a good moral character in children still have to go through the filter of a child's distinctive makeup.

The teaching of values and virtues is not an isolated practice. It is not a course students can take or a book they can read. It evolves out of our day-to-day interactions with our children. It has to do with how we empathize with others, how we handle our own stress, and how we choose to spend our valuable and limited time. It grows from our choice of words in our self-expression and from our personal explanations of how things seem to us on a day-to-day basis.

Unfortunately, building character takes considerable effort, especially if we are trying to break old patterns left over from our own childhood. If our own parents were critical and overbearing, for example, it's going to be a challenge to overcome that in order to model compassion and flexibility. In reality, we can use our own childhood trauma to set the stage for how we want our "new families" to be.

HONK!

Gus

There are several different directions we can head with this. I can tell you what other authors have selected as priority values or I can expound on my personal beliefs. In the end, though, YOU will have to inquire within yourself. Look at what you think you believe in and compare it to how you are living your life.

Think they'll manage to blunder their way through life?

> "The child learns to see his parents as more than human piñatas, full of goodies he has only to hit away at to get. He learns to see them as moral beings with standards and values that are more important than his own immature wishes, and he begins to internalize these standards and values, making them his own, developing a conscience in the process."
> — Dr. Barbara Lerner

Arthur, Age 9

OTHER WRITERS' OPINIONS

It is intriguing that authors with different backgrounds and outlooks show so much overlap. For example, what one person identifies as Fidelity, another may term Loyalty; what one calls Hospitality, another may call Helpfulness or Caring. Let's look at consistent themes.

Classic philosophers taught that virtues and values are **not abstract concepts** but personal **ways of acting**. These habits and practices then determine how we turn out and how we impact our world. Plato, Cicero and Aquinas all believed that moral life was based on four key virtues:

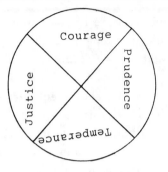

The Reverend James F. Keenan (1996) believes that what we **do** determines what we **become.** His four key virtues are: Justice (treating everyone equally), Fidelity (regard for family and friends), Self-care (regard for self) and Prudence (discerning and balancing life).

Unell and Wyckoff (1995) explore twenty "teachable virtues." These include the following (in alphabetical order):

Caring	Honesty	Responsibility
Cooperation	Humor	Self-discipline
Courage	Loyalty	Self-motivation
Courtesy	Patience	Self-reliance
Empathy	Peacemaking	Tolerance
Fairness	Resourcefulness	Trustworthiness
Helpfulness	Respect	

Mandy, Age 7

Cramer (1995) lists thirteen values most frequently identified as "core values" by her workshop participants. These are as follows:

Achievement	Intellectual Stimulation
Altruism	Intimacy
Autonomy	Meaning
Beauty	Personal Power
Challenge	Respect
Creativity	Security
Honesty	

Five Skills Needed by Every Person in "Sales"

1. **Sincere interest in others.** Listen to what they need.
2. **Ability to focus on one thing at a time.** No distractions!
3. **Sense of humor.** Laugh with others, and at yourself.
4. **Humility.** Take pride in yourself, but stay off the pedestal.
5. **Good self-confidence.** Belief in yourself bolsters customers' confidence in you.

— Selling Power, April 1997

Character Counts! Coalition is an organization dedicated to promoting old-fashioned values in America. Tom Selleck, a board member and occasional spokesperson, describes the group's "six pillars of character" (Doughtery 1997):

❖ Trustworthiness   ❖ Fairness

❖ Respect   ❖ Caring

❖ Responsibility   ❖ Citizenship

Dr. Niyo (1999) talks about the values he learned from his mentor as those he is trying to pass on to his students: honesty, hard work, compassion and facing your fears.

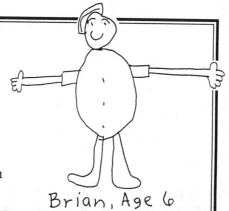

"What lies behind us and what lies before us are tiny matters compared to what lies within us."

— Ralph Waldo Emerson

Brian, Age 6

Finally, author Stephen Levine (1997) has examined "life review" values. These are "living lessons" learned by his work with terminally ill patients, often those afflicted with HIV-AIDS. Think for a moment how you would spend the next year if you knew it was all the time left in your lifetime. Levine suggests the following:

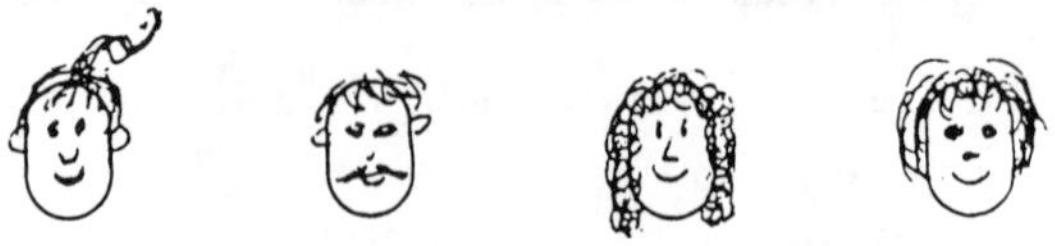

1. **Forgiveness:** Using visualization, forgive people in your past for harmful acts, and seek out people whose forgiveness you want.

2. **Gratitude:** Cultivate joy and help others share happiness by emphasizing the high points of life — anything from fresh flowers to birthdays.

3. **Singing:** Open your heart to a tune and sing it every day, all or in part.

4. **Journaling:** Keep a daily notebook. Write about your moods, your dreams, your setbacks, your plans.

"I hope I will be able to confide everything in you (the diary), as I have never been able to confide in anyone, and I hope you will be a great source of comfort and support."

—Anne Frank, *The Diary of a Young Girl*

Alan, Age 9

"Think deeply
speak gently
love much
laugh often
work hard
give freely
pay promptly
pray earnestly
and be kind."
— Anonymous

MY CHOICES (Can we have the envelope, please?)

My personal list is of course biased by my profession as a psychotherapist with children and by my own experience as a parent. Given
that, I'll share my "Top Three Virtues."

1. COMPASSION

This quality is in fact a combination of many virtues, including
Empathy, Helpfulness, Caring and Tolerance. Compassion is knowing
that everyone has past wounds and that we all suffer in some way.
Compassion is accepting others' shortcomings with tolerance. It is
giving unconditionally to help others. It is patience, nurturing and
sensitivity to others' feelings.

Much of the day-to-day behavior to teach and model Compassion comes
from lessons already covered in this book. Remember that the single
greatest predictor for a child to feel empathy for others is a sense of
attachment to at least one adult. When children make mistakes, we
focus on the behavior not their "badness." We discipline in a fair,
consistent way. We listen, listen, listen. We express our feelings ("I
messages") rather than accuse. We set boundaries by labeling behavior
and giving fair warnings. We limit television and spend time genuinely
interacting. We praise, not shame, our children.

"To live is not to live for
one's self alone;
let us help
one another."

— Menander

James,
Age 10

➤ Help Others

Compassion means going beyond our own needs to think of others, expecting nothing in return. Compassion truly is one of the times to do what you **say**, not just say it. It may be helping at your child's school or mowing the lawn for your church. Consider volunteering time at the YMCA, an AIDS center or a homeless shelter. Children can donate their used toys to charity or run favors for friends or relatives without expecting to get paid. In our home, compassion for abused and abandoned animals is a value that is demonstrated by donating time and money to the Humane Society and similar organizations. (This also explains the ridiculously large pet population at our house.)

"There is no higher religion than human service.
To work for the common good is the greatest creed."
— Albert Schweitzer

Tyler, Age 6

❥ Avoid Prejudice and Criticism

Watch what you say about others' color, weight or clothing. Vicious thinking can become a life-long habit that does no one good.

REAL LIFE: A local city newspaper, The Orlando Sentinel, carries a twice-weekly column called "Ticked Off." Readers mainly call in brief complaints anonymously that are then printed in the paper. Without going into the pros or cons of such a feature, I'll just say I continue to be amazed at what little empathy people have for each other and how little it takes to trigger some people's anger. Some of the complaints are truly vicious about seemingly trivial events . . .

*"I'm really ticked off at my husband for blowing his nose in the shower. HONK!" (If a man can't blow his nose in the privacy of his own home — in the **shower** no less — where can he?)*

"I'm ticked off at those noisy ice-cream trucks that cruise through neighborhoods. If I want ice cream, I will go to the store." (Has this individual never had the childhood joy of chasing down an ice-cream truck, mid-summer to savor a cold, creamy delight?)

"I'm ticked off at the women who outline their lips with lip liner but don't fill them in with lipstick. Don't you know how stupid you look." (Imagine if a real problem confronted this person!)

"When you are kind to others, it not only changes you — it changes the world. Cumulative acts of kindness change the emotional climate in which we live and teach people to see the world differently. When we go out of our way to be kind to someone, in large ways or small, our reward is the knowledge that we have redeemed the world."

— Rabbi Harold Kushner

Haley, Age 6

❧ Look for New Perspectives

In your day-to-day living, look for opportunities to show children there are often many sides of a story. For example, the grumpy cashier at the check-out counter may indeed be a person with a negative disposition . . . or she may be worried about a sick child at home . . . or how to get her car fixed with few funds. Help children see that "being different is OK."

TIP: For a delightful twist on seeing the other perspective, check out The True Story of the 3 Little Pigs . . . By A. Wolf *(Scieszka 1989). Here, the wolf gets a chance to tell his side of the story, and he insists he was set-up. For example, he did not huff and puff, he simply had a bad cold and "sneezed a great sneeze."*

2. <u>OPTIMISM</u>

An optimistic attitude is priceless! Optimistic children bounce back from adversity rather than wallow in it. They learn how to persist when things get tough. Caregivers can teach children as young as kindergarten to be optimistic, to look for the "silver lining" even on a dark cloud. If all else fails, we can always teach children "This too shall pass." We can also focus on what lessons they have learned about life that will help them in the future — or what things they can do or think to make themselves feel better.

REAL LIFE: Randy was a 7-year-old youngster with a recurrent tumor. Although it was not life-threatening, it was extremely painful and required repeated surgeries out-of-state. His parents first brought him to me because of his extreme discouragement. He was developing a "Why bother?" attitude about the next surgery.

My initial focus with Randy was HOPE. Given that this is an awful situation and it is not fair, what good can we find in it anyway? Following are some excerpts from one of our homemade books. I put Randy's feelings into the text, and he drew the pictures.

Randy is going to have surgery. He is not happy. He is a little scared. Mostly he is MAD!

Randy really HATES the tumor. He wishes it would just disappear!

There is one thing that is very good news. Randy's doctors are excellent! In fact, Dr. G█████ is the BEST doctor in Boston!

After Randy recovers, he will be able to run and play and do sports then he will be like all the other kids again.

Seligman (1995) in his excellent book, *The Optimistic Child*, refers to Optimism as "psychological immunization." Even in studies of animals, those who were taught how to actively control or "master" the bad things that happen to them (in this case, mild electric shock) never gave in to helplessness. They never became passive or "hopeless" because they had learned and believed that things could get better.

Pessimism has become rampant in our society. Not coincidentally, the rate of depression has also soared. Dr. Seligman reports that the rate of depression is ten times higher now than in the 1950s. A depressed person feels miserable and loses productivity at work and school; even physical health can be affected.

❧ Teach Up-Talk

Our **inner** dialogue affects our **outlook**! The things we say and think throughout the day sink into our subconscious and affect the way we feel and act . . . and the way others feel and act toward us. People with a negative outlook tend to feel depressed and dissatisfied with their lives. On the other hand, "**Up-Talk**" — **positive self-talk** — is a powerful tool for instilling Optimism.

Experts used to believe that it was necessary to explore the origins of feelings in depth before they could be changed. Now we know **people can change the way they feel by changing the way they act first!** For example, children who were taught to deliberately smile at other people (even when they did not feel like it) significantly increased their positive outlook and self-esteem over another group of children who were told not to smile unless they felt like it.

"I'm sad. The rain feels like crying. Maybe tomorrow will have the rainbow."
Carrie, Age 6

❧ Fish Picture

Remember children learn a great deal from concrete examples. I use the following metaphor in my practice constantly. Try it!

In a quiet moment, sit down and look at the picture on the next page with your child. If you've already set up some habits of time together and good listening skills, that should be easy. Rather than point out the "moral" or "lesson" here, try to draw out the child's interpretation of this analogy to real life.

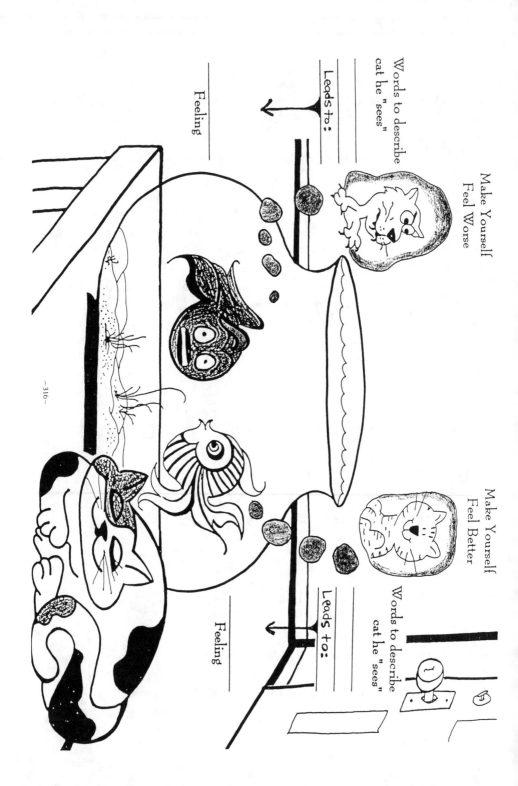

Make Yourself
Feel Worse

Words to describe
cat he "sees"

_____

Leads to:

_____

Feeling

_____

Make Yourself
Feel Better

Words to describe
cat he "sees"

_____

Leads to:

_____

Feeling

_____

-316-

Key Issues are:

① What kind of cat is that really? (We don't know. It looks OK. It's just sleeping, not bothering anyone.)

② How does the grey fish **see** the cat? What are some words we could write in the blank? (Mean, Vicious, Evil, Dangerous . . .)

③ If that's what he's **thinking**, how is he making himself **feel**? (Worried, Upset, Anxious, Mad . . .)

④ What about the striped fish? What are some words to describe how he **sees** the cat? (Fun, Playful, Harmless, Cheerful . . .)

⑤ So how is what he's **thinking** making him **feel**? (OK, Not Worried, Good Enough, Satisfied . . .)

⑥ Try to make the connection that it is not so much what **REALLY HAPPENS** to us as what we **THINK** about it that affects us. **Up-Talk makes us feel better!** Give some examples from your own life. Depending on your child's age, have him or her draw a picture or talk about a real incident and two different ways of looking at it.

REAL LIFE:
Here's a picture by
8-year-old Ryan
depicting two
different ways of
seeing his bicycle
accident.

❧ Be Realistic

People who tend to look for the worst usually find it — even in their very attempts to change! Negative thinking can be as much of a **habit** as smoking cigarettes or biting fingernails. Unfortunately, when a child tries to "just be positive" and then blows it, he or she may end up thinking even more derogatory and negative thoughts: "I'm hopeless" or "I can never do anything right". That's normal. Just don't stay with it — MOVE ON! Remember, you and your child are IMPROVING every day.

> "Each of us makes his own weather, determines the color of the skies in the emotional universe which he inhabits."
>
> — Fulton J. Sheen

Susie, Age 7

Wow, that's **7** more than last week! It <u>is</u> getting easier & easier!!

❧ Set an Example

One of the surest ways to build optimism and perseverance is to demonstrate that trait yourself. Do it openly. For example, if you have joined an exercise class, stick with it and notice small changes aloud instead of complaining about your weight. If you have cut down from one pack to ½ a pack of cigarettes a day, **give yourself credit out loud** instead of harping on how hard it is to quit.

❥ Teach the 2 = 1 Equation

This means it takes two positive comments or thoughts to equal one negative one. If you find yourself blurting out, "She has a big nose," quickly add, "but she has gorgeous eyes and a nice smile." If your son complains "The beans are too salty," help him find two good things he does like about the meal. The trick is to "jump start" the positive thinking without accusing or sounding like you are preaching. Negative thinking will take time and deliberate effort to change.

REAL LIFE: Fourteen-year-old Robert was brought to my office because his parents were worried about how irritable and negative he had become. As an example, they spoke of a recent evening going out to eat. Because of his grumpy attitude, they let him pick the restaurant. (Think about our Slot Machine from Step 3 - LIMITS. Was this teen getting a "payoff" for his nasty mood?) Robert not only was allowed to select the meal — pizza — but he was even allowed to choose all his favorite toppings. Yet when the pizza arrived, he still found fault: there wasn't enough pepperoni or there was too much sauce.

If you can make yourself miserable over a pizza, just imagine how difficult real crises are going to be. As it turned out, this pattern had been developing in Robert since early childhood. By catering to him to avoid his bad moods, his parents had unwittingly developed the trait of negativity. It was not until he hit adolescence and the emotions were intensified that they became concerned enough to seek professional help. It's a good thing, too, as Robert's attitude was leading him to a sense of despair — a sense of helplessness and hopelessness with the world.

❥ Label Down-Talk

Identify negative thinking and make a note to stop it. Every time you say a negative comment, tell yourself, "That's a "**Down-Talk**" (or a bummer or put-down), cancel that." Then think of a more realistic comment. For example, change the "bummer" comment of "I never do anything right" to "I made a mistake." Teach your child to change the negative comment of "No one likes me" to "Those kids are being rude."

*REAL LIFE: Sandra and her mother who were working on the issue of rudeness were taught to play the "**Buzzer Game**." For several weeks, their job was to monitor each other when they were together. If one said something negative, the other would "Bzzz" like on a game show. They kept score and had fun with it. Pretty soon, they were buzzing themselves and stopping themselves before they started.*

BEFORE

AFTER

"me and my mom"

Sandra, Age 9

"All of us"

Two aspects of these drawings are especially interesting:

①   In the "Before" drawing the characters are slanted at an angle which can suggest a feeling of **instability**. Notice the "After" drawings have more vertical characters.

②   Sandra even chose to include her younger brother, Scott, in the "After" drawing, suggesting the positive talk was contagious.

♪ Learn From Mistakes

This approach beats blaming ourselves for failing hands down.
Remember to reinforce effort more than product. A favorite example is
Edison's invention of the light bulb. Rather than seeing his first 200+
attempts as "failures," he said they were **learning experiences** — he then
knew what **not** to do! We must recognize children when they **try hard**
even if total success is still out of reach. Children need to learn that they
have the **stamina** to overcome periods of frustration, conflict and anger
to develop persistence and diligence.

"Everything that is happening
at this moment is a result
of the choices you've made
in the past."

— Deepak Chopra

Kathy, Age 7

*TIP: Show children how to learn from mistakes, how to take an active
approach instead of stewing about setbacks. For example, after a poor
spelling test, ask "What's a better way to study?" or "How can you practice
differently?"*

Mike, Age 6

"Mishaps are like knives that
either serve or cut us as we
grasp them by the blade or
the handle."

— James Russell Lowell

❧ Create Fun & Relive Happy Times

Optimism is based a great deal in real-life experience. You might think of your life as a videotape. Rewind often to "the good parts." Replay your favorite vacation or the first step your baby took, even if he's a handful now at 16. Let children go back to their **Accomplishment Album** to replay their successes and improvements.

HINT 📖: For more about the **Accomplishment Album**, see Step 1 - Praise.

"Much unhappiness results from an inability to remember the nice things that happen to us."

— W. N. Rieger

Trevor, Age 6

If you're in a rut, do something active to create excitement and break up the routine. Get out a game you haven't played in a while (or make up new rules to an old game!) Have pizza for breakfast and scrambled eggs for dinner, go a different route to school or work, part your hair on the other side, or wear your underwear inside out! Take a sightseeing trip or drive out to the airport just to ride the tram and watch the planes.

"Going to the Airport"

Justin, Age 7

REAL LIFE: Dr. E is a successful clinical psychologist in town. I see her at least once a month when we get together with our group of friends for Girls' Night Out (GNO). Sometimes there are 4 of us, sometimes there are 15. We may meet at someone's home for snacks or at a restaurant after work for dinner. Always it's a chance to catch up with the goings-on in our friends' lives. Usually, someone has good news or a funny story. At times, someone needs advice. Occasionally, someone is going through a crisis and needs support.

So why would Dr. E have a **slumber party**? Why not? Imagine a dozen professional women in their 40s and 50s at a sleep-over like teenage girls. What fun! The unexpected adds spice to life!

"Children, on average, laugh about 400 times a day. Adults only about 15 times. Scientists who study humor want to know why 385 laughs disappear."

— Delthia Ricks

Eric, Age 10

❥ Find Your Sense of Humor

While humor admittedly has a dark side when it is used to hurt or
degrade, overall research consistently shows the benefits. Laughter
and humor . . .

- ✦ enhance social interaction (making and keeping friends)
- ✦ facilitate learning
- ✦ decrease stress and anxiety
- ✦ help ease pain
- ✦ make difficult situations easier to handle
- ✦ lower blood pressure
- ✦ increase muscle flexion
- ✦ help the immune system by increasing natural killer cells that
  destroy viruses and tumors (Ricks 1996)

> "You cannot hold back a good laugh
> any more than you can the
> tide. They are both
> forces of nature."
>
> — William Rostler

Laura, Age 7

Rapp (1951) in his discussion of the origins of humor notes that
laughter was actually recommended by doctors to their patients at the
turn of the century to help with a variety of physical ailments. Laughter
was used to stimulate the lungs, respiratory system and heart. More
widely known is the writing of Norman Cousins (1979) who utilized
reruns of "Candid Camera" and old Marx brothers films to cure himself
of deadly diseases.

Although we wouldn't want to send the message that "life is a joke," sense of humor is one of the strongest **Protective Factors** to make children resilient in the face of adversity. Laughing at ourselves and at the world around us can help us make it through the tough times and enjoy the good times even more.

HINT 📖: To review all of the **Protective Factors,**
see the section titled Resilience: The Brick House.

"Among those who I like or admire, I can find no common denominator, but among those whom I love, I can: all of them make me laugh."

— W.H. Auden

Lauren, Age 7

Realize that humor is very contextual. What is funny depends on the age of the child, the gender and past events. Researchers have found that **incongruity** is the common thread in humor at all ages. It means there's a difference between what is expected and what is experienced. **Novelty** is also important because it piques our interests and can make us laugh.

KIDS' JOKES AND RIDDLES
(Answers on the next page)

① What goes "Boo-hoo, boo-hoo, PLOP. Boo-hoo, boo-hoo, PLOP?"
② What did Tarzan say when he saw the elephants coming?
③ What did Tarzan say when he saw the elephants coming with sunglasses on?
④ What's a computer's favorite snack?

FUNNY FACTS

Ancient Egyptians shaved off their eyebrows to mourn the deaths of their cats.

Months that begin with a Sunday will always have a "Friday the 13th."

Barbie's measurements if she were life size: 30-23-33.

Assuming Rudolph was in front, there are 40,320 ways to arrange the other eight reindeer.

Answers to Jokes & Riddles on Previous Page:
① Someone crying their eyes out.
② "Here come the elephants."
③ Nothing — he didn't recognize them.
④ Chips.

"If you have a negative thought that lasts for
more than 15 or 20 seconds, you'll start
drawing more negative thoughts,
because, research suggests,
it brings on changes in your brain chemistry."
— Susan Olson, Ph.D.

One of my favorite tricks with a new but obviously nervous child in counseling is to switch to a voice with an unusual accent. For a small child, I may pick up a puppet and go into a goofy routine. An older child usually giggles and lightens up to my witch accent and threat to "turn you into a toad." Adolescents are initially shocked then thaw to my guttural British accent and sometimes respond with their own made-up voice. The point is it is unexpected and it eases tension, and sometimes we even joke about "who really needs help."

Troy, Age 15

Angie, Age 9

Self-effacing humor is especially helpful in tough situations. One example is a speaker who has to face a tough crowd. Right off the bat, she might start with an unexpected twist such as "My assistant gave me some advice before coming down here tonight. She told me I looked fine and not to worry. She said don't try to be smart, funny or charming. Just be yourself."

"You must do the things you think you cannot do."

—Eleanor Roosevelt

Sarah, Age 10

3. <u>BELIEF-IN-SELF</u>

This is a hard value to label because, like Compassion, it has so many facets. It encompasses a variety of personal power virtues such as Resourcefulness, Autonomy, Security, Achievement, Self-motivation, Honesty and Self-discipline.

Instilling these beliefs overlaps with much of what we have already learned. Self-discipline results from setting goals, being consistent and giving responsibility. Self-reliance develops from **Up-Talk** and from spending creative time mastering projects, schoolwork or hobbies. Resourcefulness grows out of being **listened to** (not lectured) and **guided** (not nagged) to make appropriate choices.

"He that respects himself
is safe from others.
He wears a coat of mail
that none can pierce."

Mark, Age 7 — Henry Wadsworth Longfellow

Edith Grotberg, the head of an international resilience project, helps people organize their belief-in-self into three strength areas (Blum 1998).

1. I HAVE (strong relationships, role models, rules at home, support).
2. I AM (a person who has hope and faith, cares about others, is proud of myself).
3. I CAN (communicate, solve problems, seek good relationships, gauge the temperament of others).

➤ Visualization & Seed Thoughts

Einstein said we use only 10% of our brain. We can put some of the rest of it to work for us by consciously deciding to do so.

> "There is nothing either good or bad,
> but thinking makes it so."
>
> — William Shakespeare

Fanning (1989) uses **VISUALIZATION** as a powerful tool for change. He reports that five minutes of visualization can cancel out hours, days, even weeks of negative thinking or acting. **Three five-minute sessions a day can change a habit that took years to form and reinforce!**

> "Man's rise or fall, success or failure,
> happiness or unhappiness depends
> on his attitude . . . a man's
> attitude will create the
> situation he imagines."
>
> — James Lane Allen

Lilly, Age 7

Everybody visualizes. You visualize whenever you daydream, remember a past experience, or think of someone you know. It's a natural, largely automatic activity like breathing or walking. By practicing, you can improve your existing powers of visualization. You can harness this automatic activity and use it consciously to improve your life.

As I tell my clients, visualization is basically "seeing a movie in your head." For best results, you have to first completely relax your body. Go someplace quiet where you will not be interrupted. Get comfortable and focus on your breath. Let your breathing become slow and deep through your nose. To get more relaxed, try slowly counting backwards from 50 to 1, or imagine you are on a long, safe stairway and stepping down, slowly, slowly, slowly (perhaps counting the steps from 20 down to 1).

Some people like to imagine they are in a safe, comfortable place. It may be the beach, the mountains, a meadow or a special room. Try to see (hear, feel, smell, taste) as many details as possible about this place. Give yourself permission to take the time to be comfortable and relaxed.

At this point, you can create what you want to have happen. It is as if you are "programming your subconscious." More simply, you are planting **"Seed Thoughts."** In my office, I have had shy children visualize themselves gradually becoming more and more friendly. Children with quick tempers visualize themselves remaining calm instead of getting agitated. Poor students visualize themselves focusing, concentrating and remembering as they study.

This technique is powerful, but it must be done repeatedly and in addition to other change agents. It **augments and enhances** everything you do, but it **doesn't replace anything**. You will not prosper by mind power alone. It doesn't work that way. Visualization can let you imagine yourself breezing through a job interview, and it will probably help relax you. Success, however, is more likely if you also practice your self-presentation with a friend, bone up on relevant facts you'll need to know, and/or talk about your fears with a professional counselor. (Fanning 1989).

A model I typically use to explain visualization is to draw the child in front of me with a "brain" and "sub-conscious."

We usually talk about the way they **want** things to be (goals) compared to how they are now (starting point). Examples from sports are good because professional athletes often use visualization to enhance their performance. They may visualize the perfect golf swing, the basketball going from their hands to inside the hoop or their own endurance in a long race.

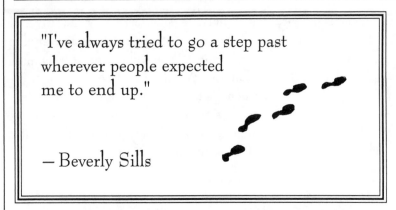

"I've always tried to go a step past
wherever people expected
me to end up."

— Beverly Sills

*REAL LIFE: Theresa was a 30-year-old professional who sought
counseling for her upcoming divorce. Although she felt convinced that this
was the right step, she felt anxious to the point of being immobilized when
she thought of actually going to court and facing a judge. In counseling, we
"mentally rehearsed" the scene dozens of times: in my office, on audiotapes I
made for her, during her own relaxation exercises. We played out all different
possibilities: "See yourself feeling self-confident and brave even if this or that
happens . . ." Throughout the day she repeated her **Seed Thought**: "I am
becoming stronger and more self-confident every day."*

*By the time of the actual event, Theresa described it as "so easy it was
almost boring." She reported extreme self-confidence. All the practice seemed
like "memories," and she was just doing it "one more time."*

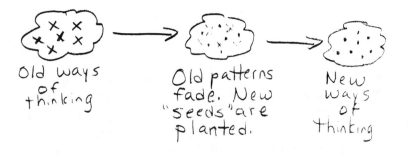

Old ways of thinking → Old patterns fade. New "seeds" are planted. → New ways of thinking

*TIP: Teach children how to utilize their subconscious by starting simple. Help them pick a **Seed Thought**. Repeatedly throughout the day (in a spare moment) say your positive self-statement and remind your children to say theirs. Typical **Seed Thoughts** may be: "Every day, it is easier and easier for me to notice the good things around me" or "Every day, I like myself better and better." Say it at a stop light. Say it in the shower. Say it again ten times before bed. You'll be planting the seeds that will help wipe out old weeds of despair.*

"Every day, I like myself better and better!"

☙ Problem Solving

Learning to **Hand**-le **Problems** leads to autonomy and achievement. We already explored this as a tool for coping. Let's see how it applies to Belief-in-Self.

HINT 📖: To review the **Hand**-ling **Problems**,
see Coping Tools in Step 6 - RESPONSIBILITY.

REAL LIFE: Ten-year-old Andy was a major disappointment to his father. Andy was timid, intellectual and artistic. His father, who had grown up with five brothers, was a sports fanatic. At school, Andy's grades were slipping and his teachers reported he seemed "depressed." At home, there was much bickering, and Andy's mother reported she felt stuck in the middle, between her husband and son. Look now at Andy's family portrait as animals. See how he eloquently depicts the family dynamics with his art.

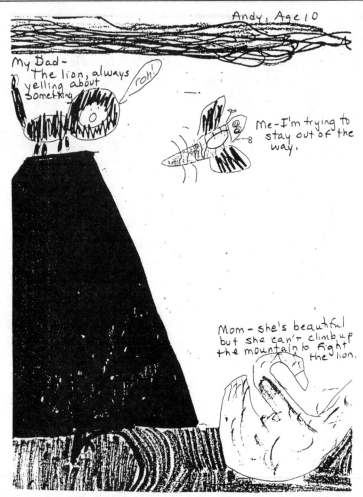

NOTE: This issue could have been approached in a variety of ways including the strategies in Step 5 about time together. Because this family was fairly chaotic, I deliberately chose a <u>**Hand**</u>-ling Problems approach to give them a blueprint they could apply to other situations.

① **Identify the problem.** We used **Ear Mirrors** to hear each person's side of it. To summarize the session, Andy saw the problem as his dad not liking him, not wanting to spend time with him and always criticizing him. Andy's father saw the problem as Andy being "too wimpy" and ineffective in his pursuits. He also thought that Andy was too dependent on his mother for constant help and that his interests and activities were "too feminine." It took some effort with **Ear Mirrors** to pull out a final problem issue we could all agree on: "Andy and Dad have different interests and talents. They get frustrated about it and blame each other."

HINT 📖: For more details on **Ear Mirrors,**
　　　　　　see Step 2 - LISTENING.

② Ask: "What have we already tried?"

Partial list:

- Dad tried to teach Andy how to pitch and hit.
- Andy had asked Dad to help him cook a surprise dinner for Mom.
- Dad had enrolled Andy in tennis lessons (which he hated).
- Andy had started going to his room when Dad got home so there wouldn't be a fight.
- Dad had invited Andy to watch TV sports with him.

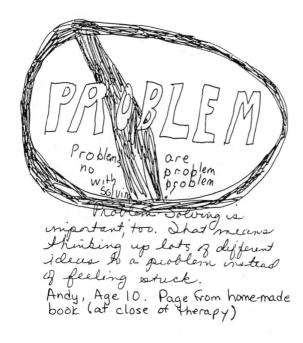

Andy, Age 10. Page from home-made book (at close of therapy)

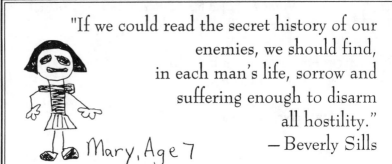

"If we could read the secret history of our
enemies, we should find,
in each man's life, sorrow and
suffering enough to disarm
all hostility."
— Beverly Sills

Mary, Age 7

③ **Brainstorm: What else could we do? What else?**

- We could try to find an activity we both like.
- We could take turns picking something to do together every weekend.
- We could watch TV sports together and make small bets to predict the winner.
- We could do one game or puzzle together each week.
- We could use the "2 = 1" rule (See the section on Optimism in this very chapter).
- ETC.

④ **Check it out.** In this case Andy and his Dad agreed they could both enjoy swimming but then they couldn't decide on a time and place to do it together. They liked the idea of taking turns and being less blaming with each other.

⑤ **Pick the best answer.** Andy and his dad agreed to use an odd/even day technique. On even-numbered Saturdays, Andy would pick an activity. On odd-numbered Saturdays, Dad would. They would agree to be "friends" and not criticize each other, especially during their shared activity. They would try to find one nice thing to say about each other every day (they even made a scoreboard).

⑥ **Try it.** They did.

⑦ **Check it out again. How did it go?** They got off to a rocky start as old patterns snuck in over the best intentions. Often on Dad's day, Andy had a pressing homework project, or on Andy's day, Dad might have had to do yard work. (This is where you model your talent for negotiation!) At our next session, Dad agreed to help Andy with homework and Andy agreed to help Dad with chores, but their activity together was top priority! They also switched from the daily compliment system to the **Buzzer Game**.

HINT 📖:   For more details on the Buzzer Game,
see **Label Down-Talk** under Optimism
in this chapter.

NOTE:

Parents can always get creative with this too. Remember to **create fun!**

OK. I'll give you 5 cents more if you correctly name the states that border Oklahoma.

REAL LIFE OUTCOME: Andy's teachers reported he seemed less timid and increasingly self-confident. His mother reported great relief in Andy's new-found ability to "connect" with his father. Lots more work still needed to be done, but this was a good start.

"We can do no great things — only small things with great love."

— Mother Teresa

Chris, Age 6

❧ Integrity

This means more than just being trustworthy with others. It also means being honest with yourself, standing up for your own beliefs and values. Children with integrity are less likely to lie to avoid punishment or impress others.

Point out honest acts of other people. Connect honesty with rewards and a sense of self-satisfaction. Show how dishonesty leads to grief, not just in our own lives, but all around us (in the news for example). Model you own integrity even when things get rough.

REAL LIFE: One of the hardest decisions I ever faced was testifying in court about an adolescent accused of attempted murder.   Fourteen-year-old Juan admitted to chasing his stepmother with a machete.   I was at first hesitant to even be in the room alone with him.   After I worked with him, though, I was convinced his behavior was a survival reaction.   He had felt his own life was threatened by a weapon (stepmother's gun) which was never found by the police.

On the stand, I had to make a commitment that I believed Juan would not be a danger to other teenagers. A safer route would be to simply agree to send him to a facility with hard-core juvenile offenders. I believed if that happened though, Juan would never be salvageable. On the other hand, I had no guarantee he wouldn't hurt other children in a least-restrictive environment.

Despite repeated grilling by the prosecuting attorney, I stood my ground because I did believe that Juan was well-adjusted overall. He did not show the pattern of maladjustment I typically see in a juvenile defendant.

"Do not let what you cannot do
interfere with what you
can do."
— John Wooden

I don't mind telling you, I sweated it out. I believed in this boy and had stood up for him on the stand. If he did get violent and hurt someone, I would be responsible. As it turned out, my position was verified only a few months later. Juan's stepmother was arrested for aggravated assault with a weapon. She committed suicide shortly thereafter. Juan was then released to the custody of his father, and allowed to resume his normal life.

YOUR TURN

The home is the most critical area where values are instilled. Even teenagers who disagree with their parents over myriad smaller issues typically hold firm to their parents' moral values. Most adolescents have similar values as their parents for major issues (Associated Press 1997; Hill 1987). Rejection of parental values is usually temporary or superficial. "Adolescent rebellion" actually amounts to little more than a series of minor skirmishes. Fewer than 1 out of 5 teens have such severe rebellion, they show blatant conflict in the family and hostility toward society (Offer, et al. 1989).

"Character building begins in our infancy and continues until death."

— Eleanor Roosevelt

Betty, Age 9

Passing on our values should not be a haphazard approach. For example, are we unwittingly passing on the value of "artificial urgency"? That means we have to rush, rush, rush all the time. We phone from our cars on our mobile phones and fax information rather than mail it. We "beep" people to find them instantly. What we do shows what we think is important. Are we putting as much effort into things we **say** are important but may not really **show**?

❥ Forced Choice

Use a twist on an old "**Forced Choice**" technique to help clarify your values, and have some fun. On many personality tests and vocational inventories, the individual is required to choose between only two options. Sometimes both are very appealing, and sometimes, neither is. For example, a question to clarify extrovert vs. introvert tendencies might ask: "Would you rather a) visit with a small group of friends for the evening, or b) attend a large, noisy party with lots of new people."

> "It matters not
> how long you live,
> but how well."
>
> — Publilius Syrus

Laura, Age 7

REAL LIFE: When my daughter and I played this "game," she asked me questions such as . . .

"Would you rather step into a dark cave with snakes or lay down in a tub of slugs?"

"Would you rather get your finger slammed in a door or have your best friend see you pick your nose?"

When it was my turn, I asked . . .

"Would you rather have the kids at your school think of you as cool and popular or smart and kind?"

"Would you rather get $100 to spend for yourself or know that $200 was donated to a needy family?"

This kind of self-exploration can be fun, but more importantly it leads to a deeper understanding of values we may never have otherwise tapped into.

❧ Deep Thinking

If you were forced to write your "top five virtues" what would you choose? You may want to get some ideas from the various writers at the beginning of this chapter. Reflect on your own childhood. How did that affect the values you have today? How does the work you do or your career reflect your values? Think of how you show your values through behaviors on a day-to-day basis.

Remember the study that analyzed what people said they valued?

HINT 📖: To review the chart, see **Budgeting Time** in Step 5 - TIME.

Americans said they placed the highest value on the following activities: sex, playing sports, fishing, enjoying art or music, and going to a bar or lounge. Playing with and/or hugging children placed sixth after all of these in the top ten list. More shocking was the way Americans

REALLY spent their time. Being involved with their children was not even in the top ten. The top six activities were: sleeping, working, watching TV, eating at home, getting dressed and cooking. Eating out and shopping were higher on the list than spending time with children.

*TIP: Imagine you have a relatively minor emergency — your car battery died (at night, in the rain of course) or your child was hitting balls and one accidentally crashed through your new neighbor's bay window. Figure out the cost in dollars, time and heartache. Then say words of **gratitude** you didn't really have to deal with that (although you are strong enough if you had to). Then make a donation to your local humane society (or other good cause) for what that would have cost you in either dollars or time.*

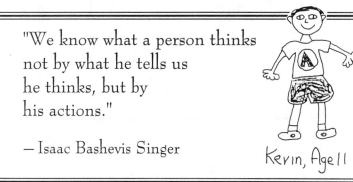

"We know what a person thinks not by what he tells us he thinks, but by his actions."

— Isaac Bashevis Singer

Kevin, Age 11

❥ Lifestyle Check-up

Conduct an analysis of your own values and lifestyle. Give yourself an opportunity to assess how congruent your time and your values are. Compare what you **SAY** is important to what you **SHOW** others through your behavior. You can use that information to better align your values with your life.

REAL LIFE: A recent experience in my practice forced me to confront my own values head-on. I was contacted by a national television show with an exposé-type format. I initially understood the topic to be about aggressive children, and the object was to help frustrated parents better understand and find help for their children. Some of the parents I'd worked with agreed to be interviewed. I was thrilled with the concept of reaching out to other parents with difficult children, to give them hope and ideas for intervention.

*As things progressed, however, expectations shifted. The producers wanted hidden cameras in the homes, to catch the children in acts of violence. It would be acceptable even to "provoke" the children so that there would be "dramatic visual impact." I understood the media point-of-view, but the **higher purpose had gotten lost.** I had to be true to myself. I declined. (No big deal for the network; they found another therapist to take my place.)*

"I will neither yield to the song of the siren nor the voice of the hyena, the tears of the crocodile nor the howling of the wolf."

— George Chapman

Bonnie, Age 8

The day I told a close friend the above story (with both regret and bitterness I admit), he just smiled and said "me, too." As a real-estate broker, he had been offered some very much needed money "under the table" to avoid giving the office a percentage.

The following program may not suitable for those of you who have higher values.

Sometimes we just have our inner voice to guide us . . . and the external rumble can make that hard to hear. Part of the issue is not just to analyze your values but have the backbone to walk your own path. To stand alone, to have vision, takes courage.

❥ Set an Example

We can teach or encourage children with specific behaviors that reflect
our values, but they learn best by seeing, trying it and being recognized
for it. We need to clearly think of the goals we have for our children and
decide what behaviors would lead there.

Erin, Age 11

TIP: *For the next week or so, ask various friends and acquaintances what
are the three things they value most in a person. You'll learn a lot. When I
did this I heard answers ranging from "generosity, tolerance and love" to
"creativity, courage and achievement." Then look to see if people are living
their truths.*

❥ Examine Spiritual Values

Recall that Faith is one of the **Protective Factors** for resilient children.
How often a family attends church actually makes a difference in their
probability of drug use too (Shapiro 1996). Is religion just for church
on Sunday? Or do you regularly pray with your children?

HINT 📖: To review the importance of Faith, see the
section titled Resilience: The Brick House.

David, Age 9

Tappidy! Tappidy!

"You cannot teach a man anything.
You can only help him find it
within himself."

— Galileo

I am not favoring one belief system over another. My experience has shown me, however, that children who believe and trust in a Higher Power often have an added source of solace in difficult times. That Higher Power may be, as the Creed of Alcoholics Anonymous says, "whatever you conceive it to be." It may be God, guardian angels, an inner guide, intuition or just "positive energy."

REAL LIFE: 13-year-old Patty felt overwhelmed with the demands of her young life: Drug use by an older sibling, a series of her mother's boyfriends whom she herself hated, learning disabilities which led to school frustrations and the apparent beginnings of an eating disorder. As part of our therapy we utilized **Visualization** *including a Higher Power. Patty was so pleased with this approach, she wrote it down to give to her friends! The following is an excerpt from her own writings:*

As you sit there you and relax. you
feel a God. You feel his warmness. You
know he is there with you. You know that
he is right next to you. You can not
see him thow. He is sitting right with you
waiting for you to talk so he can
listen. God is your best friend and he always
lisens he always seemes to understand. As
you sit there you can God you can
picture in your mind mind God smiling and
giving you a huge. God Loves you and he
is always happy when you come to this
place so you two can visit. You began
to talk to God telling him whatever is on
your mind that you want to discuse with
him. Sometimes God will respond only
when you want to listen or sometimes he or
you will just do all the talking. What
ever is nessasary. Now give yourself
as much time as you need to be with
God. now gather this wonderful place
of God and yours. And store it in
your memory so you can take it out at
anytime. Leave it just the same way as
the way you left it last.
                    Patty, Age 13

REAL LIFE: Seven-year-old Lacy came to see me already diagnosed by her pediatrician as "school phobic." Worse, her problem was increasing so that she became very anxious just leaving her home for fear something bad would happen to her. Even enticements to go to an amusement park or special playground were adamantly refused.

To make a long story short, Lacy had been terrorized by some bullies at her previous school. Adults who were informed told her not to exaggerate and ignored her pleas. Her parents had the mistaken impression that their calls were taken seriously and interventions made. With highest possible intentions, they continued to force her to school each day, believing she would "outgrow" it.

> "Nothing in life is more wondrous than faith — the one great moving force which we can neither weigh in the balance nor test in the crucible."
>
> — William Osler

Kim, Age 8

When the truth came to light, witnesses actually saw Lacy being physically held down and taunted with profanity by a gang of cruel older boys. Her parents immediately withdrew her and enrolled her in a private school.

Even though her physical being was now safe, the psychological scars remained. Lacy had panic attacks in her new school and still refused to leave the safety of her own home. It's a credit to her parents that they were able to get her out of the house to seek professional help.

Traditional therapy may have dictated some type of "Desensitization Process." For example over a series of sessions, I would have taught Lacy how to tighten, then loosen, her muscles to relax her body. We may have practiced deep breathing and counting. I might have had her imagine gradually more stressful situations in my office, where it was safe and she was relaxed. Alternate therapies might have utilized EMDR (lateral eye movements) or TFT (tapping techniques) to uncover and resolve trauma. Other therapists may have utilized hypnosis or neuro-linguistic programming approaches.

After talking with Lacy and her mom, though, I believed that this child needed some immediate relief and reasonable logic was not going to work. Parents had repeatedly assured her she was "safe now" and "nothing else bad would happen." Her subconscious did not believe it. After getting mother's permission, I used a novel approach: Since the current fears and anxiety were no longer based on something concrete and tangible, the coping mechanism didn't have to be either. We went for the Higher Power.

Lacy told me how she believed that God watches everything and that she did have guardian angels, although she didn't understand their function, particularly as they had not prevented her pain. When asked, she acknowledged she had never really asked them to. She then told me her grandfather had died several years ago, and she believed he was in heaven, too, with the angels.

Lacy, Age 7
Guardian Angel (who else can you trust?)

In a very powerful therapy session, Lacy and I lit a candle, turned off the lights and said prayers. We used a guided visualization (see the section on Visualization in this chapter for more ideas). We asked that Lacy be filled, surrounded and protected by God's love and her grandfather's affection. Whenever she closed her eyes and concentrated, she could bring her Special Guardian Angel — her grandfather — down to wrap beautiful, soft wings around her shoulders. I also gave Lacy a precious stone called "Angelite" which she could hold in her hand for more strength and power. Afterwards, she drew a picture of her angel with such a sense of relief on her face, I thought I'd cry.

I received a phone call two days later from Lacy's mom. It was "like a miracle." Lacy was her "old self." She kept her special stone with her in a special pouch around her neck and paused at times for prayer and reassurance. But mainly, she just got on with her life — playing in the neighborhood, going out for pizza and even getting to school with an adequate disposition. Of course, her safety built on itself. The more she extended herself, the more "normal" she became.

The point here is that Lacy's power to change came directly from a foundation of spiritual values. At a time when children are exposed to so much "grime" through the media, it's a wonderful opportunity for us to show them "the light."

FINAL NOTE

In this chapter, as throughout the book, we have considered how we can help children be stronger and more capable. By closely examining our values, we become the best possible archers, setting our sights on the mark to send children forward toward the future.

"Your children are not your children . . .
they come through you but not from you,
and though they are with you
yet they belong not to you . . .
you are the bows from
which your children
as lifting arrows
are sent forth."

— Kahlil Gibran

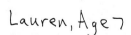

Lauren, Age 7

Part Three:

THE PIGGY BANK

Secrets of the Third Little Pig

Hope:
THE
FOUNDATION
FOR THE HOUSE

"Hope is believing you have both the will and the way to accomplish your goals."

– C. R. Snyder

Kathy, Age 7

REAL LIFE: Recall 10-year-old Steven from our discussion about RISK FACTORS. He was the delightful youngster who methodically destroyed my room while declaring "Sorry" after each "accident." His case was striking because he used anger and defiance as weapons to hurt others, while his older brother displayed resilience by his use of charm and perseverance.

At our third session, I was able to maneuver Steven to come to my room by specifically telling him NOT to join his father and I as we had "adult things" to discuss. Of course, he jumped right up and ran to my room. During this session, there was a major power struggle as Steven tested my authority. He plopped down in a chair, pulled his baseball cap down over his eyes, and folded his arms in front of his chest. All ready for counseling. Right!

I told Steven he did not have to talk but he did have to remove the cap or turn it backwards so we could see his face. The limit was set: cooperate with that one task or leave. Remember: Label it, give a warning and mean it. I gave him a chance to do it without losing face, too. I chatted with his dad during the two-minute time frame I'd set.

HINT 📖: For more details on labeling behavior, see Step 3 - LIMITS.

At the end of the time, Steven had, of course, neither removed his cap nor removed himself from my room. Eventually, I pulled Steven's chair out into the hall and locked him out of my room. I'm sure colleagues in my office were thrilled when Steven began kicking and pounding on my door. Soon his screaming included profanities.

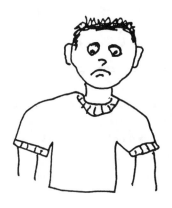

*"What am I going to do with him?" groaned Steven's dad. "I can't stand it anymore. It's gotten to where . . ." But he couldn't finish his thought. He didn't have to. I knew instinctively: He did not **like** his own child anymore! He still had **a father's love** for his son, but he did not **like** Steven, even dreaded being with the boy. I imagined Steven's dad coming home from work exhausted only to wish he could retreat back there after about ten minutes.*

*If you were a therapist, how would you handle it? There are infinite possibilities. I felt my **first task** was to give Steven's father HOPE. "Believe it or not, this may turn out to be one of our best sessions once the dust settles!" I said brightly. I explained that Steven was learning about my limits and my need for respect. As I gave his father some "homework" to spend specific time with his child, I focused again on HOPE.*

HINT 📖: For more details on spending time together, see Step 5 - TIME.

"This is very exciting. Steven is going to change – and you are, too. You'll be very surprised and pleased in the end. Just don't expect miracles overnight." After the session, as I watched them walk past my window to their car, Steven's cap still far down over his face, I silently wished my words of encouragement and hope would stay with Steven's dad until more tangible results were seen.

> "Keep your face to the
> sunshine and you
> cannot see the
> shadows."
>
> — Helen Keller

Ben, Age 5

REAL LIFE OUTCOME: It has been over a year, and I still see Steven about once a month for a "check-up." At first, our weekly sessions were "challenging" to say the least. True to form, Steven got worse before he got better. It's hard for me to identify the most important change factor. Rather, I compare the therapy to a tapestry woven of many strategies (most addressed somewhere in this book) and plenty of snags along the way.

One of Steven's favorite activities now is to take on the role of the therapist, sitting in my chair, and have me be a defiant, pouting client whom he tries to help. Steven still has some "rough edges," but on the whole, he is a much happier, cooperative and personable young man.

Danny, Age 6

HOPE MAKES ALL THE DIFFERENCE

Until you or your child (or ideally both of you) believe that things can and will get better, we cannot make much progress. I have worked with many children with whom I truly believe the strongest curative factor — the thing that made them **GET BETTER** — was HOPE! They believed that things WOULD get better and they did.

"Hope is the thing with feathers
That perches in the soul,
And sings the tune without the words,
And never stops at all."

Travor, Age 6

— Emily Dickinson

Children who have had one bad experience (i.e., a bite by a dog or an accident in a car) can become quite phobic about that one thing (dogs or cars). My first task is usually to reassure them with stories about other children who have had similar or even worse experiences and gotten better! I show them other children's artwork depicting their anxiety at first and their relief later.

Both
Drawings
by
Beth,
Age 8

Note sense of hopelessness at at beginning of therapy.

Note entirely different affect 3 sessions later. The legs are more even with the torso, suggesting a stronger sense of balance.

A favorite technique is to fold a piece of paper in half and have children draw on the left side how it feels right now (upset, sad, worried, nervous, and so on). On the right side, they draw how they would like to feel (OK, calm, safe, happy, brave).

BEFORE AFTER

Jennifer, Age 16 (Painting)

The contrast in this adolescent's painting is not only
in design but in color.
The drawing on the left is drab in shades of brown and grey.
The one on the right is bright with yellows and greens.

Then I try to convince them, "No problem. I've done this plenty of times. You'll be feeling better soon." (I am always careful not to guarantee the perfect cure or to put a time limit on the anticipated change because everyone travels at a different pace.)

*TIP: Review the section of **Oops Eavesdrop** in Step 1 - PRAISE. This is a great way to bridge the gap to **caregiver-instilled hope**. Get someone on the phone and have your child "accidentally" hear how excited you are about the new behavior plan or what wonderful things you've heard about your new counselor (or even what you've read in this book!).*

WHAT DO THE EXPERTS SAY?

For decades, researchers have found that "no particular therapeutic school or technique can claim superior efficacy" (Duncan 1997). Therapists use all types of strategies from Freudian theory to behavior modification. Your therapist might use groups, psychodrama, art, medication or visualization. Most therapists have an array of favorite tools, and the best ones are always learning more.

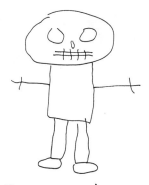

Benjamin, Age 5

Although there are over 250 different types of therapy (a shocking statistic!), "none stands head and shoulders above the rest . . . [it] amounts to little more than the competition among aspirin, Advil® and Tylenol®. All of them relieve pain and work better than no treatment at all" (Duncan 1997).

A comprehensive review of 40 years of research found that specific techniques and strategies in therapy accounted for only 15 percent of clients' improvement, **roughly the same proportion ascribable to HOPE** (Lambert, in Duncan 1997).

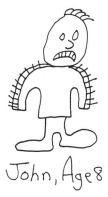

John, Age 8

Obviously, not all children go to therapy, so hope is a strong foundation for any kind of change. For those in therapy, though, there is another factor that makes a huge difference. In fact, this issue accounted for 30 percent of improvement in therapy. Can you guess it? It's the **relationship** between therapist and client. To be effective, the therapist must be "well-liked" and have "good rapport." Children in particular must believe their helper is warm and caring.

> "My therapist is different from other grown-ups . . . he takes time and consideration into answering my questions. He thinks about the advice toward the situation, instead of blurting out something like, 'Don't let it bother you.'"
>
> — Jack, Age 14
> (In Markowitz 1997)

FEELING RELIEF

Time and again, caregivers have come in saying that just since that first session, they could tell a dramatic difference. The child seemed less agitated, more in control or whatever. There's no magic here. The child was **feeling relief** and was **showing it!**

"'Tis always morning somewhere in the world."

– Richard Henry Horne

Angie, Age 10

Children who are tested because of school problems and are found to have learning disabilities can also experience this sense of hope and relief. Usually, they show up with some hodge-podge of concerns such as not listening, not completing work, not following directions, or seeming to be smart but not performing up to ability level.

When we are able to put a **hopeful label** on it (dyslexia or SLD – Specific Learning Disabilities), we can reframe it in **Up-Talk**. The glass being half-full not half-empty is a good analogy here.

Finally, the child can be shown that, "It's not my fault" or "I'm not dumb (or stupid or lazy)." This does not mean learning disabilities can become an **excuse** for any poor school performance. It does mean there is a **reason** for not working up to potential. Changes have to be made in both the way the child approaches school work and in the way caregivers at home and school operate.

REAL LIFE: Eight-year-old Jordan accompanied her parents to a consultation session to review her test results. I had already discussed the findings in detail with her parents at a previous conference.

```
Learning by Looking ☀
Ability
Math

Average — Middle

Reading
Writing

Learning by Listening ☽
```

*By folding a piece of typing paper in half, we identified the Middle (or average). Then, step by step, we drew lines. I drew a line across the page to show Jordan she had "a good head on her shoulders" (strong ability). Her math was good (above average), but her reading and writing were weak (below average). Most importantly, I showed Jordan she had L.D. — **Learns Differently** (in fact, the D "officially" stands for Disability in most school systems, but I find this too negative a term). The tests showed Jordan is an outstanding **Visual** learner with some of her skills here at college level! On the other hand, she is very poor in **Auditory** processing of information. Listening skills were on kindergarten level! No wonder she was having trouble understanding and following directions adults gave orally.*

*A breakthrough seemed to come when Jordan looked at a handout of famous people who **Learn Differently.** There was a picture of the genius Albert Einstein who was considered a "dumb student." He did not learn to talk until age 4 and did not learn to read until age 9. Jordan was stunned . . . and relieved! Now there was an explanation of why she was so frustrated in school. We could make a plan, get her help, emphasize her strengths. I will never forget her beaming face as she walked out the door mumbling "Me and Albert Einstein — we're LD."*

THERE'S EVEN MORE TO IT . . .

The impact of HOPE is not just in making us feel better in time of stress. It actually helps in school achievement and career success, too. A recent study compared the academic achievement of freshman students identified as either high or low on HOPE. Results showed "hope was a better predictor of their first-semester grades than were their scores on the SAT . . . [WOW!] . . . Given roughly the same range of intellectual abilities, **emotional aptitudes** made the critical difference" (Goleman 1995).

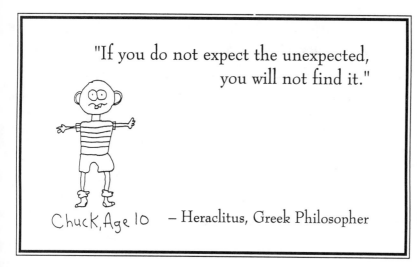

"If you do not expect the unexpected, you will not find it."

Chuck, Age 10 — Heraclitus, Greek Philosopher

*REAL LIFE: We can use the tool of **Visualization** to raise our hope! James Mapes, a highly successful business entrepreneur and consultant used visualization in an extraordinary experience. On a seven-day rafting trip with 11 other people, Mapes was confronted with his fear of heights. One of the scheduled activities was a rock climb.*

*The instructor taught everyone climbing strategies and safety techniques. Most importantly he had the group **envision themselves successful**. He told them to **"see themselves at the top."** This would help their subconscious minds to find the way up.*

HINT 📖: For more details on **Visualization**, see Step 7 - HIGHER VALUES.

Mapes tells how he was initially frightened but became more and more comfortable as he climbed safely in his harness. More than halfway up, he panicked! He could not find a finger hold! He became dizzy and desperate and kept repeating in his mind the negative thought "I'm going to fall."

Suddenly he remembered the instructor's words, and he visualized. He got a clear picture in his mind of himself standing at the top of the cliff. He kept repeating, "See yourself at the top." The change was like an altered state — he found his way forward and up to the top! His positive image had given him courage and **hope** *(Mapes 1996).*

I made it!

C.M.

"Hope means one will not give in to overwhelming anxiety, a defeatist attitude, or depression in the face of difficult challenges or setbacks."
— Daniel Goleman

Bonnie, Age 8

Every day Bonnie is getting better and better.

This drawing was made at the beginning of our work together on the issue of enuresis (bed wetting).
Note the tiny arms and lack of hands suggesting feelings of inadequacy and helplessness in her world.
Even so, there is a smile . . . perhaps suggesting hopefulness?

> "Hope puts a smile on our face when the heart cannot manage. Hope puts our feet on the path when our eyes cannot see it. Hope moves us to act when our souls are confused about the direction."
> – Author Unknown

Julie, Age 10

WHAT'S TOOTHPASTE GOT TO DO WITH IT?

As a closing thought I would like to present an analogy to a tube of toothpaste. If you were sitting in my office right now, I'd say something like this . . .

"Here, __(fill in your name)__ . I am giving you this special tube of toothpaste because it's the most magnificent thing I've come across. It does everything — you wouldn't believe! It has fluoride and tartar control and all kinds of things to protect your teeth. It can even reverse the damage of cavities. But the neatest thing of all, Friend, is how it brightens your smile! It is truly awesome. This toothpaste has special ingredients to make teeth actually **sparkle.** It will be as if you have stars on your teeth every time you smile!"

Well, you think, this is really exciting. Very special. Of course, you're happy to give it a try. We agree to meet back in one month to see how things are going.

Next time I see you, you are stone faced and refuse to open your mouth at first. When you do, I am appalled! This is TERRIBLE! Your mouth is filthy. There's an awful dingy tint on your teeth, and your breath is foul. It looks like there are even little bits of green stuff hanging off some of your teeth. You are obviously very agitated and your teeth are pathetic.

I am stunned! How could this have happened? Your teeth did not get better. They did not even stay the same! They got **worse**. WORSE! How is that possible?

At first, I am speechless. Then I find my voice and ask very gingerly, "Did you brush well with it? Did you use it at least twice a day? Did you spend enough time to carefully brush each tooth?"

"What?" you cry out. "Use it? NO, I didn't use it! I know how to brush my teeth. I don't have to do it all the time. I set the toothpaste right by my bed and it is there for whenever I need it."

So, you see the fallacy . . . and the parallel I hope. All the information in this book — from the expert tips to the children's wisdom — will not help you at all unless you USE them. If you simply put the book aside because "I know how to . . . it is there when I need it," it will do you very little, if any, good at all.

Laura, Age 7

FINAL NOTE

There is only so much we as caregivers can do anyway to improve children's chances of thriving in this world. They are in our care for such a limited amount of time, let's do everything in our power to make them stronger, happier and more resilient.

"Do everything right, all the time, and the child will prosper. It's as simple as that, except for fate, luck, heredity, chance, and the astrological sign under which the child was born, his order of birth, his first encounter with evil, the girl who jilts him in spite of her excellent qualities, the war that is being fought when he is a young man, the drugs he may try once or too many times, the friends he makes, how he scores on tests, how well he endures kidding about his shortcomings, how ambitious he becomes, how far he falls behind, circumstantial evidence, ironic perspective, danger when it's least expected, difficulty in triumphing over circumstance, people with hidden agendas, and animals with rabies."

—Ann Beattie

Jimmy, Age 8

Secrets of the Third Little Pig

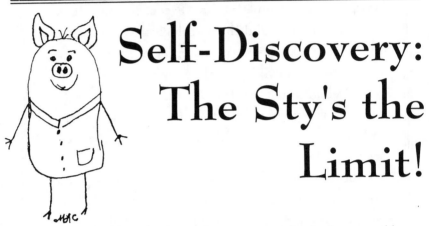

Self-Discovery: The Sty's the Limit!

Using this book shows the drive of your spirit to be the best possible caregiver you can be. Trust yourself, and never stop seeking truth.

Things come up in our day-to-day living that force us to call on our inner strength. Following is an article I wrote recently about overcoming a trauma in my own life. Not until I reread it did I realize I was automatically using some of the tools in this book (visualization and positive outlook).

Also in this section you will find some activity sheets from the companion workbook soon to be published. You can use the **Sentence Seeds** pages to help you focus. They can reveal what areas need attention and work . . . where you need to put some energy. You might also see areas that are already OK . . . and give yourself a well-deserved pat on the back.

The **Pretend Portraits** are a fun way to explore personalities. As you've seen throughout the book, art and animals seem to go together to help children express themselves.

These discovery ideas can be done on paper or verbally, as an activity or informally. Get CREATIVE!

SATURDAY SPECIAL

Surviving serious injuries

'This will make a great story some day'

By Charlene Messenger

SPECIAL TO THE SENTINEL

I have always believed that human beings are remarkably resilient creatures. We are given trials and burdens to help us learn and grow, to become strong and wise. Our lives actually become richer and our outlooks more sensitive. It was not until a devastating accident, however, that I learned the true meaning of stamina and faith.

Three summers ago, I was vacationing in northern California, visiting Lassen Volcanic National Park. Although I followed other hikers on the crust of a geyser, it was *my* foot that broke through and sank into the boiling mud. The next few moments still seem frozen in time. Screaming hysterically, I tore off my shoe. A layer of skin came right off with it!

I was overwhelmed with excruciating pain. Then, to my horror, I saw the crust breaking up around my daughter. We successfully stumbled to safe ground. Leaving me there, she ran to a nearby mountain and gathered a pile of snow in her shirt. The snow's freezing cold numbed my burning skin.

By keeping snow packed around the injury, I was able to hobble along. The fun, 20-minute hike to the geyser turned into a hellacious attempt to leave as I limped, cried and stopped to gather more snow. We made it to the car, then to the Ranger's station. Expecting some relief, I was instead given forms to fill out and told to discard the snow because it was "unsanitary."

As the freezing numbness faded, the pain returned like countless hot needles jabbing into my foot and lower leg. That hour's drive to the nearest hospital seemed interminable. In a whirlwind of pain and anguish, my mind whipped around words I had overheard — circumferential burn, infection, possible amputation. Pictures flashed through my brain of a stump where my foot should be. I saw myself hobbling around my office on an artificial limb. My fears turned into dragons whose fiery breath lashed out to sear

About this page . . .

"Saturday Special" asked its readers: How have you coped with an illness or injury? Tell us your story of courage, inspiration. These essays, the fifth in a series, are among the responses.

Screaming hysterically, I tore off my shoe. A layer of skin came right off with it!

my mind, matching my charred skin.

Enough! I had to stop the madness. I deliberately tried to project myself into the future. I imagined telling this scenario as "a great story" one day. I saw my friends laughing as I said, "And then, you wouldn't believe what happened. ..." I imagined myself with a bandaged foot, asking others, "Guess what I did over vacation?" or telling new acquaintances that I enjoy "crust-busting" as a hobby.

Amazingly, I found that taking my mind to a future time and place made the present bearable, distancing me somewhat from the agony. The moment-by-moment suffering almost became transformed to a "memory" on which I was looking back.

Arrival at the emergency room brought the relief of morphine, and I collapsed into tears and exhaustion. The next few months were torturous: hospitals, doctors, physical therapy, medication, bandages, crutches, even a wheelchair. When most discouraged, I tried to view the present from the future, telling myself, "This will make a great story some day."

Today, the obvious scar from my injury could be considered ugly, but I see it as a blessing that I am now whole and healthy. And I have, as you see, been able to turn it into an entertaining tale after all.

Charlene Messenger is a school psychologist who practices in Orlando.

BIG PIGGIES

(Adult Level)

My favorite memory with my child is _____

The best thing about my child is _____

The worst day I can remember is _____

The most frustrating thing about my child is _____

If I could say anything, the one thing I'd really want my child to understand is

_____

If I were given an extra hour each day, I'd spend it _____

If I could wish for anything, I'd wish _____

My favorite family holiday (Christmas, Hanukkah, Halloween, Etc.) was

_____

The biggest difference between this family and the family I grew up in is

_____

My favorite family activity is _____

When I was a kid, I really liked _____

When I was a kid, I really hated _____

My child is just like me when it comes to _____

My child is opposite me about _____

To give my child **PRAISE** and encouragement I often _____

People in our house **LISTEN** and pay attention to _____

I prepare myself for the difficult task of setting **LIMITS** for my child by

_____

Some of the ways I send messages of **LOVE** to my child include

_____

I make arrangements to spend **TIME** with my child by _____

I teach **RESPONSIBILITY** to my child through _____

The three **HIGHER VALUES** I feel most strongly about are _____

_____

LITTLE PIGGIES
(Not-Adult-Yet Level)

I like_____

I am best at_____

I hate_____

I am not so good at_____

My family is different from other families because

_____

The best vacation our family ever had was_____

If I could change anything about my life I'd change

_____

My favorite birthday was_____

My favorite thing to do as a family is_____

If I could wish for anything, I'd wish:

1._____

2._____

3._____

If I were stuck on a desert island, the three people I'd want with me are:

1._____

2._____

3._____

When I get angry_____

I feel really loved when_____

My favorite day was when_____

Someday I want to_____

THE WHOLE PIGGY FAMILY

Put It Into Words Game

You can use dice or jacks to make the following *feeling sentences* your family's own personal "put it into words" game. For example, whatever number you roll on the die, you must complete a sentence for that number. Help your children by writing their answer in if they can't write yet.

Have fun working together to make up specific rules to invent a totally new game. Or, you might combine this list with some other board game you already enjoy . . . just add the rule that you must fill in a *feelings sentence* in order to move your turn or get an extra point or whatever you choose.

1. When you _____ I feel _____
    I always feel _____ when _____

2. I can tell you're SCARED when _____
    I feel SCARED when _____

3. I can tell you're MAD when _____
    I feel MAD when _____

4. I can tell you're HAPPY when _____
    I feel HAPPY when _____

5. I can tell you're SAD when _____
    I feel SAD when _____

6. I can tell you're _____ when _____
    I feel _____ when _____

Pretend Portraits

Children do not live in isolation. People around them have temperaments too! Everyone in the family (or group or class or whatever, depending on what kind of caregiver you are) has a **distinct** personality.

Give everyone a **sheet of paper** and **pencil** . . . and maybe some **markers** and **paint.**

Everyone draws everyone in the group as an animal.

Think about what different animals stand for. Even less-prized animals have their attributes. Some ideas are on the next page.

Some ANIMAL PERSONALITIES to help you brainstorm . . .

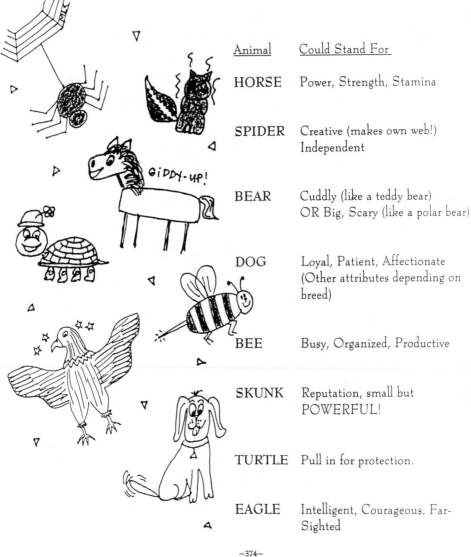

Animal	Could Stand For
HORSE	Power, Strength, Stamina
SPIDER	Creative (makes own web!) Independent
BEAR	Cuddly (like a teddy bear) OR Big, Scary (like a polar bear)
DOG	Loyal, Patient, Affectionate (Other attributes depending on breed)
BEE	Busy, Organized, Productive
SKUNK	Reputation, small but POWERFUL!
TURTLE	Pull in for protection.
EAGLE	Intelligent, Courageous, Far-Sighted

ow, have everyone **look** at each other's drawings. **GUESS** which
imal stands for each person in the family (or group).

lk about your **"personalities."**

Curious

clever

Talk about your **STRENGTHS**.

Dependable

Talk about your **WEAKNESSES**.

Sneaky

5.:   You can also do the family portrait as **plants**.
Are you a **tall pine**?
Are you a **prickly cactus**?
Is there a **delicate rose bush** in your family?

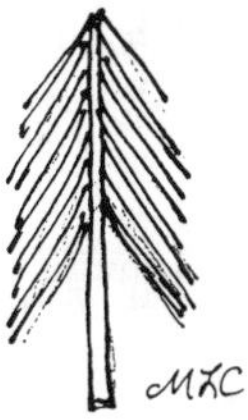

MKC

IAT I LEARNED:

_____

_____

_____

_____

Perpetual Calendar:
Abby, Age 6
WISDOM FOR THE DAY

Here's a special surprise for the 2nd edition: a collection of perpetual calendars! These calendars are reusable — which means you pick the correct calendar, copy it, then fill in the right month and year. The print had to be small to fit the pages of this book, but they enlarge great.

Look for more calendar pages in the soon-to-be-released activity book. Right now, there is one calendar for each of the 7 Steps, which just happens to match one for each starting day of the week.

Here's how to get started:

1. Find the correct calendar for the month you want based on the day of the week it starts. For example, December 1999 starts on a Wednesday so that would be the Love calendar. December 2000 starts on Friday so that would be the Responsibility calendar.

2. Copy the calendar, and don't forget you can **enlarge** it to see the words better.

3. Fill in the blanks at the top with the correct month and year.

4. Cross off or cover up day 31 if that month only has 30 days. (And, of course, 29 & 30 for February unless it's a Leap Year.)

5. Read the Wisdom for the Day first thing each morning and see how it can be applied to your life.

TIP: Tape a small version to your steering wheel. You can't help but reread it at every red light.

Phoebe's Piggy Portion of PRAISE Secrets

SUNDAY	MONDAY	TUESDAY	WEDNESDAY	THURSDAY	FRIDAY	SATURDAY
No matter how difficult a day it may be, a child will be sure to do **something** you can compliment. Show that you notice and that you care.	1 Most of us don't realize how much we need recognition, and how uplifted we are when we receive it . . . Take the wonderful opportunities you have to build each other's self-image and self-confidence.	2 Sincerity is what gives praise its power.	3 We want to build children's confidence in themselves, not just their ability to please others.	4 Growing up means that there are lots of challenges and disappointments that lie ahead . . . praise is a powerful tool for helping young people feel good about themselves.	5 Use **Kind Eyes** to rephrase the negative. If a neighbor calls your baby cranky and difficult, reframe it to "feisty" ~ a more positive attribute, implying alertness, zest and strength of character.	6 When we are supportive, positive and appropriately complimentary, we are making a valuable investment in children's sense of self.	7
8 Children especially are eager to hear praise and encouragement.	Use the **Invisible Signal** to praise your child. This is a nonverbal sign of approval. Possibilities include affectionately rubbing a child's hair, patting the shoulder, winking or giving a thumbs-up.	9 Most caregivers do not err in the direction of too heavy praise given without thinking, but rather in withholding praise or giving insincere praise.	10 Immediate recognition is powerful, but so is **reliving the experience**. Think of it as "rewinding the tape" and watching an **Instant Replay**.	11 The habit of giving credit regularly (even perhaps especially) in the little things will contribute to a happy home life.	12 Children tend to be hard on themselves. Praise can help children focus ~ to develop into what we knew was there all along.	13 Effusive praise, bordering on child worship, can certainly lead to arrogance.	14
15 Using **Sentence Seeds** is a great way to jump-start recognition. I am amazed at how my . . . I enjoy it so much when the two of us . . . It wasn't easy, but you sure . . .	A simple "I'm proud of you," and an explanation of why, will go a long way.	16 Recognition does not need to be just a routine part of interaction with children.	17 **Effort Approval.** Praise the child for the **process** ~ the feelings and thoughts that went into the work.	18 An important task for caregivers is to provide a great deal of nurturing to children's fragile egos.	19 Global praise such as "That's **good**" has less impact. Use a **Detail Magnifier**, to be specific about the activity and the effort.	20 An **Accomplishment Album** is a great way to focus on a child's progress and improvements. Fill up a photo album with highlights of recognition.	21
22 Recognition and encouragement have got to be two of the main ingredients in anyone's emotional first-aid kit.	Too heavy praise given without thinking can make a child dependent on external rewards, rather than developing self-satisfaction from learning.	23 Informal words of praise in everyday conversation are natural and eagerly accepted.	24 **Oops Eavesdrop.** Nothing carries more weight than accidentally overhearing something good about yourself. You were not meant to hear it, so it must be true. Make it happen for your child.	25 Generally, positive commenting does not spoil a child ~ unless the praise is extremely excessive or given indiscriminately, that is, regardless of what the child does.	26 What children need (in fact, what we all need) in order to truly blossom is support and encouragement.	27 Positive recognition is an art with far-reaching effects.	28
29 Honesty is critical if recognition is to succeed.	Children are quick to recognize false praise, and it does more harm than saying nothing at all.	30 Nothing adds impact to praise like getting close and smiling. A hug is an added bonus.	31			

~377~

More of Phoebe's secrets are available in Dr. Charlene Messenger's book, **Secrets** of the *Third Little Pig: 7 Steps to Build a Child's Inner Strength.*
Call 1-877-PIG-BOOK, 1-877-744-2665 to order. Visit us on the Web: brighterpathways.com

Phoebe's Piggy Portion of LISTENING Secrets

Month _____ Year _____

SUNDAY	MONDAY	TUESDAY	WEDNESDAY	THURSDAY	FRIDAY	SATURDAY
	1 The give-and-take of good listening must be established early in order to carry over into later years and other relationships.	**2** Sentence Seeds are a great way to get started . . . My favorite vacation ever was . . . If I could wish for anything, I'd wish . . . The one thing I'd love to change is . . .	**3** Try using Ear Mirrors while listening . . . reflect back to the child in your own words what you thought you heard.	**4** Children's body language often speaks of feelings they will not or cannot put into words. A giggle, a tear, or a shrug can tell a lot.	**5**	**6** Remember, when people listen with their minds already made up, they are not hearing with their hearts.
7 Watch anyone's face closely while listening and you will see many signs of the feelings within . . . If you seem bored while listening, children will pick up on it immediately.	**8** As you listen, be aware of your own attitudes and values and how they fit with what the child is saying and feeling.	**9** Out of listening grow the arts of negotiating and problem-solving.	**10** Poor listening can lead to poor morale and even depression, not only in childhood but in later adult life.	**11** Sometimes it takes a conscious effort to understand and care about what a child is saying. Make your concern obvious to the child through body language.	**12** Be ready to listen without forcing a child to reveal.	**13** Don't try talking with a child when either of you is angry. At that point, feelings are out of control and not much will be accomplished.
14 By actively listening to a child, we are sending a message that "You are worth my time."	**15** Show acceptance of a child's feelings, whatever they are - up or down. We are not saying we approve. We are simply showing we understand.	**16** Put it Into Words: I feel _____ when _____. It makes me want to _____.	**17** When we are truly listening, we hear beyond the actual words. We attend to the feelings.	**18** Barriers to communication that are established early in a child are hard to break later ~ remember the adult that is developing within.	**19** Listen to the tone and the quality of what a child is saying . . . Hear between the lines.	**20**
21 Sometimes it is hard to wait patiently listening when you know what you want to say . . . Try the **Talking Stick** . . . Whoever holds the special stick will speak and be listened to.	**22** Give children time to express themselves. Sometimes their feelings change so rapidly, it's hard to guess what's really going on.	**23** All children have something important to say . . . Unfortunately, the typical adult simply does not spend enough time listening.	**24** Remember to praise or encourage . . . Even when we've had a difficult conversation, we can thank a child for talking or for trying to come up with a solution.	**25** Allowing children to disagree shows we are strong; admitting we don't have all the answers shows we are **human**; and being willing to help find a solution shows we are **supportive**.	**26** Pick a good time and a private place to address a touchy subject. When children have had a bad experience, give them time to think it through without bombarding them with questions.	**27**
28 Make eye contact. Look directly at a child while listening, leaning forward and getting close to pay attention.	**29** Do not pretend to have all the answers. Allow some disagreement.	**30** To avoid misunderstandings and hurt feelings, use **Feedback**. Ask a question about **what you thought you heard** the child say. Did you mean . . . ? Are you saying . . . ?	**31** Children who are listened to and who learn to listen become sensitive to others . . . they perceive their own ideas as important, but also learn to see others' perceptions.			

~379~

*More of Phoebe's secrets are available in Dr. Charlene Messenger's book, **Secrets of the Third Little Pig: 7 Steps to Build a Child's Inner Strength**. Call 1-877-PIG-BOOK, 1-877-744-2665 to order. Visit us on the Web: brighterpathways.com*

SUNDAY	MONDAY	TUESDAY	WEDNESDAY	THURSDAY	FRIDAY	SATURDAY
		1 When setting limits there are some areas where caregivers feel very strongly and must simply **put their foot down**, and there are other areas where they can be more flexible.	**1** Boundaries or limits help children develop a sense of security. They know they can count on someone to guide and protect them, even if at the time they are angry and resistant.	**2** Children may even use the caregiver's rules as an **excuse** when they feel peer pressure to misbehave . . . "**My parents would kill me!**"	**3** Setting limits means being **strong not rigid.**	**5** When children are allowed to be completely self-absorbed, they never learn to truly love or value others.
Ignoring the disobedience once you've labeled it is as bad or worse than never setting the limit in the first place.	**6** Many limits, such as curfew, need to be set in advance. Decide what is reasonable, make it very clear, then **stick by it.**	**7** When children are learning new rules, it might seem "worth it" to go ahead, misbehave and face the consequence. But when there is a reward in play as well, they often stop, think and make the more positive choice.	**8** As much as children outwardly protest limits, deep down they come to recognize that we care enough to risk a conflict.	**9** Children will test caregivers to see just what the restraints are —how far they can go and what will happen "if."	**10** The key to setting effective limits is to clearly know and state your position. The tricky part is to **say what you mean and mean what you say.**	**12** When young people know that we are in charge, that limits are not excessive and that there is consideration for their feelings, they come to accept and even appreciate the structure.
The lack of limits in today's society has made it harder than ever for teenagers to cope with the complex mix of challenges they face (drugs, violence, sexuality, alcohol).	**13** Sit down and go over the rules and consequences when things are relatively calm. Family meetings are great for this.	**14** When setting limits, be prepared for some resistance from the child . . . In fact, children often become worse before they get better.	**15** There are some things you can prohibit but not prevent. . . . children still have the free will to decide. With limits, however, violations will have specific consequences.	**16** Limits help build self-discipline and improve impulse control.	**17** When you discipline, you want to get in, make your point and get out. That leaves it up to the child to make a decision to cooperate or not.	**19** Warnings are a method of teaching **self-control.** Just **one warning, though!**
20 You can randomly reinforce appropriate behaviors with the **Slot Machine mentality** . . . Children never know when they'll get an unexpected surprise for cooperating.	**21** Too many rules can be overwhelming, and too many restrictions can inhibit a child. That is why it is critical to pick which things are truly important.	**22** The job of setting limits is one of the hardest for caregivers.	**23** Children who never learn the meaning of the word "no" . . . do not learn to say no themselves when later presented with outside temptation, such as drugs or shoplifting.	**24** Be careful of the **Black Hole.** This phenomenon happens when children somehow get so far "in debt" with their consequences, they can never see the light at the end of the tunnel.	**26** When there are no limits or the limits are constantly changed or not enforced, children will flagrantly disobey in order to force the adults to do something.
27 Many times the real issue is not whether the child gets to do a particular behavior but rather "**Who is in control?**"	**28** It is wise to have a preset list of consequences.	**29** Caregivers must be prepared to be unpopular in the short term for long-term payoffs.	**30** Most children come to appreciate sensible boundaries with clear consequences.	**31**		

*More of Phoebe's secrets are available in Dr. Charlene Messenger's book, **Secrets** of the Third Little Pig: 7 Steps to Build a Child's Inner Strength.*
Call 1-877-PIG-BOOK, 1-877-744-2665 to order. Visit us on the Web: brighterpathways.com

Phoebe's Piggy Portion of LOVE Secrets

Month ♡ ⋅ ♡ ⋅ ♡ ⋅ ♡ ⋅ ♡ ⋅ ♡ ⋅ ♡ ⋅ ♡ Year ♡ ⋅ ♡

SUNDAY	MONDAY	TUESDAY	WEDNESDAY	THURSDAY	FRIDAY	SATURDAY
Somewhere along the line, our love includes stepping back, trusting and being there when they fall down. This is the most unselfish kind of love.	5 The root of poor self-image in adulthood is often **conditional love in childhood,** that is love with strings attached.		1 The messages of love you send to children can include displays of affection and prompt attention. They can be as simple as being available and as difficult as teaching respect.	1 A smile, a hug, or a simple "I love you" can go a long way in fostering self-esteem - especially if it's given for no special reason other than "because you're my kid."	2 Infancy appears to be the most critical period to establish attachment. When a caregiver picks up and soothes a baby, the child gets gratification and out of this satisfaction grows trust.	4 The term attachment refers to the emotional **bonding** between children and significant adults. It starts at birth and continues throughout life with constant, gradual changes.
12 By being aware of the importance of secure **attachment,** we can take the first steps toward changing our behavior to become warmer, more supportive and more available.	13 A child's life can be one of exploration and wonder - don't forget to join in.	7 Releasing resentment is not a favor we do for others. It is a key to our own well-being. It frees us from being stuck in the past with old pain.	8 Reading to children is clearly a message of love. Even older children and teens can enjoy special reading time. It sets up a beautiful family tradition.	9 When caregivers are supportive and available, children respond by being more capable human beings. In this way, our messages of love help children become more competent, self-confident and resilient.	11 The challenge to caregivers is sending your message of love so children recognize it and grow from it.	
19 A caring mother shows her love to her infant by being sensitive and responding to his signals.... Bonding through displays of love starts very early in life, in fact immediately after birth.	20 Parents of students who do the best are involved with them and show interest in their grades and homework.	14 When a child comes home to an empty house, a special note on the counter or a phone call from you (ideally at the same time every day) can instill feelings of security.	15 Children should feel that they are just as important as their caregivers' careers - not competing with them.	16 For no reason at all, dare to listen to some music together, go for a walk in the woods, or have an indoor picnic.	17 Children of loving caregivers are more affectionate and cooperative and are better able to handle challenge.	18
26 We can usually force a child to mouth the words, "I'm sorry," but we cannot make a child truly feel sorry. The best we can do is model forgiveness and teach empathy.	27 A responsive caregiver shows love to older children by reading the cues, showing support, and offering - not forcing - the opportunity to talk.	21 Ask yourself what are some of your happiest memories from your own childhood? Were they big events or simple shared times? Ask yourself too, what kind of deposits you are making in your child's memory banks?	22 Happy early memories become treasures that can trigger stability and reassurance in tougher later years.	23 By being warm, supporting and loving, you can help a child become more competent and happy. It takes commitment to invest time and energy to display your love.	24 Try to teach children to avoid bad mouthing or getting revenge.... Teach them that something else might be going on "under the surface" of a person's unkind behavior.	25
	28 Adolescents least likely to get in trouble with the law or drop out of school are those whose caregivers provide supervision after school - even if it is not "on site."	29 Children's development is a continuous process. They need love and nurturing when they grow older just as they did as babies.	30 What we really teach our children is what is in our hearts ~ our unexpressed feelings. This carries much more weight than what we say or even do.	31		

~383~

More of Phoebe's secrets are available in Dr. Charlene Messenger's book, *Secrets of the Third Little Pig: 7 Steps to Build a Child's Inner Strength.* Call 1-877-PIG-BOOK, 1-877-744-2665 to order. Visit us on the Web: brighterpathways.com

Phoebe's Piggy Portion of TIME Secrets

Month _____ Year _____

SUNDAY	MONDAY	TUESDAY	WEDNESDAY	THURSDAY	FRIDAY	SATURDAY
				Healthy families view time as a controllable commodity. They value time together and allow it to be spent only on quality activities. How would you like your children to remember shared time together?	**1** Be prepared for a few complaints until people get used to **family time**. Start simple, perhaps only an hour together. Make sure you have a specific activity – a family walk, drive to the park, board game, baking, etc.	**2** Try a family meeting…. Share how you are feeling rushed and bothered about lack of time together and would like to change that … Block out a family time for the following week or two.
3 Children are like sponges. They absorb that to which they are exposed … If we as caregivers are not instilling our values in them, where are children picking up theirs?	**4** The average father spend less then five minutes a week giving individual attention to each child in the family. **Don't let this be you!**	**5** Family Calendar…. Mark off at least I day for a family time … Teach children to budget their time … Put on adult appointments … Record accomplishments.	**6** If children are used to the ritual of you sitting on the edge of the bed a few minutes every night to chat, it will seem perfectly normal when they are older – a time when other adults are complaining their teens "never talk."	**7** Certainly vacations are a good way to relax together, but there are plenty of ways to share time around the house – … baking cookies, riding bikes, gardening, putting photos in albums or painting with watercolors.	**8** It is no easy task, but as adults we can set priorities and budget time in a positive way. Let's examine our values and see if we are spending our time on what we truly believe is important.	**9** Leisure time does not have to cost money. It can mean a trip to a library, beach or picnic.
11 Working and creating together helps people communicate and accomplish things. It also sets the scene for cooperation for those times down the road when emergencies arise.	**11** Some topics to increase communication during dinner or on a walk may be an interesting experience from the day, a new joke or story, or what each person is reading or working on at present.	**12** Don't make the mistake of assuming that a busy family is a joyful family. There are many outside activities which can rob a family's time together. Try one night a week of no outside activity!	**13** TUIT No more excuses – you now have a Round Tuit.	**14** If backtalk and rude attitude are a problem at your house, you probably don't enjoy the time you do spend with your children. You might consider a Response Cost system.	**15** All the minutes spent in the car traveling to and from places is a perfect sharing time. Use your active listening skills to allow children to share their inner selves – wishes, secrets, fears or worries.	**16** Try not to allow hurried schedules to threaten dinnertime together. This is one guaranteed opportunity to share the day's events. If necessary, block out certain nights of the week for dinner together.
18 The television can become an electronic hypnosis machine, with children daily absorbing whatever is on the screen. It can devour valuable time and prevent the development of healthy human relationships.	**18** Give yourself a time to unwind when you first get home. Call it **Transition Time**…. you will be surprised at the comfort you yourself can derive from the bonding time that follows with your child.	**19** Car time with older children can be spent practicing school skills aloud, such as foreign language terms or math facts. Some children prefer to spill their deeper issues when you are driving … there is less discomfort of eye contact.	**20** Whatever activity everyone finds enjoyable, try to block out a routine time, such as once a week, every other week, or the third Saturday of the month. USE YOUR FAMILY CALENDAR!	**21** Shared projects can include planting and maintaining a garden or cleaning out the garage or attic. Almost all children enjoy making things, and so crafts are a good choice.	**22** Just as certain amounts of money can be designated for bills, groceries, savings or entertainment, time can be budgeted and designated for certain activities.	**23** To increase communication during dinner, you might allow children to invite friends to join on a rotating basis. Try playing a word game after dinner before clearing the dishes.
25 Whatever your bedtime ritual, start it when children are young and do not abandon it when they reach adolescence.	**25** Meal preparation and cleanup are excellent times to teach and interact with young people. Keep it fun and involve everyone. Even small tots can set place-mats and napkins or tear lettuce for the salad.	**26** Time together improves communication, shows love and helps resolve problems. With our time, we are helping children on their life journey.	**27** If we are perplexed about just how much we can fit into a day, a big step will be to free up time where we can. Time management experts repeatedly advise: JUST SAY NO.	**28** Children need time with their primary caregivers. Even teenagers want more time with their caregivers…. The average working couple spends only 30 seconds a day talking with their children!	**29** Watching the news on TV or reviewing the newspaper together may be appropriate. You might be surprised at the positive response you will get from a child.	**30** Worrying is a huge time waster. Make the best decisions you can … follow through … learn from your mistakes, then move on. Give yourself credit for your efforts as well as accomplishments.
						31

~385~

*More of Phoebe's secrets are available in Dr. Charlene Messenger's book, **Secrets of the Third Little Pig: 7 Steps to Build a Child's Inner Strength**.*
Call 1-877-PIG-BOOK, 1-877-744-2665 to order. Visit us on the Web: brighterpathways.com

Phoebe's Piggy Portion of RESPONSIBILITY Secrets

Month _____ Year _____

SUNDAY	MONDAY	TUESDAY	WEDNESDAY	THURSDAY	FRIDAY	SATURDAY
					1 Children should be encouraged to carry a level of responsibility in accordance with their maturity. Start very young with simple tasks.	**2** Despite the limitations of any given age, we want children to feel good about what they can do, not upset about what they cannot do.
3 As caregivers, we will have to be willing to accept discomfort and even conflict at times, as we help children with the issue of responsibility.	**4** When a child successfully completes a job, get the child to talk about that unbeatable sense of accomplishment.	**5** Instilling responsibility means giving children chores, including taking care of their belongings and contributing to the family team. It also means being responsible for yourself and making amends when necessary.	**6** Parents should not feel guilty about their careers. They just need to show how each member contributes to the family through work, school and chores.	**7** Time for training a child on a new task should be relaxed. You may even want to mark special Learning Days on the calendar to anticipate the practice time together.	**8** Responsibility helps people feel better about themselves. It also helps children get a bigger sense of their world and their impact on it.
10 By beginning with small tasks and building up, children gradually learn how to handle responsibility. In this way, responsibility becomes a habit.	**11** Especially with a new task, demonstrate and work along with the child for a while. It is very hard to train a child when there are definite time limits and everyone is rushed.	**12** Children vary tremendously in their development, and caregivers can look at their strengths and weaknesses to help select age-appropriate chores.	**13** Support a child's sincere efforts even if the child doesn't necessarily bring the desired results. Praise the process of doing the job, not just the final product.	**14** Every time we do something for children which they are capable of doing themselves, we take away the opportunity to develop competency.	**15** Focusing on the family as a TEAM where each person's contribution is important helps children feel they are performing a beneficial service.	**9** Children's sense of responsibility grows directly in relation to how responsible they percieve others are to them.
17 By trying new things and meeting new people, children have more opportunity to stretch their independence. Encourage children to take part in organizations and activities.	**18** Accepting responsibility is not the same as blind obedience. An obedient child does strictly as told - no more, no less. . . A resilient child is resourceful and independent in judgment when necessary.	**19** Let children do what they are capable of doing. Do not pamper them by performing tasks they can do for themselves. Give them chores, including taking care of their belongings and contributing to the family team.	**20** When children do refuse to take assigned responsibility, many times caregivers can simply withdraw from the conflict and allow the "Natural Consequences" of irresponsibility to happen.	**21** A chalkboard, message center, chore chart or wall calendar helps establish a system of reminders without the adults having to "nag."	**22** You might set up a "penalty fund" for each chore neglected. A nickel from their allowance goes into a special change box to be donated to charity.	**16**
24 As you read or watch TV with your child, look for responsible role models and comment on how the hero solved the problem, stood up to adversity, or admitted a mistake.	**25** Responsibility means that it is not enough to say "I'm sorry" when we make a major mistake. We must show our remorse and attempt to rectify it. We Make Amends.	**26** Animals offer excellent means of developing responsibility. Please do not buy a pet solely for this purpose though! A pet should be brought into the home as an addition to the family, not as a "lesson" which may or many not work out.	**27** Children too often see their parents as successful adults without noting the daily struggles and decision we have to work through. Show, teach and model problem-solving techniques.	**28** You are teaching by example. Remember promises you make to your child and commitments you make to others - take them seriously!	**29** Help children to see that a mistake is not a failure, but in fact is an opportunity to learn.	**23**
31 Failure is inherent in growing up, but we must be careful about expecting children to do things they are not capable of doing. . . . Tasks can be modified so a child will meet success.						**30**

More of Phoebe's secrets are available in Dr. Charlene Messenger's book, *Secrets of the Third Little Pig: 7 Steps to Build a Child's Inner Strength.* Call 1-877-PIG-BOOK, 1-877-744-2665 to order. Visit us on the Web: brighterpathways.com

Phoebe's Piggy Portion of HIGHER VALUES Secrets

Month _____ Year _____

SUNDAY	MONDAY	TUESDAY	WEDNESDAY	THURSDAY	FRIDAY	SATURDAY
						1 By closely examining our values, we become the best possible archers, setting our sights on the mark to send children forward toward the future.
30 Resourcefulness grows out of being listened to (not lectured) and guided (not nagged) to make appropriate choices.	**31** Find Your Sense of Humor. Laughing at ourselves and at the world around us can help us make it through the tough times and enjoy the good times even more.					
2 Watch what you say about others' color, weight or clothing. Vicious thinking can become a life-long habit that does no one good.	**3** The best attempts to mold a good moral character in children still have to go through the filter of a child's distinctive makeup.	**4** In the midst of all the emotional litter in today's society, it is more important than ever that we as caregivers make a commitment to develop not only children's minds and bodies but their souls and spirits as well.	**5** Set boundaries by labeling behavior and giving fair warnings. Limit television and spend time genuinely interacting.	**6** An optimistic child is priceless! Optimistic children bounce back from adversity rather than wallow in it. They learn how to persist when things get tough.	**7** The home is the most critical area where values are instilled. Even teenagers who disagree with their parents typically hold firm to their parents' moral values.	**8**
9 Part of the issue is not just to analyze your values but have the backbone to walk your own path. To stand alone, to have vision, takes courage.	**10** Learn from Mistakes. Children need to learn that they have the stamina to overcome periods of frustration, conflict and anger to develop persistence and diligence.	**11** Building character takes considerable effort, especially if we are trying to break old patterns left over from our own childhood. We can use our own childhood trauma to set the stage for how we want our "new families" to be.	**12** Set an Example. We can teach or encourage children with specific behaviors that reflect our values, but they learn best by seeing, trying it and being recognized for it.	**13** My experience has shown me that children who believe and trust in a Higher Power often have an added source of solace in difficult times.	**14**	**15** Passing on our values should not be a haphazard approach. Are we putting much effort into things we say are important but may not really **show**?
16 Sometimes we just have our inner voice to guide us. . . . and the external rumble can make that hard to hear.	**17** Integrity means more than just being trustworthy with others. It also means being honest with yourself, standing up for your own beliefs and values.	**18** Compare what you SAY is important to what you SHOW others through your behavior. You can use that information to better align your values with your life.	**19** Point out honest acts of other people. Connect honesty with rewards and a sense of self-satisfaction. Show how dishonesty leads to grief, not just in our own lives, but all around us - in the news, for example.	**20** If you were forced to write your top 5 virtues what would you choose? Reflect on your childhood. How did that affect the values you have today? Think of how you show your values through behaviors on a day-to-day basis.	**21** In your day-to-day living, look for opportunities to show children there are often many sides of a story . . . the grumpy cashier may really be worried about a sick child at home.	**22**
23 Self-discipline results from setting goals, being consistent and giving responsibility.	**24** By helping children focus on caring about themselves, their family and those around them, we help them feel happier and more satisfied with their lives.	**25** The teaching of values and virtues has to do with how we empathize with others, how we handle our own stress, and how we choose to spend our valuable and limited time.	**26** The teaching of values grows from our choice of words in our self-expression and from our personal explanations of how things seem to us on a day-to-day basis.	**27** Children with integrity are less likely to lie to avoid punishment or impress others.	**28** Through words, but most of all by actions, we transmit lessons about what we care about. Why not make a conscious decision to teach a child higher-level values?	**29**

~389~

More of Phoebe's secrets are available in Dr. Charlene Messenger's book, *Secrets of the Third Little Pig: 7 Steps to Build a Child's Inner Strength*.
Call 1-877-PIG-BOOK, 1-877-744-2665 to order. Visit us on the Web: brighterpathways.com

"No set goal achieved satisfies. Success only breeds a new goal. The golden apple devoured has seeds. It is endless."

— Bette Davis

Your Story:
THE FOURTH LITTLE PIG?

Dr. Messenger is currently working on other projects which will expand on the main theme of this book: resilience, bouncing back, refusing to be defeated. Specific topics will include "Single Parenting" and "Adolescents." Dr. Messenger is especially interested in how much our thoughts and attitudes affect our destiny. Many people believe "you are what you think." Yet optimism is hard to maintain in a whirlwind of chaos. As Dr. Messenger says about her accident (see the article on page 369 of this book), **"only by being literally 'stopped in my tracks,' did I finally settle down and write the book that I had been intending to write for years."** Sometimes in looking back we come to see "if that (fill in the blank 'bad' thing) had never happened to me, then that (fill in the blank 'good' thing) would never have come about."

If you have a story of how you or someone you know has risen above adversity that you would like to donate for consideration to be included in her next book, we would love to hear from you. Please understand that your story will be held in strictest confidence, and names and specific identifying information may be changed to protect confidentiality. If you have a TIP you think would be helpful to other caregivers as they interact with children that you would like to donate to our library of tips and possible future publication, we would love to hear from you too!

Please be sure to let us know how to get back in touch with you. If your submission is selected for publication, we will want to contact you for permission.

You can e-mail us at **messenger@brighterpathways.com**. You can fax us at 407-895-0306. Be sure to visit our web site **brighterpathways.com**. Write us at Brighter Pathways, Inc., 210 South Bumby Avenue, Suite A, Orlando, FL 32803. Call us toll free at 1-877-PIG-BOOK (1-877-744-2665). Central Florida residents can call us at 407-895-0540. We look forward to hearing from you as together we continue to **Brighten Children's Pathways.**

References

A SNOUTFUL OF SOURCES

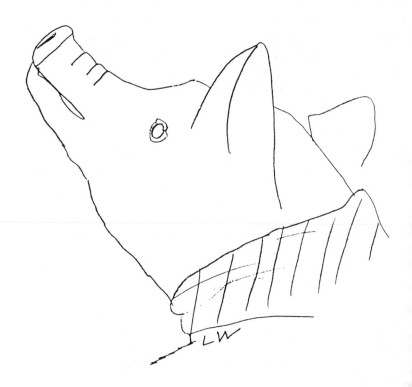

Aldwin, C., Sutton, K., and Lachman, M. 1996. "Most People Claim Past Traumas Foster Resilience," *Journal of Personality*, 64:4, 837-871.

American Demographics, in *Signs of the Times*. November 1993, 6.

Ames, Louise Bates, and Ilg, Frances L. 1982. *Your One (or Two, Three, Four, Five or Six)-Year-Old*. New York: Dell.

Associated Press. 1997. "Study: If Parents Don't Give Up, Teens Listen," *The Orlando Sentinel*, September 10, 1997, A1, A7.

Barkley, Russell. 1987. *Defiant Children - A Clinician's Manual for Parent Training*. New York, NY: Guilford Press.

Beck, A. & Katcher, A. 1983. *Between Pets and People: The Importance of Animal Companionship*. New York: Putnam.

Berk, L.S. Tan, S.A., Fry, W.F., Napier, B.J., Lee, J.W., Hubbard, R.W., Lewis, J.E., & Eby, W.C. 1989. "Neuroendocrine and Stress Hormone Changes During Mirthful Laughter." *The American Journal of the Medical Sciences*, 296:7, 390-396.

Berk, L.S., Tan, S.A., Napier, B.J., & Eby, W.C. 1989. "Eustress of Mirthful Modifies Natural Killer Cell Activity." *Clinical Research*, 37, 115A.

Benson, P.L., Galbraith, J., & Espeland, P. 1995. *What Kids Need to Succeed*. Minneapolis: Free Sprit Publishing.

Bienenfeld, Florence, Ph.D. 1987. *Helping Your Child Succeed After Divorce*. Claremont, CA: Hunter House, Inc.

Birns, B. 1976. "The Emergence and Socialization of Sex Differences in the Earliest Years." *Merrill-Palmer Quarterly*, 22, 229-254.

Bleuler, Manfred. 1978. *The Schizophrenic Disorders*. New Haven, CT: Yale University Press.

Bliss, Edwin C. 1976. *Getting Things Done: The ABC's of Time Management*. New York: Charles Scribner's Sons.

Block, Jack. 1995. "On the Relation Between IQ, Impulsivity, and Delinquency," Journal of Abnormal Psychology.

Bloom, B.S. 1964. *Stability and Change in Human Characteristics*. New York: John Wiley & Sons, Inc.

Blum, Deborah. 1998. "Finding Strength: How to Overcome Anything." *Psychology Today,* May/June, 32-73.

Bradshaw, Charles and Gilbert, Dave. 1991. *Too Hurried to Love*. Eugene, Oregon: Harvest House Publishers.

Brazelton, T.B. 1982. *On Becoming A Family: The Growth of Attachment*. New York: Bantam Doubleday Dell.

Brazelton, T. Berry. 1989. *Toddlers and Parents*, Revised. New York: Dell.

Brazelton, T. Berry, M.D. 1996. "The Pretty One, the Smart One, the Loser: Why Any Label can Hurt a Child's Self-Image." *Family Circle*, August, 30, 34-35.

Brazelton, T.Berry, M.D. 1997. "Nation Needs to Support Parents as they Rear Tomorrow's Citizens," *The Orlando Sentinel*, May 28, 1997, E-3.

Brickel, C.M. 1986. "Pet Facilitated Therapies: A Review of the Literature and Clinical Implementation Considerations." *Clinical Gerontologist*, 5, 309-332.

Brofenbrenner, Urie. in **Vissel, Barry & Joyce** (ed.) 1986. *Models of Love: The Parent-Child Journey*. Aptos, CA: Ramira Publishing.

Brown, C.C. (Ed.) 1984. *The Many Facets of Touch*. New Jersey: Johnson & Johnson Baby Products.

Bushman, Brad J. 1999. "Catharsis, Aggression, and Persuasive Influence Self-Fulfilling or Self-Defeating Prophecies?" *Journal of Personality and Social Psychology*, January 1999 Vol. 76, No. 3, 367-376.

Buscaglia, Leo. 1972. *Love*. Fawcett Crest Books: Charles B. Slack, Inc.

Butler, Katy. 1997. "The Anatomy of Resilience." *Networker*, March/April, 22-31.

Cline, Foster, M.D. 1992. *Hope for High Risk and Rage Filled Children - Reactive Attachment Disorder*. Evergreen, CO: EC Publications.

Cline, Foster, M.D. and Fay, Jim. 1990. *Parenting with Love and Logic - Teaching Children Responsibility*. Colorado Springs, CO: Pinon Press.

Cline, Dr. Victor B. 1980. *How to Make Your Child a Winner, 10 Keys to Rearing Successful Children*. Walker Publishing Co., Inc.

Cohen, Patricia. 1994. "Experts Re-Examine Parental Influence," *The Orlando Sentinel,* February 4, 1994, E-1,4.

Coie, J.D., Watt, N.F., West, S.G., Hawkins, J.D., Asarnow, J.R. Markman, H.J., Ramey, S.L. Shure, M.B., & Long, B. 1993. "The Science of Prevention: A Conceptual Framework and Some Directions for a National Research Program." *American Psychologist*, 48, 1013-1022.

Condry, J.C. & Condry, S. 1974. "The Development of Sex Differences: A Study of the Eye of the Beholder." Unpublished manuscript. Cornell University, Ithaca, NY.

Cousins, Norman. 1979. *Anatomy of an Illness as Perceived by the Patient: Reflections on Healing and Regeneration.* New York: Norton.

Covey, Stephen R. 1989. *7 Habits of Highly Effective People.* New York: Simon & Schuster.

Cramer, Kathryn. 1995. *Roads Home: Seven Pathways to Midlife Wisdom.* New York, NY: William Morrow.

Dane, Pati. 1997. "Many More than 101 Dalmations Abandoned After National Pet Craze," *The Orlando Sentinel,* September 10, 1997, A1, A4.

Deisler, Francis J. 1997. "News: Mixed Bag for Kids: Deaths Down, Abuse High." *National Association of Forensic Counselors News,* Winter, 3.

Dennis, W. 1960. "Causes of Retardation Among Institutional Children: Iran." *The Journal of Genetic Psychology,* 96, 47-59.

Dennis, W. and Sayegh, Y. 1965. "The Effect of Supplementary Experience Upon the Behavioral Development of Infants in Institutions." *Child Development,* March, 36.

Diagnostic Criteria from DSM-IV. 1994. American Psychiatric Association. Washington, D.C.

Dillon, K.M., Minchoff, B., & Baker, K.H. 1985. "Positive Emotional States and Enhancement of the Immune System." *International Journal of Psychiatry in Medicine,* 15, 13-17.

Doll, Beth & Lyon, Mark. 1998. "Risk and Resilience: Implications for the Delivery of Educational and Mental Health Services in Schools." *School Psychology Review,* Vol. 27, No. 3, 348-363.

Dornbusch, SM, Ritter, PL, Leiderman, PH, Roberts, DF, & Fraleigh, MJ. 1987. "The Relation of Parenting Style to Adolescent School Performance." *Child Development,* 58, 1244-1257.

Doughtery, Margot. 1997. "Tom Selleck: Gentleman Farmer." *Ladies' Home Journal,* October 1997, 52,54.

Douma, Allen J. 1998a. "The Family Doctor," *The Orlando Sentinel,* January 11, 1998, F-8.

Douma, Allen J. 1998b. "Update on Drug Abuse," *The Orlando Sentinel,* December 13, 1998, F-10.

Douma, Allen J. 1999. "Update on Kids' Accidents,"*The Orlando Sentinel,* May 30, 1999, F-8.

Dreikurs, R. and Soltz, V. 1987. *Children: The Challenge.* New York: Penguin Group.

Duncan, Barry. 1997. "Stepping off the Throne." *The Family Therapy Networker,* July/August 1997, 22-31, 33.

Dyer, Dr. Wayne. 1985. *What Do You Really Want for Your Children?* New York: Avon Books & William Morrow

Efran, Jay, Greene, Mitchell & Gordon, Don. 1998. "Lessons of the New Genetics." *Networker,* March/April, 27-32, 35-41.

Eftimiades, Maria. 1997. "Heartbreaking Cries: Kids without a Conscience." *People,* June, 46-53.

Egeland, B., Carlson, E., & Stroufe, L.A. 1993. "Resilience as Process." *Development and Psychopathology,* 5, 517-528.

Eisenberg, A., Hathaway, S., and Murkoff, H. 1989. *What to Expect the First Year.* New York: Workman Publishing Co. Inc.

Engelhardt, Lisa and Sontag, Lyn. 1998. *Talking with your Kids about Forgiveness.* St. Meinrod, IN: Abbey Pres

Englemann, S. and Engelmann, T. 1966. *Give Your Child A Superior Mind.* New York: Simon & Schuster, Inc.

Faber, A. and Mazlish, E. 1980. *How to Talk So Kids Will Listen and Listen So Kids Will Talk.* New York: Avon Books.

Fanning, Patrick. 1989. *Visualization for Change,* Second Edition. Oakland, CA: New Harbinger Publications.

Ferraro, Susan. 1999. "Sobering Look at Alcoholism." *The Orlando Sentinel,* March 2, 1999, E-1, E-4.

Field, T.M., Sandberg, D., Garcia, R., Vega-Lahr, N., Goldstein, S., & Guy, L. 1985. "Pregnancy Problems, Postpartum Depression, and Early Mother-infant Interactions." *Developmental Psychology,* 21: 6, 1152-1156.

Field, T.M., Windmayer, S., Greenberg, R., & Stoller, S. 1982. "Effects of Parent Training on Teenage Mothers and Their Infants." *Pediatrics,* 69:6, 703-707.

Florida Department of H.R.S. 1986. *What Everyone Should Know About Child Abuse.* Channing L. Bete Co., Inc South Deerfield, MA.

Folkins, CH and Sime, WE. 1981. "Physical Fitness Training and Mental Health." *American Psychologist,* 36:4, 373-389.

Friedman, H.S. 1992. *The Self-Healing Personality.* New York: Henry Holt.

Friedmann, E., Katcher, A., Lynch, J.J. and Thomas, S.A. 1980. "Animal Companions and One-year Survival of Patients After Discharge from Coronary Care Unit." *Public Health Reports,* 95: 307-312.

Frisch, H. 1977. "Sex Stereotypes in Adult-infancy Play." *Child Development,* 48, 1675.

Fromm, Erich. 1956. *The Art of Loving.* New York, NY: Harper & Row, Inc.

Garbarino, James. 1995. *Raising Children in a Socially Toxic Environment*. San Francisco, CA: Jossey-Bass.

Garmezy, N., & Masten, A.S. 1994. "Chronic Adversities." In M. Rutter, L. Herzov, & E. Taylor (Eds.), *Child and Adolescent Psychiatry*, Third Edition. Oxford: Blackwell, 191-208

Garrison, W.T., & Earls, F.J. 1986. "Epidemiological Perspectives on Maternal Depression and the Young Child." In E.Z.Tronick & T. Field (Eds.), *Maternal Depression and Infant Disturbances*. San Francisco: Jossey-Bass.

Garth, Maureen. 1992. *Moonbeam, A Book of Mediations for Children*. Australia: Collins Dove a Division of HarperCollins Publishers, Inc.

Gibran, Kahil. 1968. *The Prophet*. New York: Alfred A. Knopf.

Ginott, Haim. 1965. *Between Parent and Child*. New York: Macmillan Co.

Ginott, Haim. 1969. *Between Parent and Teenager*. New York: Macmillan Co.

Goleman, Daniel. 1995. *Emotional Intelligence, Why It Can Matter More Than IQ*. New York: Bantam Books.

Greene, Ross, Ph.D. 1998. *The Explosive Child*. New York, NY: HarperCollins Publishers.

Greenfield, S., Kaplan, S., & Ware, J.E. Jr. 1985. "Expanding Patient Involvement in Care: Effects on Patient Outcomes." *Annals of Internal Medicine*, 102, 520-528.

Guarendi, Ray, Ph.D. 1985. *You're a Better Parent Than You Think*. Englewood Cliffs, New Jersey: Prentice Hall.

Hadley, Josie & Staudacher, Carol. 1989. *Hypnosis for Change*, Second Edition. Oakland, CA: New Harbinger Publications.

Hales, Dianne. 1997. "You Can't Fake Feeling Good . . ." *Ladies' Home Journal*, October, 130, 132, 134.

Hall, N.R., Altman, F. and Blumenthal, S. (Eds.). 1996. *Mind Body Interactions and Disease*. National Institutes of Health.

Hart, Dr. Louise. 1987. *The Winning Family: Increasing Self-Esteem in Your Children and Yourself*. New York: Dodd, Mead.

Hersch, Patricia. 1998. *A Tribe Apart: A Journey into the Heart of American Adolescence*. Fawcett Columbine.

Hill, J.P. 1987. "Research on Adolescents and Their Families: Past and Prospect," in E.E. Irwin (Ed.). *Adolescent Social Behavior and Health*. San Francisco: Jossey-Bass.

Hockenberry, M.H. 1989. "Guided Imagery as a Coping Measure for Children with Cancer." *Journal of the Association of Pediatric Oncology Nurses*, 6:2, 29.

Hubbard, J., Realmuto, G.M., Northwood, A.K., & Masten, A.S. 1995. "Comorbidity of Psychiatric Diagnoses with Posttraumatic Stress Disorder in Survivors of Childhood Trauma." *Journal of the American Academy of Child and Adolescent Psychiatry*, 34, 1167-1173.

Jenkins, Peggy. 1992. *The Joyful Child: A Sourcebook of Activities and Ideas for Releasing Children's Natural Joy*. Tuscon, Arizona: Harbinger House, Inc.

Johnson, Marilyn. 1997. "Oprah Winfrey: A Life in Books." *Life*, September, 44-48, 53-54, 56, 60.

Joyce, Amy. 1999. "Teen Girls Vulnerable at Work," *The Orlando Sentinel*, April 28, 1999, E-1, E-4.

Kagan, J., Snidman, N., Sellers, M.J., & Johnson, M.O. 1991. "Temperament and Allergic Symptoms." *Psychosomatic Medicine*, 53, 332-340.

Kasl, Charlotte Davis 1994. *Finding Joy*. New York: HarperCollins Publishers, Inc.

Keenan, James F. 1996. *Virtues for Ordinary Christians*. Kansas City, MO: Sheed & Ward.

Kelly, Marguerite and Parsons, Elia. 1992. *The Mother Almanac*, Revised. New York: Doubleday.

Kincher, Jonni. 1995. *Psychology for Kids II*. Minneapolis, MN: Free Spirit Publishing.

Kohn, A. 1990. *The Brighter Side of Human Nature: Altruism and Empathy in Everyday Life*. New York: Basic Books.

Kushner, Harold S. 1996. *How Good Do We Have to Be?: A New Understanding of Guilt and Forgiveness*. New York, NY: Little, Brown and Company.

Kushner, Malcolm. *The Light Touch: How to Use Humor for Business Success*. New York, NY: Simon & Schuster.

Lakein, Alan. 1989. *How to Get Control of Your Time and Your Life*. New York: Signet.

Landers, Ann. 1997. "Dear Ann Landers," *The Orlando Sentinel*, September 11, 1997, E-3.

Langer, E.J. & Rodin, J. 1976. "The Effects of Choice and Enhanced Personal Responsibility for the Aged: A Field Experiment in an Institutional Setting." *Journal of Personality and Social Psychology*, 34, 191-198.

Layton, Molly. 1998. "Ripped Apart." *Networker*, Nov-Dec 1998, 24-31.

Leach, Penelope. 1981. *Your Baby & Child*. New York: Knopf.

Lerner, Barbara. 1999. "Killings Show Moral Void that Psychology Cannot Fill," *The Orlando Sentinel*, May 2, 1999, G-1.

Levine, Stephen. 1997. *A Year to Live: How to Live This Year As If It Were Your Last.* New York: Crown Publishers.

Locke, S.E. & Heisel, J.S. 1977. "The Influence of Stress and Emotions on the Human Immune Response." *Biofeedback and Self-Regulation*, 2, 320.

Longster, Samantha. 1997. "Tiresome Tongue Lashings: What is it with all this Rudeness?," *The Orlando Sentinel*, August 22, 1997, X-1.

Loomans, Diane. 1996. "Gloria Estefan." *Body, Mind, Spirit*, June/July, 45-49.

Luks, A. & Payne, P. 1992. *The Healing Power of Doing Good.* New York: Fawcett Columbine.

Luther, S.S. 1991. "Vulnerability and Resilience: A Study of High-Risk Adolescents. *Child Development*, 62, 6 612.

Lykken, Thomas, Ph.D. 1994. "Experts Re-Examine Parental Influence," *The Orlando Sentinel*, February 4, E-1, E-4.

McKay, Matthew, Ph.D. and Fanning, Patrick. 1987. *Self-Esteem.* Oakland, CA: New Harbinger Publicati

Magid, Ken and McKelvey, Carole. 1987. *High Risk - Children Without A Conscience.* New York: Bantam Bc

Malatesta, in Trottei, R.J. 1983. "Baby Face." *Psychology Today*, 17:8, 14-20.

Mapes, James J. 1996. *Quantum Leap Thinking: An Owner's Guide to the Mind.* Beverly Hills: Dove Books.

Markowitz, Laura. 1997. "A Kid's-Eye View of Therapy." *The Family Therapy Networker*, July/August, 22-33.

Masten, A.S. 1994. "Resilience in Individual Development: Successful Adaptation Despite Risk and Adversity. M. Wang & E. Gordon Eds.), *Risk and Resilience in Inner City America: Challenges and Prospects.* Hillsd NJ: Erlbaum, 3-25.

Masten, A.S., Best, K.M., & Garmezy, N. 1990. "Resilience and Development: Contributions from the Stuc Children Who Overcome Adversity." *Development and Psychopathology*, 2, 425-444.

Masten, A.S., & Wright, M. 1997. "Cumulative Risk and Protection Models of Child Maltreatment." In B. Rossman & M. Rosenberg (Eds.), *Multiple Victimization of Children: Conceptual, Developmental, Research a Treatment Issues.* Binghamton, NY: Haworth Press.

Masten, Ann, Ph.D. 1997. "Resilience in Children at-Risk." Center for Applied Research and Educational Improvement, College of Education and Human Development, University of Minnesota.

Masten, Ann, Ph.D. and O'Connor, Mary, Ph.D. 1989. "Vulnerability, Stress, and Resilience in the Early Development of a High Risk Child." *The Journal of the American Academy of Child and Adolescent Psychic*

Mickley, J.R., Soeken, K., & Belcer, A. 1992. "Spiritual Well-being, Religiousness and Hope Among Wome with Breast Cancer." *Image - The Journal of Nursing Scholarship*, 24:4, 267-272.

Miller, K. 1985. *Ages and Stages: Developmental Descriptions and Activities.* New York: Telshare Publishing.

Montagu, A. 1986. *Touching: The Human Significance of the Skin,* Third Edition. New York: Harper & Row.

Moore, Thomas. 1996. *The Re-Enchantment of Everyday Life.* New York: HarperCollins Publisher.

Moore, Thomas. 1996. "The Enchanted Child." *Body, Mind, Spirit*, June/July, 80.

Mose, Melissa. 1997. "Confessions of a Self-Mutilator." *JUMP*, September/October, 58, 60-61.

Moyer, I. 1983. *Responding to Infants: The Infant Activity Manual (0-30 Months).* New York: T.S. Denison a Co., Inc.

Myrick, Robert D. 1981. *Children Helping Children: Teaching Students to Become Friendly Helpers.* Minneapol MN: Educational Media Corp.

National Center for Education Statistics (NCES). 1985. "The Relationship of Parental Involvement to Hig school Grades." (Publication No. NCES-85-205b). Washington, DC: U.S. Department of Education.

Neifert, Marianne, M.D. 1997. "Raising a Self-Confident Child." *Parenting*, June/July, 86-90.

Niyo, Yosiya. 1999. "Doc Miburn's Prescription." *Reader's Digest*, April, 25-26, 29-30, 36.

Offer, D., Ostrov, E., & Howard, K.I. 1989. "Adolescence: What is Normal?" *American Journal of Disease Children*, 143, 731-736.

Olson, M., Sneed, N., Bonadonna, R., Ratliff, J., & Dias, J. 1992. "Therapeutic Touch and Post-Hurricane Hugo Stress." *Journal of Holistic Nursing*, 10:2, 120-136.

Papalia, Diane & Olds, Sally. 1978. *Human Development*, Fifth Edition. New York: McGraw-Hill, Inc.

Parker, Kathleen. 1999. "Father Should Have No Right to Out-of-Wedlock Child," *The Orlando Sentinel*, February 28, 1999, G-3.

Parker, Kathleen. 1999. "National Narcissism Sparked Columbine," *The Orlando Sentinel*, April 28, 1999, E-

Paul, Henry A. 1995. *When Kids are Mad, Not Bad.* New York: Berkley Books.

Pearce, J.C. 1986. Talk in Los Angeles to the Council for Excellence through Self-Esteem.

Pennebaker, JW. 1991. *Opening Up: The Healing Power of Confiding in Others.* New York: Avon.

Peterson, C. and Bossio, L.M. 1991. *Health and Optimism.* New York: Free Press.

Peterson, Karen S. 1989. "The Ultimate Challenge," *USA Today,* April 13.

Pfohl, Bill, Psy.D. and Ferstl, Shawna. 1996. "Selecting Computer Software for Children - Guidelines for Parents." *National Association of School Psychologists,* June.

Pfohl, Bill, Ed.D. and Ferstl, Shawna. 1996. "Helping Children Use Computers: A Guide for Parents." *National Association of School Psychologists,* September.

Rapp, Albert. 1951. *The Origins of Wit and Humor.* New York: EP. Dutton, Pg. 170.

Ricks, Delthia. 1996. "Researchers Encourage Laughter for Better Health," *The Advocate,* November 5, 5A.

Robb, Mrs. Charles. 1997. "Happy Tails," *Pet Talk.,* 22: 2, 1.

Robinson, John P. 1977. *How Americans Use Time.* Praeger Publishers.

Rodin, J. & Langer, E.J. 1977. "Long-term Effects of a Control-relevant Intervention with the Institutionalized Aged." *Journal of Personality and Social Psychology,* 35, 897-902.

Rubin, Lillian. 1996. *The Transcendent Child: Tales of Triumph Over the Past.* New York: Basic Books.

Rutter, Michael, in Butler, Katy. 1997. "The Anatomy of Resilience." *Networker,* March/April, 22-31.

Schaefer, Charles E. and Di Geronimo, Teresa Foy. 1994. *How to Talk to Your Kids About Really Important Things.* San Francisco: Josey-Bass Publishers.

Scheier, M.F. & Carver, C.S. 1987. "Dispositional Optimism and Physical Well-being: The Influence of Generalized Outcome Expectancies on Health." *Journal of Personality,* 55:2.

Scheier, M.F., Weintraub, J.K., & Carver, C.S. 1986. "Coping with Stress: Divergent Strategies of Optimists and Pessimists." *Journal of Personality and Social Psychology,* 51:6, 1257-1264.

Schulman, Michael. 1985. *Bringing Up A Moral Child.* Reading, MA: Addison-Wesley Publishers.

Scieszka, Jon. 1989. *The True Story of the 3 Little Pigs! By A. Wolf.* New York: Scholastic Inc.

Sears, William, M.D. 1998. "Loving Ways to Bond With Your Baby." *Parenting,* December/January, 118-125.

Seligman, Martin E.P. 1995. *The Optimistic Child.* Boston, MA: Houghton Mifflin.

Shapiro, Francine. 1995. *Eye Movement Desensitization and Reprocessing.* New York: The Guilford Press.

Shapiro, Joseph P. 1996. "Invincible Kids." *U.S. News & World Report,* 121:19.

Sheikh, AA (Ed.) 1984. *Imagination and Healing.* New York: Baywood Publishing.

Shoda, Yuichi, Mischel, Walter and Peake, Phillip. 1990. "Predicting Adolescent Cognitive and Self-regulatory Competencies from Preschool Delay of Gratification," *Developmental Psychology,* 26, 978-986.

Sills, Judith. 1997. "Bouncing Back." *New Woman,* August, 102-103, 128-129.

Sroufe, L.A. 1983. "Individual Patterns of Adaptation from Infancy to Preschool" in M. Perlmutter (Ed.), *Proceedings of Minnesota Symposium on Child Psychology.*

Steinberg, L. 1986. "Latchkey Children and Susceptibility to Peer Pressure: An Ecological Analysis." *Developmental Psychology,* 22:4, 433-439.

Straus, Murray & Paschall, Mallie. 1999. "Corporal Punishment by Mothers and Child's Cognitive Development: A Longitudinal Study." Family Research Laboratory, University of New Hampshire. Durham, NH.

Tellegren, A., Lykken, D.T., Bouchard, T.J., Wilcox, K.J., Segal, N.L, & Rich, S. 1988. "Personality Similarity in Twins Reared Apart and Together." *Journal of Personality and Social Psychology,* 54:6, 1031-1039.

Thomas, A. & Chess, S. 1984. "Genesis and Evolution of Behavioral Disorders: From Infancy to Early Adult Life." *American Journal of Orthopsychiatry,* 141:1, 1-9.

Thomas, A., Chess, S., & Birch, H.G. 1968. *Temperament and Behavior Disorders in Children.* New York: University Press.

Trafford, Abigail. 1992. *Crazy Time: Surviving Divorce and Building a New Life,* Revised Edition. New York: HarperColins Publishers, Inc.

Turecki, Stanley and Tonner, L. 1989. *The Difficult Child.* New York: Bantam Books.

Ulrich, R. 1984. "View Through a Window May Influence Recovery from Surgery." *Science,* 224, 420-421.

Unell, Barbara C. and Wyckoff, Jerry L., Ph.D. 1995. *20 Teachable Virtues: Practical Ways to Pass on Lessons of Virtue and Character to Your Children.* New York: Berkley Publishing.

Walsh, Froma. 1996. "The Concept of Family Resilience: Crisis and Challenge." *Family Process ,* 35, 261.

Wankel, LM and Bewrger, BG. 1990. "The Psychological and Social Benefits of Sport and Physical Activity." *Journal of Leisure Research,* 22:2, 167-182.

Weiss, J. 1972. "Psychological Factors in Stress and Disease." *Scientific American*, 226:104.

Werner, E. 1993. "Risk, Resilience, and Recovery: Perspectives from the Kauai Longitudinal Study." *Development and Psychopathology*, 5, 503-515.

Werner, Emmy E. & Smith, Ruth S. 1992. *Overcoming the Odds*. Ithica, NY: Cornell University Press.

Wertheimer, Linda K. 1997. "Schools Feel Population Pinch," *The Orlando Sentinel*, November 2, 1997, K1, K

Wertheimer, Linda K. 1997. "Webster: Run-down School Has to Go," *The Orlando Sentinel,* November 1, 1997 A1, A8.

Whiffen, V.E., & Gotlib, I.H. 1989. "Infants of Postpartum Depressed Mothers: Temperament and Cognitive Status." *Journal of Abnormal Psychology,* 98:3, 274-279.

White, K.R. 1982. "The Relation Between Socioeconomic Status and Academic Achievement." *Psychological Bulletin, 91:3*, 461-481.

White-Bowden, Susan. 1987. *From a Healing Heart*. Baltimore, Md.: Image Publishing, LTD.

Wideman, John Edgar. 1984. *Brothers and Keepers*. Cambridge, MA: Holt, Rinehart and Winston.

Williams, Redford & Williams, Virginia. 1994. *Anger Kills: Seventeen Strategies for Controlling the Hostility that can Harm Your Health.* Harperperennial Library.

Wilson, Miriam. 1987. *Help for Children*, Fifth Edition. Sepherdstown, West Virginia: Rocky River.

Wolin, Steven, MD and Wolin, Sybil, Ph.D. 1993. *The Resilient Self: How Survivors of Troubled Families Rise Above Adversity.* New York: Villard Books.

Yoshikawa, H. 1994. "Prevention as Cumulative Protection: Effects of Early Family Support and Education on Chronic Delinquency and Its Risks." *Psychological Bulletin*, 115,28-54.

Young, Bettie. 1991. *Six Vital Ingredients of Self-Esteem*. New York: MacMillan Publishing Co.

Zachariae, R., Kristensen, J.S., Hokland, P., Ellegaard, J., Metze, E.,& Hokland, M. 199). "Effect of Psychological Intervention in the Form of Relaxation and Guided Imagery on Cellular Immune Function in Normal Healthy Subjects. An Overview." *Psychotherapy and Psychosomatics*, 54:, 32-39.

Zuckerman, B.S., and Beardslee, W.R. 1987. "Maternal Depression: Concern for Pediatricians." *Pediatrics*, 79:1, 110-117.

Index

PIG OUT
ON THE DETAILS

The End

Order Form: EXTRA HELPINGS
Secrets of the Third Little Pig:
7 Steps to Build a Child's Inner Strength
by Charlene Messenger, Ph.D.

~ ❀ ~ ❀ ~ ❀ ~ ❀ ~ ❀ ~ ❀ ~ ❀ ~ ❀ ~ ❀ ~ ❀ ~

Name

Address

City   State/Province   Zip

Telephone   Fax   E-Mail

1. Price Per Copy: $ 14.00*
2. Number of Copies   x _____
3. Subtotal $ _____
4. Add $4.00 Shipping & Handling
   (Plus $1.50 Each Additional Book) + _____
5. Florida Residents Only + 6% Sales Tax + _____
6. Total Check or Money Order Enclosed $ _____

MasterCard ____ or Visa ____ Card Expires __/__
Card Number: _____
Signature: _____

*($20.00 in Canada)
Discounts on bulk quantities of this book are available to corporations,
professional associations, schools, churches, and other organizations.
For details and discount information, contact the Special Sales Department at
Brighter Pathways, Inc. Publishers
Phone: 407-895-0540   ~   Fax: 407-895-0306
e-mail: messenger@brighterpathways.com
Brighter Pathways, Inc., 210 South Bumby Avenue, Suite A, Orlando, FL 32803
Call us TOLL FREE at: **1-877-PIG-BOOK** (1-877-744-2665)
Visit us on the WEB at:

brighterpathways.com